Working Together

Also by David R. Eyler and Andrea P. Baridon

MORE THAN FRIENDS, LESS THAN LOVERS: MANAGING SEXUAL ATTRACTION IN WORKING RELATIONSHIPS

Working Together

The New Rules and Realities for
Managing Men and Women at Work

Andrea P. Baridon
David R. Eyler

McGraw-Hill, Inc.
New York San Francisco Washington, D.C. Auckland Bogotá
Caracas Lisbon London Madrid Mexico City Milan
Montreal New Delhi San Juan Singapore
Sydney Tokyo Toronto

Library of Congress Cataloging-in-Publication Data

Baridon, Andrea P.
    Working together : the new rules and realities for managing
men and women at work / Andrea P. Baridon, David R. Eyler.
        p.   cm.
    Includes bibliographical references (p.   ) and index.
    ISBN 0-07-003552-0
    1. Personnel management.   2. Sex differences.   3. Interpersonal
relations.   4. Sexual harassment.   I. Eyler, David R.   II. Title.
    HF5549.B2697   1994
    658.3'042—dc20   94-9715
                                                                                       CIP

1 2 3 4 5 6 7 8 9 0   DOC/DOC   9 0 9 8 7 6 5 4

ISBN 0-07-003552-0

*The sponsoring editor for this book was Betsy N. Brown, the editing supervisor
was Olive H. Collen, and the production supervisor was Donald Schmidt. The
book was set in Palatino by McGraw-Hill's Professional Book Group
composition unit.*

Printed and bound by R. R. Donnelley & Sons Company.

To Munya and the memory of Eunice,
for all the things that mothers are.

Contents

Preface   xi

Introduction   **1**

Part 1. Understanding Gender Differences   **5**

**1. Things We Can Change and Things We Cannot
   Change**   **7**

Equal but Not the Same   10
   A Brief History   11
   Tenets of Misunderstanding   17
The Inevitability of the Mixed-Gender Workforce   19
   The Demographics of Change   20
The Challenge of the Future   45

2. The Myths and Realities of Gender Differences   **48**

Different Kinds of Differences   49
Recognizing Differences for What They Are   50
Differences between the Sexes   52
   Body Differences   54
   Brain Differences   57
   Psychological and Cultural Differences   67
Conclusions   80

Part 2. Regulating the Interaction of Gender Differences   83

3. Laws, Regulations, and Gender in the Workforce   85

The Law and Managing Gender Issues at Work   87
    1868—Equal Protection Amendment   88
    1920—Voting Rights Amendment   88
    1963—Equal Pay Act   89
    1964—Civil Rights Act of 1964   89
    1968—Executive Order 11246 as Amended by Executive
      Order 11375   90
    1972—Equal Employment Opportunity Act   91
    1978—Pregnancy Discrimination Act   91
    1980—Sexual Harassment Guidelines   92
    1991—Civil Rights Act of 1991   92
Applying the Law to Gender Issues at Work   94
    Six Court Cases on Equal Pay   95
    Six Court Cases on Sexual Harassment   107
How a Charge Is Filed   120
Conclusions   122

Part 3. Working with Gender Differences   123

4. Workplace Etiquette for Men and Women   125

Unlearning the Stereotypes of Gender   126
Why Working Relationships Are Different   127
On-the-Job Etiquette for the Sexes   129
    Topic 1 "Anthropology, Biology, and Colleague Relationships"
      Etiquette   130
    Topic 2 "Assuming You Know" Etiquette   133
    Topic 3 "Closed-Door and Locker-Room" Etiquette   136
    Topic 4 "Competition Mentality" Etiquette   139
    Topic 5 "Giving and Taking Our Lumps" Etiquette   142
    Topic 6 "Sexual Stereotype" Etiquette   146
    Topic 7 "Invitations, Approaches, and Propositions"
      Etiquette   148
    Topic 8 "Attractiveness and Power Relationship Management"
      Etiquette   151
    Topic 9 "Male Standard" Etiquette   153
    Topic 10 "Meeting People" Etiquette   155
    Topic 11 "Required Socializing" Etiquette   158
    Topic 12 "Saying and Doing" Etiquette   161
    Topic 13 "Saying It Right" Etiquette   163
    Topic 14 "Sharing" Etiquette   166
Conclusions   168

5. Managing Women and Men   170
A Credible Management Problem   171
What Management Can Do about Sexual Harassment   174
Managing the Glass Ceiling Problem   177
  Fundamental Problems   178
  Motivations for Change   181
  Self-Imposed Glass Ceilings   182
  Value of Mentoring   183
Management and the Family   184
  Women Have Changed the Workplace   185
  Workers' Needs Have Changed   187
  What Companies Can Do   188
  Keeping Policies Fair and Legal   190
Conclusions   190

6. A New Tomorrow at Work   192
New Roles and Approaches   194
Changed Managers and Decision Makers   196
Different Relationships and Attitudes   197
New Expectations   197

Endnotes   200
Bibliography   211
Index   215

Preface

Women and men spend most of their lives working. For many people, work is the source of their greatest satisfactions and most crushing disappointments. In this book we examine critical issues faced by men and women who work together as they attempt to share opportunities, careers, and lives—and to do so equitably. We look at reasons why rational, decent people turn the workplace into a battleground, with women on one side and men on the other, making life for each other a bitter contest instead of a satisfying interaction between two differently, but equally, endowed groups of human beings. And we offer positive approaches to solving the problems they face.

Our earlier book, *More than Friends, Less than Lovers: Managing Sexual Attraction in Working Relationships,* stated the reality that sexual differences come to work with us every day. We are not androgynous, and, inevitably, in the intimacy of modern working relationships, the interaction of a team will be colored by the fact that it is composed of a woman and a man. We demonstrated that, as elsewhere, sexual energy exists in the workplace, and we showed how a woman and a man could relate intimately in their *work* without romantic complications or sexual harassment problems. In this book we respond to requests that we broaden the earlier message, go beyond attraction, and address workplace sex roles in general.

A woman and a man working together are different from a same-sex business team sharing the identical experience. In working, as in the biological and emotional aspects of their lives, men and women bring different attributes to a task. Research shows that teams of men and women are more productive than same-sex teams. Given the facts that women and men *do* approach work differently and that workplace demographics show that they are working together more often, it follows that working relationships are affected by the differences between the genders. It is essential that we gain a better understanding of these differences. To begin, we must improve our understanding of each other. And that is a goal of this book.

In literally hundreds of interviews that followed the publication of *More than Friends*, we were told repeatedly that our thinking had broader applicability. That book was confined to *personal relationships* between *mutually attracted* men and women at work; the larger issue is how *all* women and men, attracted or not, might relate to one another more successfully on the job. We identified myths and realities about attraction at work, but the people with whom we interacted on talk shows and in industry wanted a broader interpretation of the myths and realities about women and men working together—how could two such different categories of employees, with preconceived and often unrealistic views of each other, possibly find a way to work together harmoniously *and* as equals on a daily basis?

The publicity tour for our book began during the week after the Hill-Thomas hearings riveted the country's attention on the issue of sexual harassment. But we learned that although most people knew that laws existed on the topic, few—including human resources professionals charged with implementing them in their companies—really grasped the big picture. Seldom was it pointed out that sexual harassment is a severe symptom of a deep problem. Women in large numbers are relatively new to the workplace as peers to their male counterparts, and both sexes have had difficulty in defining this new workplace. Some men, feeling threatened and territorial, have reacted inappropriately by discriminating and being sexually harassing. For a variety of reasons such as embarrassment, fear, or the desire not to "rock the boat," as they move up the career ladders, women have vigorously demanded equal treatment under the law only in small numbers. Until Anita Hill.

Suddenly sexual harassment was hot! Individual laws and landmark cases allowed glimpses of recognition of the broader issues, but not one person in a hundred could tie them all together and say, "Here are some of the reasons we have problems and what we have to do next." We try to do that in this book by taking the too-brief pamphlets and the too-long books and distilling them into a straightforward summary of science, law, social movements, human behavior, and management thinking that might guide us to the understanding that is the beginning of solutions. Issues this complex are seldom driven by clear-cut procedures and indisputable rights and wrongs, but there are threads of agreement among reasonable people, and it is those we identify.

After speaking before a management group one afternoon, we were somewhat taken aback when a corporate attorney reacted with dismay to our message that some of the men and women in his corporation might find each other attractive enough that they would need to consciously manage their behavior as well as their work flow. "What you're saying," he said indignantly "is that they should just have a good time together!" He didn't get it, or we didn't communicate it clearly, but we meant to say emphatically that relationships in the mixed-gender workforce have reached the point at which it is critical to contemplate managing more than the mere threat of legal action. We have to get beyond the litigation stage of conflict resolution, even though it remains an essential tool. Enduring solutions to gender-based equal opportunity problems will come when women and men learn more than simply to avoid the threat they think they pose to one another. Many of them will discover that complementary differences and abilities actually enhance their joint efforts. And yes, people who work together *should* have a good time together—they get more done and do it better!

The rights movement has been and remains an indisputable necessity. But we see danger in a negatively focused establishment of human resources personnel, corporation lawyers, and advocates who forget that they are riding a moving train—yesterday's emphasis is not necessarily appropriate for all of today's employees. With all due respect to the Pulitzer Prize–winning journalist who wrote it, Susan Faludi's *Backlash: The Undeclared War against American Women* spends too much energy on building conspiracies to explain how society is keeping women from taking their rightful place. We see a less dramatic reason for the plight of women—years of accumulated ignorance and misunderstanding. Exercises in asserting power and sensationally framing issues as Faludi has done are, for a while, constructive steps along the road to achieving change. But at some point the task has to become the less glamorous one of actually replacing myths with realities, and stereotypes with honest, contemporary role expectations based on real capabilities and limitations.

Many women and men already have acknowledged the sins of the past and recognize that much remains to be done. They want more than "thou shalt not" workshops and worst-case-scenario training films. There are large numbers of working women and men and their managers saying, "OK, you've shown us how the bad guys act. But we're not a part of that, and we'll help you fight it. Help us figure out how we can get along and avoid misunderstanding and litigation. Weed out the monsters, but teach the rest of us the positive ways of making our working relationships not just tolerable, but comfortable, and maybe even collegial. We're stuck together on the job, and getting along rather than fighting would help us get a lot more work done."

It was satisfying to introduce men and women who experienced understandable, natural, and limited attractions at work to the possibility of managed, productive, and nonromantic relationships in *More than Friends, Less than Lovers*. However, as our experience with the corporate counsel taught us, such a message can be misunderstood. To avoid that, the positive approach we advocate must be framed in bottom-line realities like: (1) women and men have no choice except to build new working relationships that are collegial, safe, and productive—our economic survival depends on it; (2) women and men are genuinely different in significant respects but are more *alike* than different, and failure to recognize *both* of these realities and make the most of them is counterproductive for individuals, advocates, and industry; and (3) shades of gray exist in man-woman workplace issues that require a range of interpretations, judgments, policies, and incentives to address individual circumstances and not just dramatic extremes.

Our own experiences as a mixed-gender business team have shown us that women and men working together have an opportunity to choose enrichment and growth rather than confrontations and limitations. It all begins with understanding that men and women are both alike and different, that their *differences* do not make them adversaries but actually give them a potential that is better and more productive than if they were the same—this is the overarching purpose of this book.

Acknowledgments

Our thanks to Jeremy Tarcher for suggesting that we write this book; Hank Stine for teaching us how; Robert A. Shapiro, Esq., Associate Solicitor for Legislation and Legal Counsel, Office of the Solicitor, U.S. Department of Labor; Jill Bogard, Director, Library and Information Service, the American Council on Education; and the Women's Bureau, U.S. Department of Labor—all for supporting our research. Appreciation is due as well to Steve Kime, our boss and colleague, for suggesting the concept of a new workplace etiquette for men and women; Bert Holtje, our agent, for finding the manuscript a commercial home; Betsy Brown, our acquisitions editor, for persisting to see the final product; and Olive Collen, our production editor, for her assistance in crafting a finished literary work.

Andrea P. Baridon
David R. Eyler

Introduction

We have worked together as colleagues for a decade, sometimes in the intimacy of business travel or writing, more often in the routine of everyday office life. Mutual respect and understanding that we each value have grown between us. Still, we are hopelessly different, alternately startling each other with fresh insights and frustrating one another with intractable differences in a fascinating dialogue of opposites. We have come to realize that, as much as we are alike in some respects, the differences will never change. We are the product of dissimilar lives—not socioeconomically, geographically, or even culturally but as a woman and a man. The combination of our separate biology and gender acculturation has made us forever different human beings.

Professionally we capitalize on our different perceptions of the world—our productivity benefits. We have a strength of pooled intellect that any two people of like minds could achieve, but we also possess a unique dimension that only a woman and a man can generate. We are each something the other cannot possibly be—not physically, not emotionally, not in the rituals of coming of age—an amalgam of traits that became the uniqueness of woman and man during the eons after we climbed from the primordial ooze together and developed as different sexes. These gender differences provide each of us a basis for screening messages others send.

In her book *You Just Don't Understand*, sociolinguist and author Deborah Tannen described the differences in expression and perception that we owe to gender. If Tannen's convincing research is to be believed, women and men have different orientations to life. She says that the point of realizing this is not to try to change one another, or to try to become the same, but to understand our gender opposites and make the most of shared lives. The task is still the same, even with a less gender-based view of why women and men are different as expressed by author Robin Lakeoff in *Talking Power: The Politics of Language*, which holds that the power imbalance between men and women, not gender, accounts for the differences.

The idea of being affected by our unique perceptions of others and their intentions toward us is not new. In the 1960s, psychotherapist

Albert Ellis popularized rational-emotive therapy. One of Ellis's main points was that misunderstanding and demonizing what we feel others are thinking can be extremely pathological. His solution was that we seek an accurate understanding of our "self-talk" (what we tell ourselves others are saying) and that we realize that self-talk may not actually be what *is* being said to us by others. Men and women have that problem with each other, as Tannen's long run on the best-seller lists attests. Yet another popular writer, Lillian Glass, says that what troubles our relationships is the "he says, she says" problem—that is, men and women base their interpretation of each other's words or actions on their own gender perspective. Often, they both "get it wrong." If the problem applied only to our social behavior, it would be one thing, but it becomes an important productivity factor when viewed in the context of shared work.

The message of psychotherapists, sociolinguists, and just plain observers of the human condition is the same: Women and men are different, and problems occur when they try to deny that the differences exist or use them to justify gender discrimination. It is time to stop demanding that men and women be the same; rather, it is time to start coping with each other realistically—responding to messages actually sent (or admitting that we need help in interpreting them) and not allowing ourselves to get stuck shouting across the barricades of real and enduring gender differences. Felice Schwartz, of the moderate women's interest group Catalyst, dared to imply in a 1989 issue of *Harvard Business Review* that the genders are different enough to warrant unique career paths. She spent a year explaining that she never uttered the words "mommy track"! In her 1992 book, *Breaking with Tradition: Women and Work, The New Facts of Life,* Schwartz continues her argument that women are different from men, but thoroughly capable of having successful careers, and adds that flexible working lifestyles are of increasing interest to both genders.

As a man-woman work team, we are convinced of our fundamental differences—as convinced as we are of our equal capacities to excel individually (if differently) in almost every aspect of our careers and lives. We have worked closely together over a long period of time, in circumstances that made it necessary for us to persist and learn to optimize our working relationship. We believe that what we have discovered personally—almost by accident—from our experience can be learned by other men and women. That is, they can form workplace relationships that make the most of what each brings to the task, letting mutual interests overcome the problems of denied opportunities and sexual harassment. They can do it by dealing with one another openly and honestly from a base of understanding that they are not the same and need not be the same to accomplish more together than they would be likely to accomplish separately.

Many books deal with the problems faced by women and men working together. Most of them focus on one or two problem areas—sexual harassment, communication, compensation, opportunity. This book is different. It explores multiple issues in the context of a rapidly changing workplace and integrates them into a comprehensive volume that is optimistic about a working environment in which men and women can and must find positive ways of sharing their working lives.

This book is written for working men and women and those who manage them, by a working woman and man who, at midcareer, have spent enough time in the organizational trenches to value practical solutions more than either passionate causes or obstinate resistance to needed change. We have put together what women and men need to know to cope intelligently with issues, such as equal pay for equal work, sexual harassment, sexual attraction in the workplace, fair hiring and promotion practices, that bedevil workers and managers alike. This book separates fact from myth, firebrand feminism from reasonable expectations of fairness; it provides day-to-day practical approaches drawn from a sea of legislation and social good intentions.

The book begins with an overview of how daily interaction between men and women at work has become an issue. The historical background covers the events, legislative responses, and social movements that have brought the issues to where they are today, including landmark events such as the movement of large numbers of professional women into the workforce.

We help readers become familiar with the essentials of the battle between the sexes in general and how it has made the workplace a more complex environment than it was even 20 years ago. The book is also a practical guide to the knowledge base that has developed around the sexes sharing work and work space. Myths and realities about how men and women are the same and different, in abilities, management styles, and so forth, are discussed, and readers are provided with the best available bases for deciding what is fair and realistic as they struggle to work and manage both fairly and effectively. In addition, we give a nuts-and-bolts introduction to the regulatory maze surrounding the issues of discrimination and civil rights, sexual harassment, and the practices of hiring, firing, and promoting people. We take great pains to distill information and illustrate points with practical explanations and examples. Managers and workers alike will finish the book with an improved understanding of the fundamental legislative mandate, and its consequences for business, respect for the impact of the legislation on personnel and organizations, and an appreciation for where future trends are leading.

After a solid grounding in the statutory rules of the game, the concluding chapters turn the knowledge to practical use. The book addresses the unique challenges of managing men and women, providing guidance on team building, making assignments, optimizing talent, ensuring a level playing field, and cultivating an atmosphere of fairness and equal opportunity. Workplace etiquette is spelled out quite differently than has been done before—not the newspaper columnists' or socialites' versions, but gut-level coping and communicating mechanisms that work when it is one-on-one in the workplace and man-woman issues come up.

We advocate change—practical, realistic, well-informed change. Knowledge, awareness, and sensitivity are the building blocks of lasting social change. This book provides the tools to understand the issues, deal with the realities, and recognize the benefits of making the most of complementary differences between the sexes as they play their enlightened roles in the mixed-gender workforce that is here to stay.

PART 1

Understanding Gender Differences

1
Things We Can Change and Things We Cannot Change

Allison and Derek work as a news team for an urban television station. She is the reporter, and he operates the camera and technical equipment. Neither is the "boss" in their working relationship; they are peers who do different, complementary jobs. Their ages, educational backgrounds, and social values are similar. His degree is in engineering, and hers is in journalism. Either could reasonably aspire to a management position. Both are romantically committed to others and have no plans to alter those relationships.

They are *much* the same but *not* the same. He finds unfamiliar locations more easily than she does but admits that she follows directions better than he does. She is quicker to anticipate an emerging news story; he understands and fixes the technical problems more readily. She moves people and paper; he moves props and heavy equipment. While they might deny it, there are times when he clandestinely appraises her romantic potential; less often, less intensely, she does the same of him. He is a bit protective of her among strangers and mildly territorial among colleagues. She vigorously maintains that she "can take care of herself"; she can and does, but she also is glad to have him around when an interview scene gets rowdy or another guy won't take no for an answer. In short, some of their behavior harkens back countless generations to long-established patterns of man-woman interaction, although fundamental assumptions are changing so rapidly that many of the explanations of yesteryear are in serious dispute today.

Allison expects to take time off to have a baby; Derek and his wife have a child whose birth caused no interruption in his career. His wife is about to return to work, and both he and Allison know few couples among their peers who are not pursuing dual careers.

Allison was pleased to draw Derek as her work partner because his technical skills were the best and the other available technician had a reputation among female colleagues as a borderline chauvinist-harasser. Derek's concerns about the men or women with whom he might be paired are different—he simply wants to work with the best. Crossing the age barrier into midlife and beyond may have a negative impact on Allison's on-camera career; but for Derek, it's basically irrelevant as long as he maintains his technical proficiency (as a male, even if he were on camera, aging would also be less of a concern for him). In spite of all Allison and Derek have in common, their uniqueness as woman and man makes their working relationship successful.

Even if their occupational roles were reversed, as well they might be today, the characteristics of this working team are representative of those found at numerous places of employment. Men and women are essentially peers and share similar lifestyles. Their opportunities and aspirations are often the same, but their abilities and limitations are different, or at least are perceived as so. Most of them realize that their working relationships with opposite-sex peers are different from those with same-sex coworkers. Men and women may be equal, but they are not the same. They come from different gender tracks, and it shows in many ways. Some of the differences will never change; others will pass as society evolves and accepts new realities.

Common sense, you say? Of course. But our relatively new mixed-gender workplace is presenting dynamic challenges for the men and women involved, and not everyone is meeting these challenges successfully. Confusion reigns. Mixed signals abound. Misunderstanding about why women and men are the way they are, as members of different genders, is rampant. Too often, we expect members of the opposite sex to be the same when they are not. Equally often, gender differences cause discomfort and make people react in ways more appropriate to social situations than to professional relationships—or in ways that are not appropriate at all. Even at their most innocent, women and men experience inexplicable discomfort with each other and find themselves pitting reason and discipline against ingrained perceptions about the opposite sex:

- They are out of their "place"
- They are sex objects
- They do not have the intellectual or emotional ability to do the job

- There must be a man-woman social relationship to exploit somewhere in this working relationship

In the midrange, they contest opportunities they should freely share:

- This is a man's (or woman's) job
- She (or he) has not had the right experiences to hold this job
- She (or he) approaches the job differently, and because the approach is different, it's inferior

And at the extreme, base instincts combine with power and translate into sexual coercion that causes working relationships to break down completely:

- I control her (or his) career; therefore, she (or he) owes me personal favors
- I have power; therefore, I am desirable

Men and women need to know each other better in order to deal rationally with such myths. Not just "Hello, I know your name, and I'm reasonably comfortable with you personally" kinds of knowledge but bedrock knowledge about their similarities and differences—anthropological, biological, emotional, social, demographic. They need to use this knowledge to understand how their gender differences affect their interaction at work, both collegially and legally.

Working relationships are clouded by traditional social perspectives. Many men and women are not good at relegating social factors to an objective secondary position in their professional relationships. And failures on this dimension are not all romantic and sexual blunders. They also include stereotypes about where people belong ("a woman's place is in the home"), what they should being doing ("men should be doctors; women should be nurses"), and how capable they are of doing it ("women aren't as good as men at operating complex machinery such as airplanes; therefore they shouldn't be commercial pilots"). Such stereotypes are part of traditional socialization that interferes with working objectivity. Although social interaction should not be eliminated or even reduced, men and women need to know enough about each other, based on objective measures, to balance the social and professional as they interact on the job.

Allison and Derek have an enjoyable and productive relationship in spite of—and, in some respects, because of—their differences as woman and man. Another business team paired in the same situation might relate awkwardly or unhappily. A successful mixed-gender working relationship arises from mutual understanding, shared appreciation for how the other person functions, and open-minded attitudes toward one another.

Although each of us "understands" the opposite sex, it is based on stereotype, heavily laced with myth and fantasy. A real working relationship requires a more fundamental basis for mutual understanding that comes from examining the man-woman dichotomy dispassionately, not from an adversarial standpoint. And it always must be done with accommodation for differences—sexual, emotional, physical—because taking advantage of the differences instead of fighting them can mean the difference between a successful working relationship and one fraught with problems.

Equal but Not the Same

Reasonable people accept that there are differences between women and men that cannot be changed, for example, the separate hands that nature dealt them. Women may never match men playing tennis, where upper body strength is key; men may never better women in marathon swimming, where buoyancy and protection against the cold favor the female body.[1] But some things *can* be changed, such as the fundamental attitudes and beliefs that cause misunderstandings about how to work with gender opposites.

We have an increasingly accepted understanding in our country, one that says that women and men are equal, and it is backed by law and driven by economic and demographic realities. But *equal* does not always mean "the same," and achieving equality among those who are different requires understanding and accommodation. As obvious as it might seem, there is an overarching concept here that must be grasped; and, if the ways men and women behave toward one another are any measure of the comprehension of this concept, many of us have failed to reconcile gender and working relationships. Jo Durden-Smith and Diane Desimone in their book *Sex and the Brain* suggest that this understanding may be well worth the effort:

> The differences between men and women—all the differences in brain and body and inheritance, in ability, fragility and immunity—are fundamental to our human biology. They are the driving force of our biological evolution and the creators, between them, of our cultural evolution. They are what tie men and women together in such a delicate, interdependent balance. If we ignore the differences, if we pretend they do not exist, we in effect cut ourselves off from one another, and from the possibility of solving together the problems of the future.[2]

There are reasons for gender differences. The overviews that follow set necessary, succinct, and irrefutable contexts for understanding why women and men are the way they are. As men and women begin to comprehend the differences, their prospects for getting along brighten.

A Brief History

To understand why the differences between the sexes have so much impact on working relationships between men and women, we need to look at how their "work" together has evolved over time. And since much of the way they behave today stems from the reproductive imperative, the first major "job" at which men and women succeeded as a team, we must start there. After sketching the past in broad strokes, we move to recent years, when the emphasis shifts from the survival-dominated roles to the equality-based ones of modern times that render the old assumptions of roles based on gender both unnecessary and outdated.

With reasons for separate domains (the workplace for him, the home for her) fading, women and men began to share life with fewer arbitrary distinctions as to what was one or the other's role. But tradition-bound behavior dies hard. Creeping egalitarianism has threatened those with the most favored status—men—and they have resisted. With their resistance have come twentieth-century social movements and legislation designed to give women the vote, establish civil rights, and provide equal opportunity. With legislation have come more resistance and the problems of sexual harassment, irrationally denied opportunity, and a chasm of misunderstanding that sometimes makes gender differences appear intractable.

While scholars differ on the proper weight to attach to history, anthropology, and biology as explanations for sexual differences, it is impossible not to begin by sketching the seemingly logical context they provide for understanding how women and men interact. As author Anthony Astrachan writes: "A number of events have changed and challenged the balance of power between men and women. In rough chronological order, they were women's working for pay in increasing numbers; the invention of the birth control pill and other high-assurance contraceptive techniques that enabled women to end the fear of unwanted pregnancy; the sexual revolution; and the women's movement."[3]

Next is a necessarily brief overview; reserve your conclusions on the issues until later, when arguments are presented more fully. But for now appreciate what has to be the starting point for viewing man-woman differences—the broad sweep of their shared experience across the ages.

The Anthropologists' View. Somewhere in the distant past, a biological event set the stage for the eternal dichotomy that is our two-gender life form—two sexes. This happened for at least one self-evident reason—reproduction, perpetuation of the species. While it may be that the creating force, in its infinite wisdom, intended something more complex, by all appearances there is an elegantly simple equality in our biological beginnings. We need one another if there are to be more of us. And so the sexes began as we see them today—different, interdependent, and essential to each other's continued existence.

A few steps more in evolutionary history, and the basis for the traditional view of gender roles appeared. Life was no longer a simple cycle of floating separately in the sea until it was time to reproduce with a partner of chance, as in some enormous square dance, uniting long enough to accomplish the task and then moving on without obligations. In order for the species to survive, sex roles were defined and a simple division of labor came about. Males were the providers and protectors, and females were the bearers and rearers of children.

To be strong and survive, men and women became selective in their breeding choices and nurturing in the development of their young. The biological imperative still ruled—the mission was to reproduce successfully—but human judgment became a factor. Choices were made among potential mates, the concept of jealousy arose, and the consequences of sexual attraction grew more complex. Competition and power entered into the equation to influence voluntary selection and override it (the strongest males got the most desirable females whether they were willingly received or not). Coercion and control on the basis of gender had begun.

With socialization came a more formal division of labor—necessary because of biological differences and the roles they naturally defined. Women continued to bear and nurture offspring as well as cook food provided by the men. They also made clothing and provided a "home," first in migratory societies and later in permanent ones. Men hunted for food, gathered materials for shelter and clothing, and protected the family and home from hostile forces. Women's and men's roles became institutionalized. Fundamental differences necessitated by physical strength and biological function became social and behavioral patterns that remain imprinted on each of us to this day. Combined with the forces of major historical events, they constitute many of the ingrained perceptions and beliefs that make workplace relationships between the sexes difficult even now.

Society evolved and changed over the ages. History shows that while men generally dominated power, women—at least sometimes—exercised it. Cleopatra ruled the Nile, the Greeks had goddesses as well as

gods of love and war, and the queens of England determined everything from morality to the course of empire, even if it took the absence
of a male heir to elevate them to the throne.

On the American frontier, women incurred a dependency that would
color their role for generations. They were bound by economic necessity, isolation, and limited choices—not always unhappy but without
practical recourse if they were. Few could start their own farms and
ranches. Becoming the proprietor of the local saloon offered the most
likely alternative if a woman wanted to start and run her own business.
Divorce was unheard of, and remarriage after the death of a husband
simply meant repeating the pattern.

The economic interdependence of that agricultural lifestyle lingered
through the evolution of an economy and social system that eventually
made such dependency unnecessary. With all the difficulties of a gender-
segregated workplace, small numbers of women began to prosper on
their own by starting businesses, entering the professions, and securing
employment that made them autonomous, with much kicking and
screaming from their men and from the majority of their female peers.
"Employment emancipated women from dependence. It also accentuated
the limits of emancipation. Although the proportion of employed women
expanded from one-seventh to one-fifth between 1880 and 1910, the over-
whelming majority of them held jobs only as a necessary economic evil,
earning less than men and often less than a decent standard of living,"[4]
writes Peter G. Filene in *Him/Her/Self: Sex Roles in Modern America.*

Long after women had the education and practical wherewithal to live
lives of economic and social independence, most of them remained stuck
in situations that allowed them only limited, domestic roles. Without
making value judgments on any lifestyle a woman chooses freely, the
motivations for the later rights movements for women who wanted a
choice and had none were accumulating and becoming apparent.

World War I was the first modern, large-scale national mobilization
that sent huge numbers of American men off to other lands. Except for
a relative handful of nurses and support people, women remained at
home and, by social default, got a taste of managing and making decisions for themselves. According to Filene:

> The century-old controversy about whether a woman should work
> became, during wartime, vividly tangible. In contrast to men's tradi-
> tional role, which seemed to be rejuvenated by the war, women's tra-
> ditional role seemed more jeopardized than ever. Certainly there
> were the angels of mercy, who rolled bandages and knitted socks.
> But there were also those who operated elevators, pounded black-
> smith anvils, handled cash in bank tellers' cages, dispatched loco-
> motives, manufactured torpedoes, and served in the numerous other

capacities that, until 1917, had belonged exclusively to men. As the United States began its second year of war, women appeared in almost every corner of the labor market. However incongruous, there they were: and, however outrageous, there they had to be if the nation was to mobilize for victory.[5]

The war fueled movements already under way. Socially active women demanded the vote and got it in 1919 and then expressed themselves in many ways—as moral crusaders of Prohibition to the dancing flappers of the liberated 1920s.

The Depression of the 1930s brought the shared tragedy of economic ruin and, ironically, freedom for women to work to support families shattered by it. "The dramatic conflict about sexual equality ended abruptly in 1930. The emergencies of the Depression and the Second World War wrote another script, in which middle-class Americans played other roles in other costumes: the patched clothing of poverty, blue collars instead of white, then military uniforms, and overalls instead of aprons. Questions of common survival, both personal and emotional, pushed the battle between the sexes off stage."[6]

Cataclysmic events like World War II and the civil rights movement forever altered the gender equation in the United States. The war temporarily blew away myths of men's work and women's work—when the men had to fight, the industry to support them had to be populated by those they left at home. A contemporary writer summarized it this way:

> Because of the sudden manpower crisis, women became a precious asset. Thus, a cosmetics salesgirl learned how to operate a 1700-ton keel binder, a beautician took over as switchman for 600 Long Island Railroad trains, women cleaned out blast furnaces in Gary, and a group of Maryland grandmothers manned the police radio in Montgomery County. In Detroit, Buffalo, Kenosha, and Wichita, more women took manufacturing jobs than had been employed in all American industries before Pearl Harbor....There she was, Rosie the Riveter, a heroine in overalls. But, even more significant, she was a middle-aged mother. In sharp contrast to the typical employed woman before the war, three-quarters of the new war workers were married, and one-third had children under the age of fourteen. They transformed the composition of the labor force. By 1945, for the first time in American history, almost a majority of all female workers were wives, most of them older than thirty-five.[7]

Women moved into the factories and businesses and developed skills and abilities that many of them didn't know they had. When the war ended, the sexes generally reverted to their prewar gender roles—he worked, she stayed at home. However, for some women, the seeds of change had been sown. They had enjoyed life in the workplace, were unwilling to step back into the past, and resisted the assumption that happy little women should blissfully endure their "places" in what had become a male-dominated social order. And they voiced their resentment—loudly.

Men reacted with confusion and tried vehemently to protect their territory—the workplace—from what they perceived as invasion by women. "On a more profound level, men resisted women's incursion because it changed a status quo they'd always known and been comfortable with. In that status quo, women were romantic partners or secretaries or, most important, wives, providing an essential support system in the home,"[8] explains Felice N. Schwartz in *Breaking with Tradition: Women and Work, The New Facts of Life.*

It should be noted that not every man was a mean-spirited oppressor; in fact, relatively few men were or are today. The problem then and now is that some people "just don't get it"! We apply this phrase to all of us—women and men alike—because there is enough misunderstanding to go around.

Following this brief reconstruction of the path men and women have traveled together from prehistory to the uneasy truce of the late twentieth century, we offer a perspective on how many myths arose and suggest the mutual understandings that will go a long way toward replacing them with practical realities. We can no more solve our problems in a one-gender vacuum than we can make babies alone.

The Contemporary View. When men returned from war in the mid-1940s, many women temporarily reverted to their roles as wives and mothers. For some, this was a welcome change for a society that had finally ended a nightmare disruption of its traditional ways of living and loving. "Even though an unprecedented number of middle-class wives had jobs, they disdained 'the career woman' and cast themselves contentedly in the role of homemaker,"[9] says Filene. But as time passed, it became clear that reversing the giant strides in social evolution that accompanied the war was not possible. Women had learned to do things on their own. Filene says that "Three-quarters of the working women said that they expected to keep on working after the war. Particularly eager were single women and those above the age of forty-five, but almost 69 percent of working wives also said they wanted to remain employed. 'I love it,' a shipyard welder declared. 'I don't know what I would do if I had to go home tomorrow and just take care of the children and be a housewife....I'd hate to do it. I love the noise and the welding and all the people in the yard.' So said the women workers."[10] Work and a paycheck bought more than groceries and makeup; they introduced women to economic independence and the possibility of broader choices in how they lived, where they lived, and with whom they lived.

Thus, giving up their jobs and returning to a dependent status was not the universally happy event for women that most men assumed it must be. Why would anyone *want* to get up and go to work if she did not have to? Because it is the basis for freedom, became the obvious answer as the postwar decades unfolded and women found their way back into the workplace without the war to add nobility to their efforts. For some women, going to work arose from the simple necessity of making a living when there was no male provider; for others, it was to pay for a higher standard of living; or, for an increasing number of women, it was to achieve the slightly scandalous objectives of independence and personal fulfillment.

The 1960s brought another liberating force to women—reasonably safe, reliable, and convenient birth control. Choice was now possible in another important aspect of women's lives that changed forever their relationships with men. Having sex no longer had to mean the likelihood of bearing a child and the social restrictions that accompany it—nine months of gestation, several years of intense nurturing, two decades of devotion during the child's growth to adulthood, and a lifetime of mother and child bonding and obligations of one sort or another. Without taking anything away from the joys of motherhood if it is a free choice, one can appreciate the life-altering burdens it imposes on women who do not want to experience the cycle. "By separating intercourse from reproduction, the pill had two profound effects. It made possible the sexual revolution, and it enabled women to discover their own sexuality and seek their own sexual pleasure on a new basis,"[11] writes Anthony Astrachan. Reproductive freedom was a prize for women that would forever alter life choices.

The civil rights movement of the 1960s was another major ingredient that changed the way women live their lives today. Although women had gained the right to vote many years earlier, civil rights laws established that they were entitled to important and practical rights that heretofore had been enjoyed only by males.

Regrettably, the by-products of these changes in women's lives were resentment and discrimination in the workplace from those who felt threatened at work and abandoned at home—men. Goodwill and common sense had little impact on loosening the grip of raw power held by the male world that was being asked, and then told, to share its privileges with others.

So what began as the economic and global political necessity of winning a great war became, decades later, a battle between the sexes in the workplace. Freedom and power grudgingly shared gave women their "place" in the working world of the 1950s, 1960s, and 1970s. It was not enough to satisfy women, and it was too much for many men determined to make the full integration of the workforce difficult. Laws led to regulations that in turn led to social action like the equal-opportunity and affirmative-action policies born in the 1960s and implemented in the decades that followed.

Initiatives to lift racial oppression merged with less urgent ones (at least according to the opinion of some people) of sex discrimination, and resentment fueled a backlash. This is how it looked to someone who observed the phenomenon:

> The changes that occurred came from the outside, enforced either by women or social-economic circumstances. And men changed grudgingly, making no more than adjustments in order to preserve as much as possible of their privilege and supposed superiority. They reacted, in other words, as most elites do in response to insurgence: defensively rather than creatively, regarding innovation as a loss of power rather than as a gain of possibilities.[12]

This was true in the early days of the movement, and it remains a concern today. Reasonable people may differ in their interpretations of the backlash. Feminist writers like Susan Faludi and other well-meaning spokespersons for women look backward with sometimes justified resentment, but through negatively focused lenses, to see problems never going away—leaving us with an eternal, mean-spirited contest between the sexes.

Ours is the more optimistic view that we have real incentives for removing the barriers between women and men and that significant numbers of men and women who share the workplace are receptive to doing just that—they are ready for practical guidelines for doing so. Faludi eloquently sketches women-hating monsters lurking in every corner of our culture, and she speaks a certain amount of truth. But others of us see the solution in fixing less sinister, though no less difficult, problems of chronic misunderstanding and unwillingness to embrace the reality of times and relationships that have indeed forever changed.

Tenets of Misunderstanding

Like nearly every other aspect of our lives, work has become a place for intimate interaction between men and women. They are in the workplace in nearly equal numbers now and, increasingly often, as peers. Inequities that were once masked by deliberately separate roles have become apparent and disputed as both sexes compete for the same kinds of success.

When we examine how women and men behave in the struggle to understand each other and define new roles, we see how the assumptions on which many of them act are wrong:

- Some insist that, if work is to be shared equitably, it must be established that men and women are the same.

- Others believe that men and women can work at the same site and at the same jobs with minimal interaction, effectively creating a "separate but equal" work environment.

Both assumptions are incorrect and must be changed to conform to these realities:

- Men and women are not the same but are highly complementary and equally, if differently, capable of accomplishing most tasks.

- It is a demographic and economic fact of life that the sexes will share their work lives as equals and be assigned to male-female job teams based on competency; there is no room for the inefficiency of gender segregation.

Men and women *have* to learn to work together. With equality in the workplace mandated by law, faulty attitudes and ill-founded beliefs about the relative places of the sexes at work must be overcome.

Women and Men Are the Same.   Whether we read feminist writers or listen to men who resist integrating women into their work teams, the message is strikingly similar: women *can* be the same as men or, alternatively, women *must* be the same as men if they are to do the same jobs that men do. The message seems to be that equality requires sameness, and it does not.

In reality, nothing could be further from the truth. Look at a man and a woman. They are conspicuously different. Test them on their physical capabilities, as many kinetic and life scientists have done. Listen to them communicate verbally, the way Deborah Tannen and other scholars of communication have. Watch emotions color their experiences, as psychologists have. Ladies and gentlemen, women and men are *not* the same, never have been, and never will be. The starting point for effectively dealing with gender differences is admitting that the differences are real.

Does it then follow that the sexes cannot have equal rights, perform tasks differently but as well, or aspire to the same kinds of success in virtually every area of life? Certainly not. We would be wise to acknowledge that women and men are different organisms, with complementary, rather than the same, ways of doing things. As we will later discuss more completely, gender differences can be compared by super-imposing two bell curves showing the performance of men and women. The *overlapping* parts (where women and men are the same) are immensely larger than the parts that do *not overlap* (where they are different). "Different but equal" becomes a more acceptable view of the man-woman relationship when one has an accurate comprehension of the relative magnitude of man-woman differences.

Women and Men Have a Choice.   Many men and women still think that the challenge of establishing new kinds of relationships with their gender opposites at work is discretionary—an option they can choose to partake of or ignore. The reality is that they have no choice. The changed gender mix in the workplace is here to stay. The point is indisputably being driven home by demographic projections that foretell a working population already in the pipeline that is dramatically less male-dominated. Women and men are going to be working side by side on the same kinds of jobs from one end of our economy to the other, and from the bottom to the top of most career ladders. They already are, and the trend is for much more of the same.

Gone are the days of saying, "I won't work or travel with a member of the opposite sex—my spouse wouldn't understand...I wouldn't be comfortable...I don't think she can carry her weight." These outmoded excuses will not wash in the contemporary workplace, where hiring and assigning people should be and, in most cases, are done on the basis of competency, not gender. To do otherwise flies in the face of the law—women and men are to work together as peers. The ideal is not yet reality, but we are moving inexorably in that direction for fundamental reasons—there are not enough men to operate the economy alone, and women have the education, the training, and other attributes needed to make us competitive in the world economy.

Men and women have no practical choice except to learn to work together. And, no, we do not have to establish that they are the same to do it. Their diversity and complementary differences will be the basis for successfully sharing careers and making the workplace more productive and enjoyable.

The Inevitability of the Mixed-Gender Workforce

The managing director of human resources at Arthur Anderson & Company, a big eight accounting firm, said in a 1992 interview that during the past five years, 40 percent of the firm's new hires were women. He went on to say what a significant change this represents for his industry.[13] And from a different perspective, at a 1991 meeting of the American Society of Travel Agents, the president of the company that operates Radisson Hotels International reported research "showing a dramatic, continuing trend in the percentage of frequent business travelers who are women."[14] His information showed that women accounted for only 1 percent of the category in 1970 but more than 30 percent in 1991. It is projected that women will account for 50 percent of business travelers by the year 2000. Without even considering how men and women relate at work, we can see from the figures that business services are being managed and marketed in ways that reflect an adaptation to the realities of changing demographics. Bright and airy decor is more prevalent than the dark, men's club atmosphere of the past, for example. Women like it, and men don't mind, according to the research. These examples reflect the impact of the changing demographics of the workplace on the business community and those who serve it.

Any way we look at it, we find that the workplace has become and will remain a two-gender domain. With fewer exceptions than ever, most jobs can be done either by a woman or a man. The ratio of men to women in the population has been declining for 50 years, with fewer men per 100 women over the time span. The participation rates of women and men in a labor force that traditionally favored men are becoming more equal. The trained workforce coming from our colleges is dramatically more female in fields not previously populated by women in large numbers. Management training programs in industry, and the working ranks from which the next generation's leaders will come, all include more women. The talented and energetic youth who will fuel our economy tomorrow are growing up and being prepared for their roles today, and gender-track patterns of the past have radically changed.

Parity has not been achieved by any means, but a significant new bulge of women ready to assume unprecedented roles is moving through the demographic snake and emerging into a workforce that is distinctly bigender—not by fiat, edict, or the luxury of choice but rather by the actuality of who is coming on line to staff the jobs of the future. The data in this chapter graphically illustrate that women and men *will* be working together in increasing numbers, and as peers.

The Demographics of Change

Even casually looking at the numbers provides instant verification of the trend toward a greater prominence of women in the workforce. Bureau of the Census and Department of Labor data paint a picture of working America with nearly equal percentages of women and men, and the trend in this direction is continuing every year in numerous occupational groups. Examine the data closely, and we discover that women, in spite of the inequities that correctly remain at issue, are increasing their earnings, taking their places in nearly every occupational field, and assuming higher levels of responsibility.

These data also can be used to show the half-empty glass. Women are progressing gradually, they are encountering obstacles and unfair practices along the way, and although the earnings gap has narrowed, they have not caught up with men doing the same work. Median annual earnings for women in real dollars for year-round, full-time work went from 63.9 percent of men's earnings in 1951, to a low of 56.6 percent in 1973, to 71.1 percent in 1990[15] and 74 percent in 1991.[16]

We do not dispute the importance of understanding these limitations. For example, Susan Faludi's book *Backlash* illustrates how general data can be refined to show apparently favorable trends that, in fact, are masking stalled progress for many women. However, we choose not to discuss at length here what is well documented elsewhere. Our purpose is to show indisputable trends that will inevitably change tomorrow's workplace with or without resistance, even with all the obstacles remaining in women's way. These overall trends, general though they may be, show progress toward an egalitarian workforce and validate the urgent need for women and men to learn to work together as peers. An unemotional look at available statistics illustrates the inevitability of the coming change.

In the Workplace. In this section, we present statistics for working women in three areas: (1) *the overall workforce*—the sweeping national picture measured by the Bureau of Labor Statistics, (2) *government*—a specialized segment of the job market seen as different from the private sector in terms of hiring, retaining, and promoting people, and (3) *business ownership*—the most independent expression of women's economic initiative. Although overlap undoubtedly exists in the categories, the data show how women are doing in different environments. Together, the three measures paint a comprehensive picture of progress for women that would be incomplete without the other two. Gains in the government sector, for example, would never be accepted as an indicator of how women are progressing in private industry, much less in developing their own businesses. A look at all three, however, is an impressive measure.

The Overall Workforce. Women still hold large numbers of traditionally female jobs in occupational groups like nursing, clerical support, and noncollege teaching, but their numbers in male-dominated fields and their professional levels within those fields are growing. The trend is toward women breaking out of their traditional stereotypes and assuming new kinds of jobs, in terms of both what they do and their level within occupational category.

According to the 1990 census figures for the entire population, 12.4 percent of all workers are in executive, administrative, or managerial positions, up from 7.6 percent in 1970 and 10.3 percent in 1980.[17] In metropolitan areas the trend is even more pronounced: 20 percent in Washington, D.C., 16 percent in San Francisco and Boston, and 14 percent or more in seven other urban areas.[18]

These fields have always included women, who constitute a growing percentage of the senior and nontraditional positions. Figure 1-1 shows where women stood in 1991 and 1983 in a number of occupational groups. While they accounted for 42.6 percent of all full-time workers in 1991, at 47 percent they accounted for nearly half of the Managerial and Professional Workers category. More than half of the Professional Specialty Occupations group—50.4 percent—was made up of women. The Health Diagnosing Occupations category, which includes physicians, was composed of 27.2 percent women. The physicians group alone was 26.6 percent women (detail not shown in Figure 1-1). More than one in three people in the Mathematical and Computer Scientists category were women; nearly a quarter of the Lawyers and Judges category was made up of women.

In 25 of the 41 occupational groups charted in Figure 1-1, the 1991 bars of the graph extend beyond those of 1983, most of them significantly, indicating dramatic increases in the percentage of women working in major occupational categories during the eight years from 1983 to 1991. With the exception of Engineering and College and University Teachers categories, the occupations that became less female were those where women welcome a better balance—Administrative Support and Clerical, Health Assessment and Treatment, Health Technologists and Technicians, and others. In general, these losses are complemented by gains in nontraditional occupational categories for women—fewer clerical positions versus more management positions, fewer nurses versus more doctors, and so on. The net loss in the total percentage of women, 43.7 in 1983 to 42.6 in 1991, is relatively insignificant compared to the favorably shifting dynamics within the occupational groups.

These statistics and the more detailed sources from which they come confirm conventional wisdom as well. More women teach below the college level than at it—71.8 versus 33.3 percent—and not many women are engineers—8.1 percent. Almost all nurses—93.3 percent—and secretaries—98.5 percent—are women, but there are few women in the construction trades—1.2 percent. If we stop there, however, we miss the equally important point that, for most of the traditionally male fields,

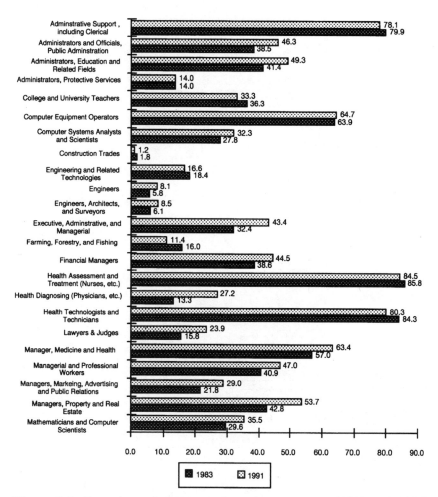

Figure 1-1. Percentage of women workers, by occupation (1983 and 1991). Note: Occupational groups were chosen to show selected, representative fields. It was not possible to maintain the subordination of categories in this simplified presentation (for example, Managers, Medicine and Health, is actually a subcategory of Managerial and Professional Workers). (*U.S. Department of Labor, Bureau of Labor Statistics, Current Population Survey, 1991 annual averages, published in* Employment and Earnings, January 1992. *Supplemented by unpublished 1992 Labor Force Statistics Table 5 and Annual Average Industry and Occupation Tables for Year Ending December 1983, Table 30.*)

such as the six major occupational categories in Figure 1-2, the trend is toward change, with the percentage of women increasing significantly in fields where they formerly had no place.

Figure 1-2 shows that the number of women employed in executive, administrative, and managerial positions increased by nearly 40 percent

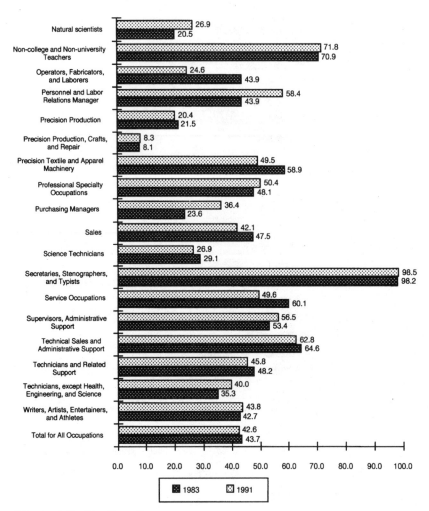

Figure 1-1. (*Continued*)

in the eight years from 1983 to 1991. For engineers, even though the absolute numbers are relatively small, the increase for women was almost 40 percent. During the same period, the number of female mathematical and computer scientists grew by about 20 percent, and natural scientists by over 30 percent. The number of women in health diagnosing occupations more than doubled, with an increase of 104 percent, and the ranks of women lawyers and judges expanded more than 51 percent.

These fields represent some of the most sought-after employment opportunities in our economy, and women are clearly gaining ground in

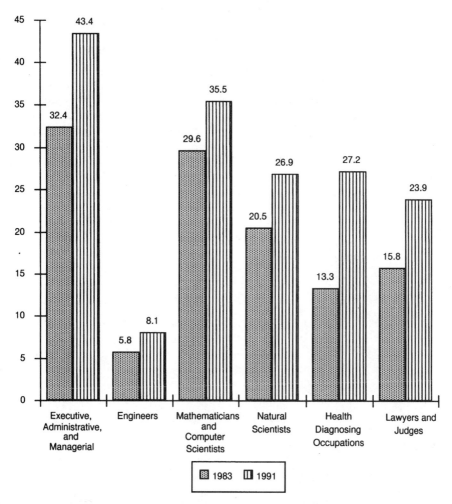

Figure 1-2. Change in the percentage of women in six major occupational categories (1983 to 1991). (*U.S. Bureau of the Census*, Statistical Abstract of the United States: 1991. *Adapted from no. 652, pp. 395–397 and U.S. Department of Labor, Bureau of Labor Statistics, Current Population Survey, 1991 annual averages. Published in* Employment and Earnings, January 1992.)

each of them. This kind of progress does not mean that the problem of disproportionately limited opportunities for women is solved. Except for the Executive, Administrative, and Managerial category, where they hold 43.4 percent of the jobs, women are still less represented in the occupational areas in Figure 1-2 than they are in the total workforce, of which they constitute 42.6 percent, according to Department of Labor Current Population Survey averages, which were the bases for the figures.

These statistics are demographic pointers in a changing workforce, and they show a trend toward women working side by side with men in increasingly equal numbers, in all kinds of occupations and at nearly all levels. Reports in 1991 that women made up 42.6 percent of the workforce have more significance than in previous decades, when such numbers glossed over the fact that while women held a high percentage of *total jobs,* they were primarily *women's jobs.* Today, more of those 42.6 percent work in *mainstream jobs,* with fewer of them pigeonholed in fields traditionally populated by women.

Government. The upward mobility of women is easy to demonstrate in the well-documented federal workforce. Figure 1-3 shows that the percentage of women in all government grades increased over the

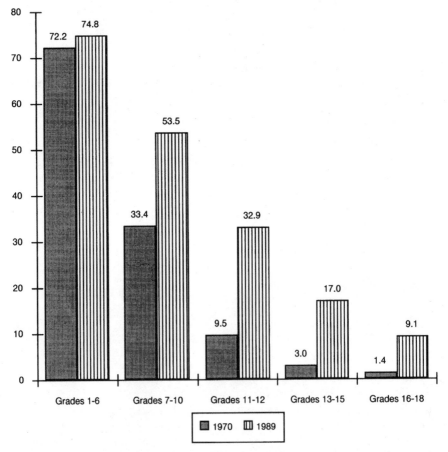

Figure 1-3. Percentage of women in federal workforce according to civil service grade (1970 to 1989). (*U.S. Bureau of the Census,* Statistical Abstract of the United States: 1991. *Adapted from no. 530, p. 329.*)

20-year period from 1970 to 1989 and that the greatest gains were at the senior levels.

Although it is apparent that most women in the federal civil service still work in the lower ranks, it should be noted that most of the available jobs are in grades 1 through 10. In 1989, 65 percent of the jobs were in the first 10 grades, and 83 percent in the first 12 grades. The number of women in the various grades shown in Figure 1-3 increased between 1970 and 1989 by the following percentages (from lowest to highest): 103, 160, 346, 566, and 650. Although smaller numbers of women work at the higher levels of the federal bureaucracy, women have made their most dramatic gains at those levels. With that said, it is important to note that 90 percent of the senior executive service positions are occupied by men, and women in the executive branch, for example, earn only 66 percent as much as men.[19] While progress is being made, obviously more is needed.

At state and local levels, women hold 41 percent of the jobs but fill only 27 percent of the official and administrative positions.[20] While women make up a high percentage of overall state and local employees, they still occupy a disproportionate number of lower-level positions,[21] according to a comprehensive study in the fall 1991 edition of *Public Administration Review*. However, bright spots existed in 1987 data provided in this study:

- In Arizona women filled 13 percent of the state's top eight civil service grades.

- In California 17 percent of city mayors were women versus 9.2 percent nationally.

- In Texas 18 percent of the heads of state agencies, 25.1 percent of all administrators, and 48.4 percent of all professionals employed were women.[22]

In a career advancement survey of the states of Alabama, Arizona, California, Texas, Utah, and Wisconsin, researchers concluded that women were promoted at younger ages and with less time in rank than men, and better than at the federal level.[23] While the authors were appropriately cautious about the progress of women in state and local government, the trend in the direction of a larger presence in more significant roles was apparent.

Business Ownership. Another measure of the advancing position of women in the economy is business ownership. The number of firms owned by women increased from 2,612,600 in 1982 to 4,114,800 in 1987, according to the *1991 Statistical Abstract of the United States*. It reported that sales and receipts for their businesses rose from a substantial $98,292,000 in 1982 to $278,138,000 in 1987, when 3,102,700 workers were employed and an annual payroll of $40,885,000 was generated. While women-owned businesses covered a full spectrum of economic activities, dollar volumes were highest in retail trade ($85,418,000), services ($61,123,000), manufacturing ($30,914,000), and construction ($20,302,000).[24] Small Business Administration figures classify 85 percent of women-owned businesses in the retail, finance, insurance, real estate, and services areas but also show that growth in nontraditional fields like engineering and manufacturing is accelerating at a rate faster than that of men.[25]

American Management Association's *Management Review* reported in its March 1992 issue that:

- Women are starting new businesses at two to five times the rate of men.

- Forty-four percent of women-owned businesses have gross sales of more than $250,000. Eighteen percent have gross sales of more than $1 million.

- The number of women-owned sole proprietorships increased by 62 percent between 1980 and 1986, from 2.5 million to 4.1 million; today women own an estimated 6 million businesses.

- Women-owned businesses grew by 35 percent in 1989–1990.

- By 2000, 40 to 50 percent of all businesses will be owned by women.[26]

The *Management Review* article concluded that since women entered the workforce in large numbers only beginning in the 1960s and 1970s, they are just now getting the MBAs, management experience, business acumen, and confidence to move into entrepreneurship.[27]

The movement of women into enterprises they own is partly a reaction to the glass ceiling, a topic discussed fully in Chapter 5. The *glass ceiling* is an invisible barrier that keeps women from advancing to the top of the corporate ladder in businesses controlled by men. But whatever their motivations, according to the numbers, women now have a significant position in the ownership of American business, and their influence is growing. They may not yet be the captains of industry, but they are assuming roles that better position them to be in the future.

Whether the measure is the overall workforce, the ranks of government workers, or owners of private sector businesses, the economic significance of women is growing. The broad measures of women's place in the economy discussed above confirm their emerging prominence in the workforce. While women will remain high-percentage workers in many of the categories traditionally defined as "women's jobs" as well, the statistics illustrate how they are making their presence felt across the board in the world of work. The importance of the statistics quoted here is their breadth and comprehensiveness. They no longer chronicle just the forced imposition of women on government agencies and contractors by regulators but the emergence of women as significant players in the general economy.

According to *Time,* the acceptance of women by the leaders of industry is increasingly viewed as a necessity and not just the politically correct thing to do. "Noble as these efforts are, the chief executives pushing open the doors to the executive suite are acting more out of pragmatism than probity. 'It doesn't make sense to cut yourself off from half the talented people in this world,' observes George Harvey, chief executive of Pitney Bowes....'If we're known as a good place to work, more good people will want to work here. That will make us more competitive, which means more sales and higher stock prices.'"[28]

Harvey's view more nearly reflects that of those who control American businesses than it did a few years ago. They see the trends and expect their employees to make workplace diversity succeed. With the Bureau of Labor Statistics forecasting a 26 percent increase in the women's labor force compared to 16 percent for men from 1990 to 2005, it is clear that the challenge of working in and managing a mixed-gender workforce will not be going away.[29]

In Colleges and Universities

Enrollments. Trends showing women moving into the mainstream that are clear in the job classification statistics of the Department of Labor and surveys of the Bureau of the Census are even more apparent in measures of the Department of Education. Figure 1-4 shows the historic path of college enrollment for women and men in the United States since the late 1860s.

- From shortly after the Civil War, when the recording of such data began, to the 1920s, when college enrollments started to increase, men led women, modestly at first and then more dramatically.

- After World War II, when the numbers of those pursuing a college education began to increase significantly, the lines of Figure 1-4 show that higher education was primarily a male enterprise.This is accounted for by forces as ingrained as the cultural practice of preparing men for leadership roles ahead of women and as progressive as the GI Bill, which opened higher education to socioeconomic classes of men who had never partaken of education before.

- In the 1960s the numbers climbed steeply, and almost in parallel, for both genders as the relative position of women stabilized.

- In the 1970s enrollments of women rose sharply as enrollments for men begin to level off.

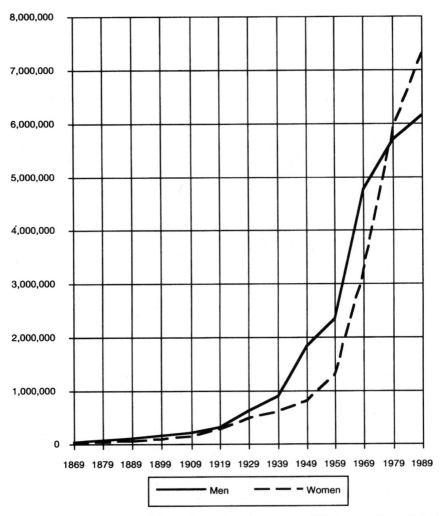

Figure 1-4. College enrollment for men and women (1869 to 1989). (*U.S. Department of Education, National Center for Education Statistics*, Digest of Education Statistics, 1991. *Adapted from Tables 160 and 161, pp. 166 and 167.*)

- In the late 1970s, the lines for men and women reached an equal point, and into the 1980s, college enrollments of women far outpaced those of men—7,302,371 women to 6,155,484 men by 1989.

The trend of women outnumbering men in colleges is projected to continue into the next century. According to the National Center for Education Statistics, "Women will continue to outpace men in higher education enrollments. By the year 2001, they [women] will number 7.9 million. [The number of men] is projected to be 6.5 million."[30]

Degrees Conferred. The most dramatic portrayals of what the American workplace of tomorrow will look like can be found in the output of its colleges and universities. At the first three degree levels, the switch from male to female dominance has already occurred. Figures 1-5, 1-6, and 1-7 graphically show this reversal occurring from the mid-1970s through the early 1980s. This trend was sustained through 1989 and is projected to continue to the end of the century. The classic X pattern of revers-

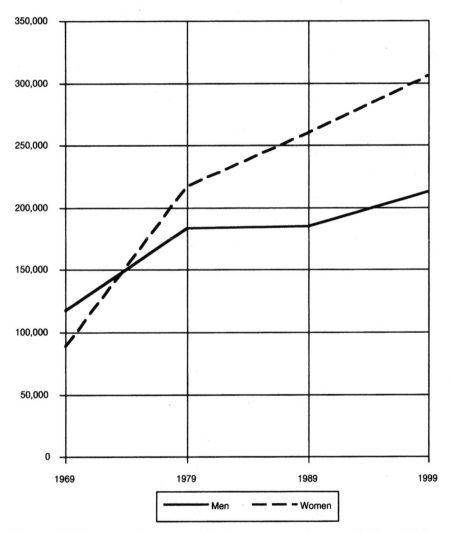

Figure 1-5. Associate degrees conferred upon men and women (1969 to 1999). (*U.S. Department of Education, National Center for Education Statistics*, Digest of Education Statistics, 1991. *Adapted from Table 228, p. 234.*)

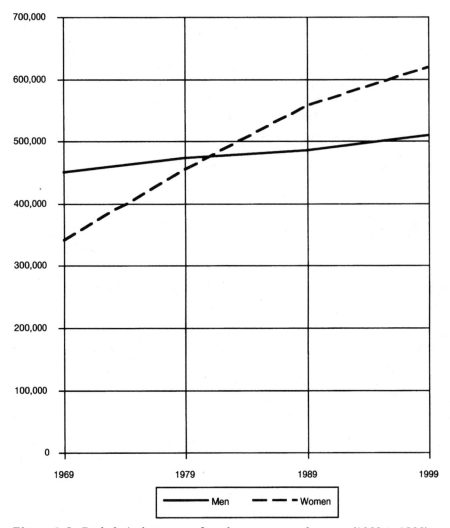

Figure 1-6. Bachelor's degrees conferred upon men and women (1969 to 1999). (*U.S. Department of Education, National Center for Education Statistics,* Digest of Education Statistics, 1991. *Adapted from Table 228, p. 234.*)

ing trends is clear in each of these graphs. In the year 2000 the American labor force should be composed of 44 percent more women holding associate degrees than men (306,000 versus 213,000), 22 percent more women holding bachelor's degrees than men (620,000 versus 509,000), and 13 percent more women holding master's degrees than men (195,000 versus 173,000).

Figure 1-8 shows the same kinds of data for first professional degrees—law and medical practitioner degrees (such as the M.D.) as

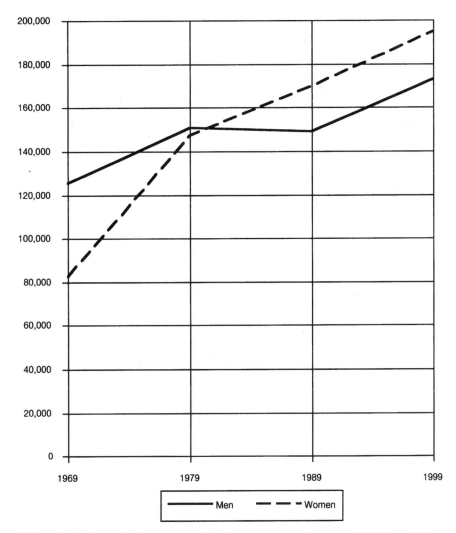

Figure 1-7. Master's degrees conferred upon men and women (1969 to 1999). (*U.S. Department of Education, National Center for Education Statistics*, Digest of Education Statistics, 1991. *Adapted from Table 228, p. 234.*)

opposed to the ritual master's and academic doctor's degrees (M.A., M.S., Ph.D., and so forth). The trend in this category shows a steady upward climb of women from the late 1960s to the end of the century. Note that men are projected to be ahead of women in absolute numbers—expected to earn 55,300 first professional degrees compared with 36,000 for women in 1999. The decline of male graduates through the 1980s then reverses in the 1990s to progress in parallel with the smaller but growing women's cohort.

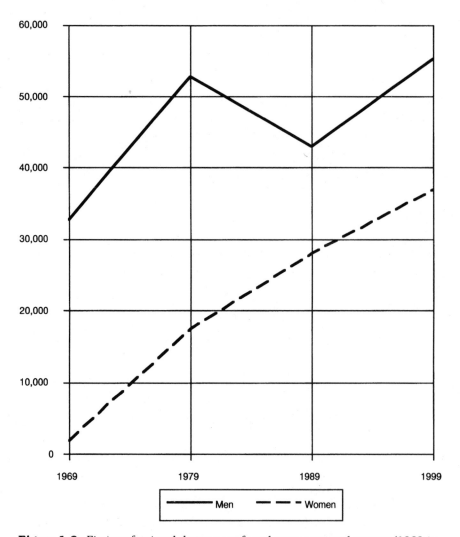

Figure 1-8. First professional degrees conferred upon men and women (1969 to 1999). (*U.S. Department of Education, National Center for Education Statistics, Digest of Education Statistics, 1991. Adapted from Table 228, p. 234.*)

The number of traditional academic doctor's degrees is shown in Figure 1-9. Female degree recipients are closing the gap; they have moved steadily upward from 1969 and are projected to continue this upward movement through the end of the century. The number of men earning doctoral degrees declined in the 1970s, rebounded slightly in the 1980s, and is projected to head slowly down again through the 1990s. Men are projected to end the 1990s with 22,900 doctor's degree recipients annually compared with 18,300 for women, again ahead in

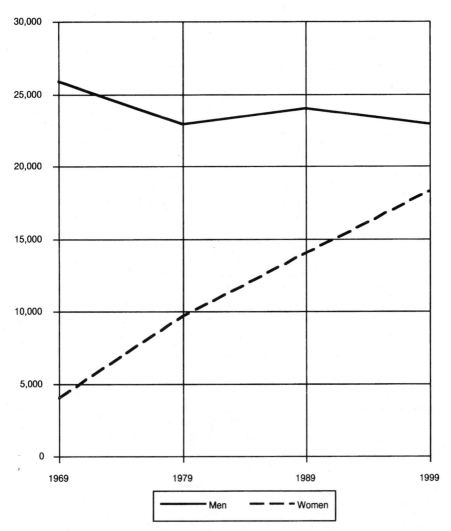

Figure 1-9. Doctor's degrees conferred upon men and women (1969 to 1999). (*U.S. Department of Education, National Center for Education Statistics*, Digest of Education Statistics, 1991. *Adapted from Table 228, p. 234.*)

the numbers but facing a reversal if the current trend continues beyond the year 2000.

Total numbers of degrees reflected by Figures 1-5 to 1-9, is one thing; percentage of degrees awarded according to field, contrasted over nearly two decades, gives an interesting perspective on the changes. As Figure 1-10 shows, bachelor's degrees awarded to women increased by 19.8 percent between 1971 (43.4 percent) and 1988 (52.0 percent). Every academic field in Figure 1-10 shows an increased share for women. For

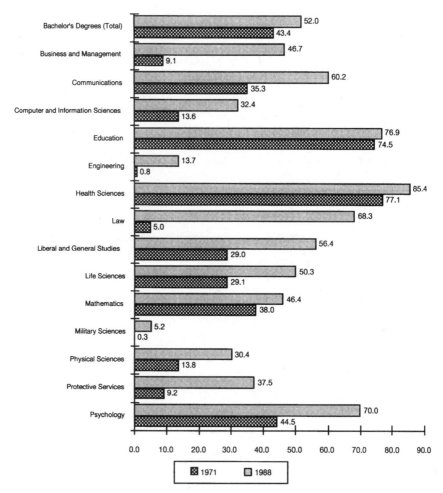

Figure 1-10. Percentage of bachelor's degrees conferred upon women, according to field (1971 and 1988). (*U.S. Bureau of the Census,* Statistical Abstract of the United States: 1991. *Adapted from no. 284, p. 168.*)

this period, increases in the percentage of bachelor's degrees conferred on women, and the percentage of increase, in several high-interest fields were as follows:

- 9.1 to 46.7 percent in business and management (an increase of 413 percent)

- 13.6 to 32.4 percent in computer and information sciences (an increase of 138 percent)

- 0.8 to 13.7 percent in engineering (an increase of 1612 percent)

- 77.1 to 85.4 percent in health sciences (an increase of 11 percent)
- 5.0 to 68.3 percent in law (an increase of 1266 percent)
- 38.0 to 46.4 percent in mathematics (an increase of 22 percent)
- 13.8 to 30.4 percent in the physical sciences (an increase of 120 percent)

Figure 1-11 illustrates similar kinds of increases at the master's degree level. Women increased their share of all master's degrees by 28 percent, from 40.1 to 51.5 percent over the 1971 to 1988 time period. In some of

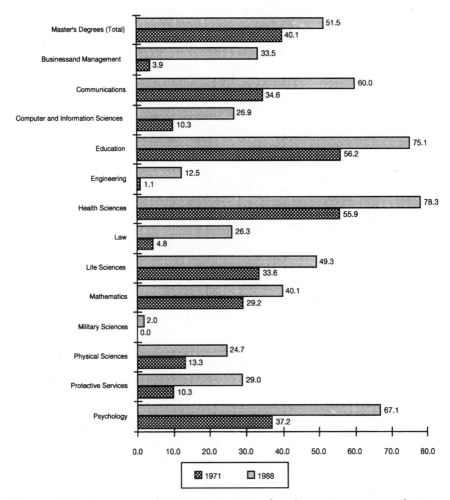

Figure 1-11. Percentage of master's degrees conferred upon women, according to field (1971 and 1988). (*U.S. Bureau of the Census*, Statistical Abstract of the United States: 1991. *Adapted from no. 284, p. 168.*)

the nontraditional fields over this time span, the increases for women receiving master's degrees were as follows:

- 3.9 to 33.5 percent in business and management (an increase of 759 percent)
- 10.3 to 26.9 percent in computer and information sciences (an increase of 161 percent)
- 1.1 to 12.5 percent in engineering (an increase of 1036 percent)
- 55.9 to 78.3 percent in health sciences (an increase of 40 percent)
- 4.8 to 26.3 percent in law (an increase of 448 percent)
- 29.2 to 40.1 percent in mathematics (an increase of 37 percent)
- 13.3 to 24.7 percent in the physical sciences (an increase of 86 percent)

The gains made by women in receiving doctor's degrees from 1971 to 1988 are delineated in Figure 1-12. Overall doctoral awards jumped 146 percent, from 14.3 percent in 1971 to 35.2 percent in 1988, with Computer and Information Sciences the only field showing a decline in the percentage of women degree recipients. For the same fields shown above at the bachelor's and master's degree levels, the changes in the percentages of women receiving doctor's degrees over the 1971–1988 time period are:

- 2.9 to 23.1 percent in business and management (an increase of 696 percent)
- 16.4 to 11.2 percent in computer and information sciences (a decrease of 32 percent)
- 0.6 to 7.0 percent in engineering (an increase of 1066 percent)
- 16.3 to 56.7 percent in health sciences (an increase of 247 percent)
- 0 to 25.8 percent in law
- 7.8 to 16.8 percent in mathematics (an increase of 115 percent)
- 5.6 to 18.0 percent in the physical sciences (an increase of 221 percent)

If college degrees in general are the gateway to the occupational mainstream for any group of outsiders seeking entry into what most of us think of as the more rewarding areas of the labor force, professional degrees are the key to prestige, status, and money. Figure 1-13 demonstrates that women moved dramatically forward in the fields of medicine, dentistry, and law during the nearly 30 years from 1960 to 1988. In each of the three categories, women jumped from bottom-rung participation to receiving one-third of the degrees in medicine, receiving more than one-quarter in dentistry, and moving toward one-half in law.

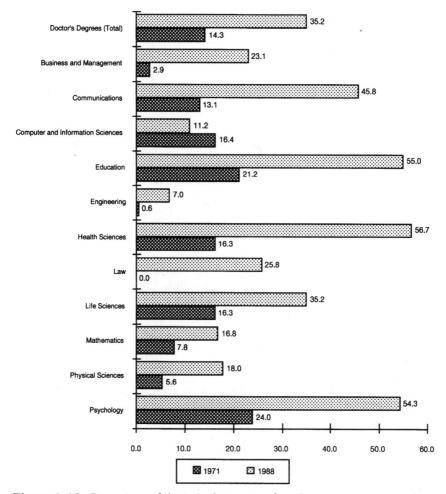

Figure 1-12. Percentage of doctor's degrees conferred upon women, according to field (1971 and 1988). (*U.S. Bureau of the Census, Statistical Abstract of the United States: 1991. Adapted from no. 284, p. 168.*)

Attitudes. Another changing perspective on women may be seen from considering data measuring the attitudes of college freshmen over the past 25 years. The Higher Education Research Institute at the University of California at Los Angeles has published such data, the results of annual surveys by the Cooperative Institutional Research Program, which was established by the American Council on Education. The study is massive, each year surveying more than 250,000 full-time students in a nationally representative sample of about 600 colleges and universities.

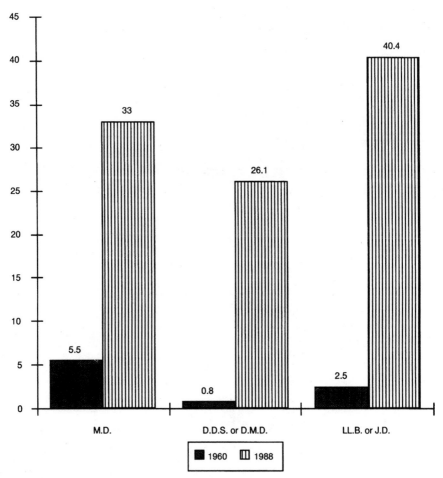

Figure 1-13. Changes in the percentages of women earning professional degrees (1960 to 1988). (*U.S. Bureau of the Census*, Statistical Abstract of the United States: 1991. *Adapted from No. 285, p. 169.*)

In the 1991 report, *The American Freshman: Twenty-Five Year Trends, 1966–1990,* researchers Eric L. Dey, Alexander W. Astin, and William S. Korn saw dramatic changes since 1966 in educational aspirations, preferences for college majors and career choices, and political and social activism. In the 25-year period, the changing role of women in American society was the most notable factor. The authors observed the following changes in the attitudes of freshmen women:

- *Large shifts in preferences for majors and careers,* away from the traditional fields of teaching, nursing, social work, and homemaking, and toward business, law, medicine, science, and engineering; also show a greater interest in pursuing advanced degrees

- *Behavioral changes,* including increased cigarette smoking, decreased use of tranquilizers, and greater participation in competitive sports

- *Attitudinal changes,* including much greater support for job equality for women and rejection of the traditional homemaker role for married women

- *Value changes,* reflected in more widespread endorsement by women of traditionally male materialistic and power goals

- *Demographic changes,* reflected in more women entering higher education[31]

Among their findings on women's career interests:

- Increased interest in engineering (tenfold increase since 1966)

- Increased interest in law (750 percent increase)

- Decline in interest in business since the mid-1980s but still five times what it was in 1966

- Rebound in interest in nursing, from a low in the mid-1980s to one-quarter higher than it was in 1966[32]

The number of students wanting to be "very well off financially" nearly doubled between 1970 and 1987, whereas the percent of students interested in developing a "meaningful philosophy of life" dropped by more than one-half. Since 1987 both of these trends have somewhat reversed, indicating early signs of a shift away from a strictly materialistic philosophy. Recently, men and women alike showed renewed interest in social action and altruism after declines in the 1970s and 1980s— reflected in their college majors and career aspirations.[33]

A glance across the trend lines of Figures 1-5 through 1-13 leaves the unmistakable impression that women will be assuming a much greater role in the trained workforce of the future. As the occupational trends indicate, women are already on the scene in many occupations; every sign points to an even larger presence in the years to come. The vivid reality of workplace and college enrollment and degree completion statistics leaves no doubt that women and men will be working together in the same fields, as peers, in the years to come.

In the Population.   Figures 1-14 through 1-18 provide several closing snapshots of where women have been and are probably going in our society. While some of them could be considered workforce statistics,

they also graphically illustrate the place of women in the general population. In their own way, each of the trends portrayed in these charts
promises a stable-to-increasing role for women. They reinforce more
broadly the messages of the previous sections—that more women are
working in, and being educated for, roles traditionally occupied by men.

   Figure 1-14 gives an overall picture of how women have steadily
become a larger part of the labor force. The projection for the year 2005
(labor force consisting of 47 percent women) is a 26 percent increase
over the 38 percent position in 1970. Women are moving toward parity
with men in the American workforce.

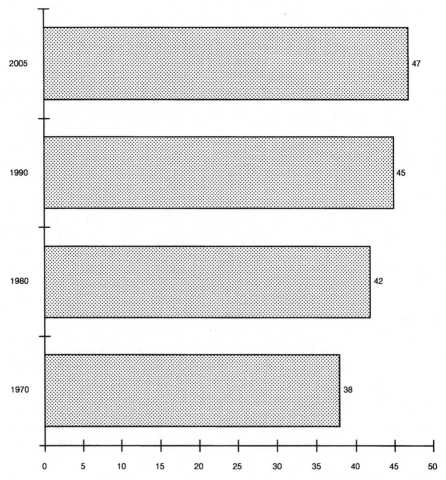

Figure 1-14. Women as a percentage of the labor force. (Facts on Women,
*"Women Workers: Outlook to 2005," U.S. Department of Labor, Women's Bureau,
January 1992, p.1.*)

Another way to look at the roles women and men play in the population is to consider their rates of participation in the labor force—the number of men versus the number of women who work or look for work. Although Figure 1-15 shows that a higher percentage of men than women work, and will continue to work, according to the projections, the trend for men is level and that of women is ascending. The difference between more than 6 out of 10 women versus 7 out of 10 men working is insignificant in terms of sharing the workplace—men and women are, and will continue to be, in the workplace in nearly equal numbers.

Figure 1-16 shows the decrease in the number of traditional stay-at-home housewives during the 15 years from 1975 to 1989, when the num-

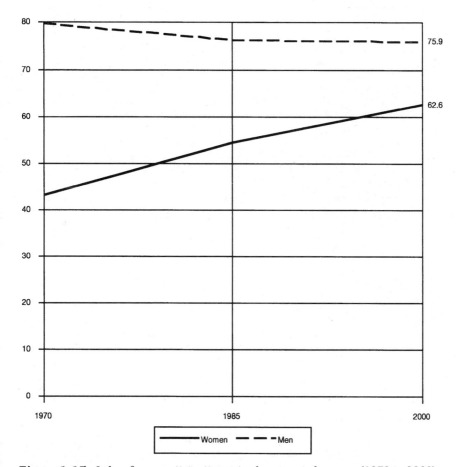

Figure 1-15. Labor force participation rates by men and women (1970 to 2000). (*U.S. Bureau of the Census*, Statistical Abstract of the United States: 1991. *Adapted from no. 632, p. 384.*)

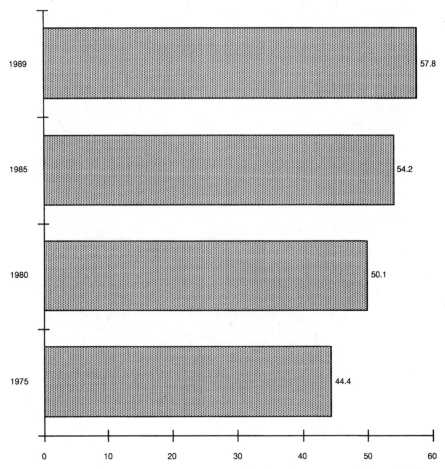

Figure 1-16. Percentage of working wives (husbands present; 1975 to 1989). (*U.S. Bureau of the Census,* Statistical Abstract of the United States: 1991. *Adapted from No. 664, p. 391.*)

ber of working wives (with husbands in the home) increased by 30 percent—from 44.4 to 57.8.

Figure 1-17 depicts one basic measure of women's influence in the population—their numbers of potential voters to influence the political process and, in turn, their place in the society. While the numbers themselves, 93.6 million women versus 84.5 million men in 1988, mean little, the fact is that women who are eligible to vote outnumber their male counterparts. This trend is continuing, giving women potential dominance in the voting-age populace that shows no signs of diminishing.

Figure 1-18 gives one last look at women relative to men in the general population. Since World War II, with the exception of a very mod-

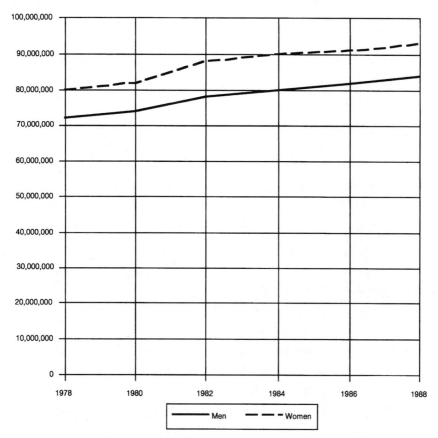

Figure 1-17. Women and men of voting age (1978 to 1988). (*U.S. Bureau of the Census*, Statistical Abstract of the United States: 1991. *Adapted from no. 450, p. 268.*)

est rebound in 1989, the ratio of men to women has been in steady decline. At least numerically, women are not a minority group.

The Challenge of the Future

Few relationships are more complex than the one between a man and a woman who spend enough time in each other's company for a biological reaction to one another to be triggered. Workforce projections remove any doubt that women and men will be spending more time together professionally in the future; equally unlikely is the possibility that human sexuality will evaporate. Therefore, as the sexes find themselves working side by side for the indefinite future, they must learn to

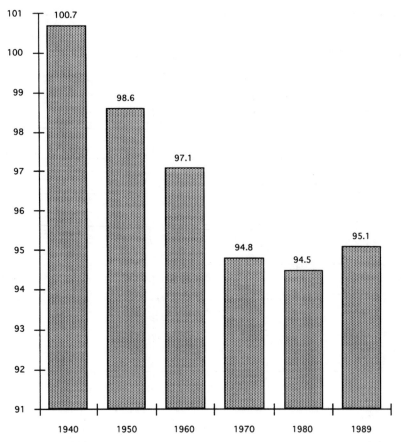

Figure 1-18. Ratio of men to women (men per 100 women; 1940 to 1989).
(*U.S. Bureau of the Census*, Statistical Abstract of the United States: 1991.
Adapted from no. 20, p. 17.)

get along as coworkers, not merely tolerate each other. To this end, they
need to:

- Increase their understanding of one another
- Acknowledge their differences, appreciate their underlying similarities, and then capitalize on the uniqueness they each bring to accomplishing a task
- Accept that there are alternative ways of reaching professional objectives together—often more efficiently and enjoyably as mixed-gender
  teams

- Agree to accept the obligation to act in good faith to change what negative behaviors and attitudes they can and to effectively manage the rest.

We all have every incentive to do these things, for, at the least, men and women have no choice but to adjust to a workplace in which they will work together as peers in virtually equal numbers. Since informed people can make the transition successfully, it is necessary to learn a great deal about one another—some of it seemingly obvious, some of it new and revealing. Examining the past helps explain today's problems. Looking to the future anticipates the changes women and men need to make if they are to successfully live the altered relationships that await them—as individuals and as members of organizations.

The challenge for us all—women and men alike—is to know one another well enough to accept a level playing field with players who are selected on the basis of their ability to perform, not their gender. In those few remaining occupations where the genuinely unique attributes of either a woman or a man are essential, let men be men and women be women—different but equal. But for the overwhelming majority of tasks women and men potentially share, their differences represent an invitation to partake of productive and complementary diversity. In such an environment, let people be people—who have no need to hide real gender differences or to exaggerate these differences to the extent that harassment, inequity, or lost opportunities for men and women to be their best together are the result.

2
The Myths and
Realities of
Gender Differences

Every time we think we've figured out how men and women accomplish the tasks of ordinary living, life teaches us another lesson about how they do these tasks differently. More often than not, they will both get the job done. Usually it's just a question of different approaches and whether the differences have anything to do with a job well done.

For example, Angela arrived at the office last winter minus her glasses and explained that she was wearing contact lenses. One of her colleagues, David, decided to get a pair for himself. A few days later, in a group of new contact lens wearers that included another man and three women, he tried to show the optometrist that he could successfully insert and remove his new lenses. As he struggled with reflexes that made a shambles of the simple technique each time his finger approached his eye, one by one the women handled the task effortlessly, leaving him and the other man behind.

David had come face to face with a difference in ability between the sexes. "Why," he wondered, "could they do it so easily, and I've been working on the same eye for fifteen minutes?" The answer is simple: most women apply eye makeup from an early age and therefore have little difficulty holding the eye open and touching it with a contact lens. For men, their first contact lenses bring a humbling recognition of skills they don't have. When this happens in the company of women who

seem to be "naturally" superior at the task, these men have an experience that has been familiar to those lacking "natural" advantages in our
society for years—they have a lower status because of skills they
haven't learned. For men, this is a frustrating role reversal in a system
where they have traditionally enjoyed "natural" superiority in most of
their encounters with women.

Different Kinds of Differences

Often the variations in ability between men and women are no more
than the result of their different experiences and opportunities. Whether
the situation is as serious as a career stopped short because a woman
can't get the line management background she needs to be a "complete"
candidate for a top job or as trivial as a man who can't insert contact
lenses, women and men face limitations in their lives that are based on
the experiences they have as members of their gender.

■ Some differences are straightforward and real—women bear children, and men don't. For a time, at least, this reality alters their living
  patterns; that is, pregnancy and childbirth impose physical limitations on women that men never endure.

■ Other differences are myths, for example, assuming that every
  woman experiences the worst-case limitations of menstruation and
  menopause and, therefore, as a group, women are inherently inca-
  pable of sustaining a professional effort comparable to that of men.

■ Still other differences are transitory "realities"—limitations that are
  real enough when they happen (David's inability to insert a contact
  lens) but not truly limitations in the sense of a "natural" incompe-
  tence (he learned to override the reflex).

Who would have imagined that years spent applying eye makeup
might give women a skill that would put men at a disadvantage? Man-
woman differences like these are common. Some of them (for example,
the way they throw a ball or sort clothes for a load of laundry) are
viewed as laughably unimportant, while others (for example, the real
impact of childbirth or menopause) are seen as genuine career impedi-
ments. In the workplace, most gender differences take a toll on the outsiders—women—who are trying to gain respect and equal treatment
from the insiders—men.

Recognizing Differences for
What They Are

To keep culturally reinforced differences from further polarizing women and men at work, they need to separate myth from reality and use the sometimes contrasting, but often complementary, talents of their genders to their mutual advantage. Goodwill, open minds, and a measure of objectivity are needed to judge the significance of gender differences fairly. Many differences cannot be scientifically proved, yet few people could deny that women and men *are* obviously different in important ways. The real question is not "Are women and men different?" but "What impact do the differences have on their abilities to succeed in the modern workplace?" In this chapter we answer some of these questions and help put gender differences into a realistic context.

If we look for reasons why women and men should stay divided into occupationally separate classes, we can find more than enough historical, anthropological, and scientific conjecture, much of it myth, to justify the practice. For example, "Women should be teachers or nurses because they are naturally more nurturing, and men should be engineers or astronomers because they are better at math." But if we look more deeply, history, anthropology, and science will show that many gender differences are either insignificant or actually complementary—that is, a woman and man can bring more to a task together than either would alone.

In her book *The Mismeasure of Woman*, Carol Tavris, a psychologist with a feminist orientation, freely acknowledges that differences exist. She says there is "a confusion between gender equality and gender sameness: the idea that to be equal in life and law, the sexes must be the same....But to deny that men and women differ in their basic natures, personality traits, and abilities...is not to deny that men and women differ at all. Of course they do. They differ in the life experiences that befall them. They differ in the work they do....They differ in reproductive processes."[1] So the real debate is over how men and women let their undisputed differences affect their lives and opportunities—how to be different but equal.

George Bernard Shaw dealt with these types of differences in *Pygmalion*. First, he showed that whole classes of people are "acceptable" or "unacceptable" depending upon how others see them—the wardrobe and Cockney dialect of Eliza Doolittle, for example. Second, he showed how the confounding differences between the sexes affect relationships—like Henry Higgins' frustrated reaction "Why can't a woman be more like a man?" as his pupil acted out her female feelings instead of fulfilling his male expectations. In today's workplace women and men repeat Higgins' mistakes every time they artificially limit the potential of the opposite sex by stereotyping its members, expecting them to react in a particular way and then, when they don't, becoming frustrated instead of seeking the understanding they need to overcome the obstacles that keep them apart.

Shaw showed us how people deal with one another on the basis of stereotyped expectations based on myth—like allowing clothing, language, and manners to define social class and measure a person's inherent worth, when, in fact, they don't. In the case of Eliza Doolittle, Professor Higgins knew that the upper classes would reject a Cockney flower girl out of hand. So to make her acceptable to society *and* himself, he decided that, if he changed what she wore and how she talked and behaved, the upper classes would welcome her. In reality, of course, the woman at the core was the same, before and after Higgins transformed her outward appearance and behavior. At the Ascot races, when an exquisitely groomed Eliza yelled, "Dover, move your bloomin' arse," in a moment of uncontrolled excitement, the veneer cracked, perceptions of her worth reversed, and she was again unacceptable in the eyes of those who relied on the myth of appearances.

The sexual revolution in the workplace had a mythical phase when women believed that looking and acting like men would help them succeed; experience proved the reverse to be true. To be successful in today's workplace, women and men must be themselves, bring their separate strengths to the job, and be productively different but equal members of the business team.

Finally, for Professor Higgins, Eliza was different in a more fundamental way. And in this regard, the situation became even more muddled for Higgins. He realized that outward differences, like class, can be altered by changing perceptions, but others, like those rooted in biology that make women and men attractive to one another, are fundamental and unchanging. And so it is in the workplace, where the sexual chemistry between women and men shouldn't be ignored. Any successful formula for managing them cannot be naive about the impact of sex on work. Thus managing men and woman effectively requires setting up workplace protocols—guidelines on how men and women should interact; it also means providing protection to women from unwanted advances or outright coercion.

Playwrights haven't been the only ones to focus on differences between the sexes. Scientist Roger Gorski, a leading contemporary scholar on the physiology of the brain, says that, to deal with gender issues intelligently, we have to be realistic about actual biological differences, even when it is popular to pretend they don't exist.

If you attribute particular behaviors or performance advantages [between the sexes]—particularly cognition—to hormone-induced changes in brain structure, to some people that's a very dangerous, sexist observation. People could certainly exploit that observation and act prejudicially in countless ways, saying females can't do this, males can't do that. But to me, since biological sex differences exist, the two sexes are better off knowing about them. One may argue about the value of societally induced sex differences, but biological sex differences are here to stay.[2]

The argument isn't over whether or not differences exist, because they do; the argument is with what the differences mean in the modern world of working together. We shouldn't overreact to the findings in either direction and take the position that (1) the findings prove why one or the other sex is superior or inferior or (2) they are inconsistent with what we believe and therefore are untrue. Instead, we need to use the revelations of science objectively as they take us closer to defining the best working relationships for women and men.

Stereotypes and myths still play a disproportionate role in our thinking. Too often we behave on the basis of long-held stereotypical views of gender differences and expectations of what the other "should" be. Sometimes these views are right (like realizing that most women's upper body strength limitations won't let them perform certain tasks, such as heavy lifting); often they're wrong (like assuming that a woman should not operate sophisticated aircraft because "women aren't good" at math, science, and navigation or "cool" under pressure).

If this were just a battle for the ego satisfaction of women and men, these issues could be taken less seriously. But when the larger task is adjusting to a new social paradigm in which women and men jointly drive the economy and culture of a great nation, it becomes important to do it right. Like many of us, psychologist Tavris sees hope emerging for a more productive way of viewing gender differences. "[T]hinking of the sexes as opposites implies that women and men invariably act in opposition to one another. It implies an underlying antagonism or conflict, the pitting of one side against the other....Yet nothing in the nature of women and men requires us to emphasize difference and opposition. We can emphasize similarity and reciprocity."[3]

With all the laws and regulations in the world bidding the change, we won't accomplish it unless we sort out the myths and realities that control relationships in a workforce that is now made up almost equally of men and women. We have to replace tradition and prejudice with realistic interpretations of capabilities and limitations if women and men are to be successful in their new working relationships.

Differences between the Sexes

What is actually known, surmised, believed, or dearly wished to be true and what is patently false blend into shades of gray differences between the sexes. Sorting out what is known about gender differences is hard, but finding agreement among scientists, sociologists, psychologists, or other experts about their significance is sometimes even more difficult—especially when we listen to them in isolation. The apparently firm ground of one scholar seems to explain something reasonably well; then along comes a challenging point of view that offers a logical reason to discount the first explanation. The conflict still centers around whether gender differences are primarily a result of biological or cultural influences—whether men and women come "hard-wired" for certain behavior, or whether they learn it—nature versus nurture. In their book *Sex: Does It Make a Difference?* Jean D. Grams and Walter B. Waetjen put the unresolved quandary this way: "Whether physiology [biology or nature] is the critical determinant of behavioral differences between men and women, or whether it is cultural definitions [learning or nurture] that determine behavioral differences and assign different jobs cannot be answered in any simple fashion. Men's greater interest and demonstrated ability in abstract reasoning and in dealing with mechanical objects, and women's supposedly greater need for affiliation with others may be due to the tasks that each sex has performed over the centuries."[4] And then again, it may *not!* A lot of thinking has been done about man-woman differences, some of it purely scientific, some of it little more than folklore. Ironically, one generation's science often sounds like the next generation's folklore, and we might wonder whether we have squandered enormous effort in trying to define that which in the end doesn't lend itself to definition.

It's tempting to set up a table with rows and columns neatly showing the myths and realities of gender differences side by side. But it is impossible to discretely quantify most categories of gender difference and place them in either the "myth" or the "reality" column. Most "differences" are so inconclusive that they cannot be categorized without listing numerous caveats and thus making an orderly presentation impossible. Thus what follows is a group of topics that provide a starting point for thinking about the nature and magnitude of differences between the sexes that have relevance to their ability to do work.

We have organized the discussion into three somewhat overlapping major topics:

- Body differences
- Brain differences
- Psychological and cultural differences

In each category, we list points and counterpoints, if they exist, from the literature on gender differences—making the case for and against gender difference. At the end of each topic, we summarize and discuss its significance for getting the job done in a modern work setting. In most cases, points that seemed dramatic in isolation are far less so when viewed with other information. With most topics, more reasons exist to agree than disagree on how meaningful the differences are between the occupational capabilities of women and men, even when contradictions regarding some of the factual details remain.

Volumes have been written on some of these topics and their alleged significance. Our sampling is illustrative and not exhaustive in either the number of topics or the depth of analysis. When one or several sources make the necessary points, we don't attempt to list more. This is a chapter-sized sample, intended to offer some understanding about the major areas of discussion on gender differences and to make them comprehensible as a whole, rather than to resolve the great debates over their meaning or significance individually. We want to lift your thinking above the impact of any individual finding (even of sensational findings) and help you gain an accurate sense of what all the information together means in terms of the practical ability of a woman or man to perform a job today.

A brief word about format. Under the headings that follow, bullets are used to flag individual points. We state the issues, identify the points, or express the conventional wisdom in *italic type* before giving the opinions of people who have studied them. Some of these opinions are simple findings of fact; others agree with and reinforce one another; still others are opposing points of view. We want you to see representative informed opinions on the issues. The end result is an overview of leading thoughts on topics that, because of limited exposure in brief articles or conversations, you may have misinterpreted as the realities of man-woman differences. Chances are that each more accurately represents just another limited contribution to the overall understanding of these complex issues.

Body Differences

Other than the obvious reproductive differences between men and women, occupational myths concerning their body differences are mostly about size and strength. For that reason, there is only one topic under this heading, and it is more a summary of generally accepted facts than contested points of view.

- *Men are larger and stronger than women, but their actual physical capabilities are not significantly different for most modern jobs.*

Medical biologist Anne Fausto-Sterling is representative of the scholars who agree that men are, on the average, larger and stronger than women. Although she is sensitive to the feminist position, she agrees that adult women weigh an average of 10 percent less than adult men. They also differ in muscle shape and body fat content. Women are 10 percent shorter than men; body fat is 25 percent in nonathletic women and 15 percent in nonathletic men.[5] Women reach their adult height during their early teens, whereas men continue to grow for an additional three to five years and usually grow taller. Growth patterns are affected by the growth hormone of the pituitary gland, which may be controlled by a differently set biological clock in women and men.[6]

In her book *Myths of Gender*, Fausto-Sterling writes:

> Height and shape differences are not absolute, but it may be that strength differences are. During development the cells that become muscle fuse with one another to form large fibers. The number of fibers in each individual becomes fixed during the first few years of life, and subsequent muscle growth consists only of increases in the length and width of such fibers. Much of the muscle size differences between males and females result from disparities in fiber growth rather than fiber number.[7]
>
> Matched for size, women have 80 percent of men's upper body strength. The upper body (arms and shoulders) strength of the average woman is about half that of the average man. The average woman has 70 percent of the average man's lower body strength, but for persons of the same weight, the woman's lower body strength may reach 93 percent of her male counterpart's. Matching only lean body weight, women's legs are 5.8 percent stronger than men's.[8]

Fausto-Sterling concludes that in a culture where women and men underwent the same kind and amount of athletic training and physical activity, the average differences between them would diminish but probably not disappear. She writes that "sports emphasizing upper body strength will probably always offer males an advantage—as long as they are played in a culture such as ours, rather than in a place like Bali [in a study she cited by Margaret Mead, the men did not do heavy lifting and had arms almost as free of heavy muscle as those of the women]. Advantages accruing to men in other sports such as running, however, may be due only to differences in leg length, rather than strength."[9]

Another reason men are stronger is that they traditionally have been trained for war. According to Grams and Waetjen, "Societies have devised additional ways to ensure that males are in fact stronger and more able to survive the stress of battle; thus it is the boys and young men who participate in sport and games. The Greek games of antiquity were reserved for males—as was war. The relation between games and war is not too hard to find; and in the words of modern psychologists, perhaps in some more rational time games can become the psychological equivalent of war."[10]

Workplace standards based on the male body can be unfair to women. One disputed area getting a lot of attention is the role of women in modern, technologically oriented fighting forces. A September 1992 study by the National Academy of Sciences concluded that "Standardized height and weight requirements in the U.S. military may have more to do with maintaining appearances than with job performance and often discriminate against women, who typically have more body fat than men."[11] Regardless of its merits in this particular case, the study is one of a growing number of arguments for changing job qualification benchmarks to fit performance requirements instead of tradition.

What we know suggests that fairness would be better served if individuals, rather than types of people, like men and women, were matched to jobs. Fausto-Sterling, for example, points out that "the amount of variation among men and among women is greater than that between sexes. Thus no two differently sexed individuals can be assumed, sight unseen, to have different heights, shapes, or strengths."[12] So even with average physical differences between the sexes known, it is still not possible to accurately judge a particular man or woman by the overall norms of gender, which may not reflect that individual's ability to do a job.

Significance of Body Differences. Scientists agree that, as groups, women and men have actual differences of size and strength. Overall, men are indeed larger and stronger than women. Whether our sexual differences are inbred or result from eons of living patterns that prepared men for more demanding physical roles is unresolved; the modern reality is one of measurable physical differences. It is reasonable to assume that the gap between the genders might narrow, but probably not disappear, with extended periods of similar cultural experiences, but the question remains largely hypothetical. The meaningful question is, "Does it matter?" And the answer, for most jobs today, is, "Not really."

So all the statistics and studies notwithstanding, the majority of men and women are within a range of size and strength that would let them perform almost any occupational task in the modern workplace. Some accommodations from the world designed for the male standard might be necessary, but there is no unbridgeable gap between the capabilities of the two genders on the basis of strength and size criteria. The limitations are cultural and economic. If it were suddenly necessary for women to do the work of men for the nation to survive, with very few exceptions, they could and would.

Brain Differences

Some scientists focus on hormonal influences in the brain as major contributors to gender differences, and some focus on other aspects, such as size and symmetry, in the brain structures of men and women. The information that follows highlights what is known about how hormonal differences and structural differences might affect the working capabilities of men and women.

Hormonal Differences. Hormonal differences are often used to establish the fact that men's and women's brains are different. Hormonal studies are a scientific way to demonstrate that there are chemical differences between the sexes. The chemical and structural differences in the brains of men and women are observable. It is not too great a step from these observations to a manipulation of facts to establish a linkage between gender and capabilities or limitations.

- *Hormones are the main reason why women's and men's brains develop in distinctly different ways.*

Roger Gorski is a professor and the chairman of the Department of Anatomy and Cell Biology of the School of Medicine at the University of California at Los Angeles and director of the Laboratory of Neuroendocrinology of the Brain Research Institute. He specializes in the study of the brain's division into distinctly male and female structures. Gorski argues that we are all basically female and that if the chromosomally genetic male were not exposed to testicular hormones, he would have a female brain and body.[13] Gorski tells us that it "is fairly common knowledge that hormones secreted by the ovaries and testes play a crucial role in shaping male and female patterns of physical appearance and development. But only recently has a revolutionary idea begun to gain credence within the scientific community: that these same hormones mold the very architecture of male and female brains along significantly different lines. And these structural differences—laid down from fetal life to adolescence—are maintained and modified by sex hormones throughout life."[14]

- *A complex balance of hormones determines sexuality.*

Melissa Hines, a UCLA neuroscientist, conducted studies suggesting that women whose mothers were given the female hormone DES during pregnancy were more apt to show male hearing patterns than those not so treated. DES is a drug that mimics the process by which the male hormone testosterone is converted to the female hormone estradiol before it masculinizes brain cells in rats. In toy preference tests on girls prenatally exposed to excessive male hormones, Hines and psychologist Sheri Bernbaum found that they preferred male toys like trucks and Lincoln logs.[15] According to Gorski, "Other researchers have shown that the metabolic conversion of testicular testosterone to estrogen is a required step in masculinizing male brains. While it seems astonishing that estrogen masculinizes the male, it does reflect a common error: that estrogen is the 'female' and testosterone the 'male' sex hormone. That's not true. What is important is the ratio of these two hormones."[16]

- *Sex-linked structural differences in the brains of rats have been reversed by manipulating their hormones, showing that the hormones account for the differences.*

According to Gorski, "The SDN [sexually dimorphic nucleus] of the hypothalamus of a rat's brain is about five times bigger in males than females, and that size difference is due principally to the number of neurons. Giving the female testosterone for a prolonged period during fetal life completely sex-reverses the nucleus. If we castrate the male just after birth or treat him with an antiestrogenic agent, his nucleus becomes more comparable in size with that of the female, so we can sex-reverse brain structure by sex-reversing steroid input during the critical development period."[17]

- *Findings in experiments on animals cannot be applied to humans without major qualifications because people's behavior is so much more complex.*

Gorski cautions us that "Animal sexuality is overwhelmingly dependent on sex hormones—much more than in humans. The differences between human and rat are so great you can't take data we've amassed on the sex behavior of the rat and freely apply them to humans....Hormones produced by the gonads circulate in the blood. But these blood levels may be almost meaningless. What counts is how the person's individual physiology transforms the hormone into meaningful signals. At present in humans it's impossible to measure the sensitivity of neuronal receptors to hormones or their products."[18]

- *Some scientific studies show that changes in hormones affect sex-linked thinking skills and behavior.*

Canadian psychologists Doreen Kimura and Elizabeth Hampson tested the verbal and spatial performance of 150 women during different stages of their menstrual cycle and found that their verbal (female) skills were heightened and their spatial perception (male) skills were depressed when the female hormone estrogen was at a high level.[19] Commenting on the importance of her findings, Kimura said, "While the fluctuations we find are interesting and significant—they tell us something about how cognitive ability patterns are formed—they are not large. Also, up to now they seem most consistent for the kinds of things women already do well. So for most women, they aren't an important factor. Of course, women vary widely in their sensitivity to these influences. For some, the changes may make them feel clumsier at some periods of the month than at others."[20]

In their tests of mood differences, Kimura and Hampson did not find significant changes in mood between the two phases of the menstrual cycle and found only one significant correlation between any of the mood components that sample things like depression, fatigue and vigor, and performance on various tasks.[21]

Psychologist Carol Tavris thinks that advertising and media obsessions with things like premenstrual syndrome (PMS) obscure the fact that the menstrual cycle basically doesn't affect a healthy woman's ability to do what she needs to do. She also points out that hormone changes affect men and that men's and women's moods and physical symptoms are more alike than different.[22] She believes that hormonal changes in women have never been reliably linked to problems in behavior or intellectual performance.[23]

Significance of Hormonal Differences.   Hormonal differences in the brains of normal men and women exist—both in their early development and during the cycles of adult living. It seems clear that the balance of hormones is the basis for sexual identity. Research shows that manipulating these hormones in laboratory animals and humans tends to prove that links exist between them and characteristics thought of as being either masculine or feminine. But scientists caution that every interesting finding about a rat cannot be directly applied to humans, whose behavior is controlled by far more complicated systems.

The bottom line is that, yes, men and women have different hormonal chemistries and, yes, they affect their behavior differently—but not uniformly or dramatically. The effects are often large enough to measure and distinguish between the sexes but usually small enough to make them relatively meaningless in performing modern jobs.

Structural Differences.   Scientists can measure the brain and correlate the differences with how people having various structural characteristics perform tasks. Men's and women's brains exhibit such differences, and there have been insinuations for generations that the differences proved the superiority or inferiority of one or the other gender. The following information highlights what is known about brain structure differences and what they mean for judging the job performance potential of women and men.

- *Male and female brains are different in size, symmetry, and structure, but there is no conclusive evidence that these differences determine intelligence.*

Medical scholars have established that men's and women's brains have a number of structural differences. Gorski says, "There is a definite list of areas in the brain showing male-female structural differences. In trying to understand neurobiology, you're much better off assuming a part of the brain is sexually dimorphic [different for each sex] until you've proven it isn't."[24] Body symmetry differences may correlate with brain hemisphere differences among women and men, suggesting the generalized nature, if not the significance, of sex differences. Canadian psychologist Doreen Kimura discovered that human bodies are generally asymmetrical—men larger on the right side, women on the left. Her tests show that body size differences seem to predict cognitive function—right-larger people are better at math, left-larger are better at verbal processing.[25]

As far back as the early 1900s, Karl Pearson, a mathematician and the father of modern statistics, challenged what he considered to be shoddiness in the brain differences research of the late 1800s. He and his students effectively ended the debate of their day with exhaustive studies that found no significant correlation between brain size, cranial measurement, and intelligence in women and men.[26]

Dick Swaab of the Netherlands Institute for Brain Research in Amsterdam says, "Men's brains are on average larger than women's by 15 percent—about twice the difference in average body size between men and women." The brains of males and females are the same size until age 2 or 3; then males' brains grow faster until age 6, when full brain size is reached. The explanation by many scientists for this growth pattern rests on the theory that all brains are female at birth and, in men, are altered when male hormones begin to act.[27]

- *Until the 1960s, when structural differences in the brains of male and female mammals were first discovered, it was the general scientific opinion that, except for size differences and hormones, male and female brains were alike.*

Oxford University anatomists Geoffrey Raisman and Pauline Field conducted the first study to demonstrate conclusively that structural differences existed in the brains of male and female mammals. They found that, in male rat brains, fewer synapses connect the two parts of the hypothalamus than in female rat brains. In the 1970s and 1980s, electron microscopes and noninvasive imaging techniques allowed scientists to conduct studies that created a "solid body of data indicating sex differences in the brains of almost every mammalian family examined so far: rodents, birds, monkeys, and—most recently and most intriguingly—human beings."[28]

■ *Comparative studies of men's and women's brains in autopsies first confirmed possible anatomical reasons for sex differences in humans in the early 1980s, but researchers are cautious about their significance.*

Christine de Lacoste, a Columbia University graduate student in neuroscience, studied nine male and five female brains in the early 1980s and discovered that the corpus callosum, which connects the brain's hemispheres, was significantly different in men and women. The connecting pathway between women's left and right hemispheres was larger than wider than in men. Hers was the first study to show that sex differences in intellect, skills, and behavior in humans might have an anatomical basis.[29]

In contrast, University of Chicago biopsychologist Jerre Levy, whose research centers on differences and interactions between the left and right sides of the brain, points out that "the variation from one woman to another woman, or one man to another man, is much larger than the average difference between the sexes....Naturally occurring individual differences among people are just huge."[30]

Nobel laureate Roger Sperry would disagree. In his research, he concluded that the weaker connection between male brain hemispheres (lateralization) resulted in greater right-brain visual and spatial skills. Women, with greater cross-communication (bilateralization) between the hemispheres, are more likely to excel in verbal skills because of less right-brain focus.[31]

But "Anne Fausto-Sterling, a medical sciences professor at Brown University, notes that male and female spatial and verbal abilities in fact constitute 'majorly overlapping curves. It is absolutely false, just wrong' to claim that either sex's performance is always better than the other. 'More than half the time there's no difference.'"[32]

■ *Differences in specific control mechanisms of the brain have been found in women and men.*

Structural differences between women and men have been found in the hypothalamus, the part of the brain that controls many basic functions such as temperature regulation, appetite, and sex drives. The shape of the area controlling circadian rhythm (the approximately 24-hour biological clock) and ovulation in women is different in men and women. The neurons in this area of the brain make different contacts in men and women, so that even though they inhabit the same part of the brain in both sexes, they may have a different function. There is also speculation that this area of the hypothalamus is a factor in male sexual preferences, possibly indicating a biological basis for homosexuality.[33]

- *While doing something similarly or even identically, women and men use different parts of their brains to accomplish the same tasks but perform at about the same level.*

Cecile Naylor, a neuropsychologist at the Bowman Gray School of Medicine in North Carolina, monitored blood flow in the brains of 30 women and 30 men who took the same spelling test. Although the test results were essentially the same, male brain activity was dramatically different from female activity. Blood flow patterns showed that many areas of the women's brains were activated during the test—they were "ablaze"—whereas activity occurred in only a few areas of the men's brains.[34] Naylor's study showed that the brains of men and women went about accomplishing the task in different ways. In other words, men and women may process the same information differently and yet come to the same or similar conclusions.[35]

Over a 10-year period, Sandra Witelson, a McMaster University professor of psychiatry, tested the left- or right-handedness of 35 female and 15 male terminally ill patients whose brains she then studied posthumously. She found that the size of the isthmus, which links the two cortices of the brain, was a significant predictor of left- or right-handedness in men but not in women. Witelson concluded that the trait must be controlled by a different part of women's brains.[36]

Neurological studies show that men and women use different parts of their brains to process verbal activities like speech. Doreen Kimura, professor of psychology at the University of Western Ontario, studied stroke victims and determined that women's verbal abilities were more equally distributed between the two hemispheres of the brain than men's but that sex differences occurred *within* the hemispheres rather than *between* them. At the conclusion of a decade-long study, Kimura discovered that injuries to the front part of the left hemisphere caused speech impairment in women, whereas damage to the back part of that hemisphere caused similar impairment in men.[37]

- *As different as the brain's regional functions are, they are complementary.*

According to psychologist Carol Tavris, "The two hemispheres of the brain do have different specialties, but it is far too simpleminded (so to speak) to assume that human abilities clump up in opposing bunches.

Most brain researchers today believe that the two hemispheres complement one another, to the extent that one side can sometimes take over functions of a side that has been damaged. Moreover, specific skills often involve components from both hemispheres: one side has the ability to tell a joke, and the other has the ability to laugh at one. Math abilities include both visual-spatial skills and reasoning skills. The right hemisphere is involved in creating art, but the left hemisphere is involved in appreciating and analyzing art."[38]

- *Men solve visual-spatial problems more easily than women.*

Psychologists like David Lohman of the University of Iowa believe that men may have a "visual-spatial scratchpad" that gives them the mental ability to retain and manipulate spatial and numeric data that cannot be solved verbally. In tests like determining where a horizontal line should be in a tilted vessel containing liquid, men answer quickly and intuitively while women often get the right result, but more slowly, using reasoning to do it. Other researchers, who emphasize social influences as large contributors to ability differences, note that greater athletic participation by men from an early age enhances their spatial skills.[39]

Men and women students differ in a number of skill areas, but there is substantial overlap, making it impossible to judge individuals by these generalized data. "Boys seem to excel in math and computational skills, whereas girls are superior in language, spoken and written. Motor coordination tests give women the edge in executing fine finger and hand movements, and in overall agility. But men tend to have faster reaction times. Male supremacy appears greatest in tasks involving spatial visualization—the ability to see, manipulate, and compute the position of a real or abstract figure in the mind's eye. Although the typical cognitive profile of women may be different from that of men, there is a huge overlap. Many women do better than men on some spatial tests, and vice versa."[40]

- *Men and women navigate differently but with equal skill.*

Animal studies suggest links between brain differences and evolutionary function. University of Pittsburgh anthropologist Steven I. C. Gaulin and University of Utah animal behavioralist Lucia Jacobs conducted a study of wild meadow voles, a species of polygamous rodents in which the males need highly developed spatial skills for navigation because they range widely to find mates. The hippocampus, the part of the brain used in spatial processing, was 11 percent bigger in the ranging voles than in their nonranging monogamous counterparts who had less need for spatial and navigation skills. Other researchers also speculate that many brain differences between the sexes are based on their evolutionary origins.[41]

Thomas Bever, a psychology and linguistics professor at the University of Rochester, ran college students through mazes and found that women rely on specific landmarks for moving through space and men use a more primitive sense of motion involving remembered vectors. "Neither style of navigation is superior….Both men and women get from point A to B just as efficiently and neither sex gets lost more often than the other…there is a great deal of overlap; some women adopt the male strategy and vice versa. 'We are talking about tendencies, not destiny,'" Bever says.[42] "[D]iscoveries of differences in the brain and behavior should not be misused for political ends. 'There are atomic differences between steel and aluminum but either can be the material for an excellent armchair. Groups may differ in the way they tend to solve a problem but have functionally equal abilities,'" according to Bever.[43]

■ *Test score results fuel the debate on gender-based intellectual abilities and on whether or not the gender gap is narrowing.*

The significance of test score differences is open to question. Table 2-1 shows SAT verbal and mathematics scores for men and women during the period 1967–1989, with men generally scoring higher than women, especially in math. Table 2-2 shows women scoring higher in reading and men scoring higher in math and science on high school

Table 2-1. SAT Verbal and Math Scores
(1967–1989)

	Verbal score (total) men/women	Math score (total) men/women
1967	463/468	514/467
1970	459/461	509/465
1975	437/431	495/449
1980	428/420	491/443
1983	430/420	493/445
1984	433/420	495/449
1985	437/425	499/452
1986	437/426	501/451
1987	435/425	500/453
1988	435/422	498/455
1989	434/421	500/454

SOURCE: U.S. Bureau of the Census, *Statistical Abstract of the United States: 1991*, no. 253, p. 154.

Table 2-2. High School Reading, Math, and
Science Scores

Subject	Men	Women
Reading	286	294
Mathematics	305	299
Science	295	282

SOURCE: U.S. Bureau of the Census, *Statistical Abstract of the United
States: 1991*, no. 255, p.155.

reading, math, and science tests. Both tests were administered to high
school students.

Julian Stanley of Johns Hopkins University began the Study of
Mathematically Precocious Youth (SMPY) in 1970. In administering the
SAT to high-ability seventh and eighth graders, he and his colleague
Camilla Benbow, who continues the work at the University of Iowa,
found a pattern that has stayed the same for 20 years: "Among 12-year
olds who score 500 or higher on the math portion of the SAT, the male-
female ratio is 2:1, rising to 4:1 at scores above 600, and 13:1 above
700."[44] One reason for the large discrepancies is *greater male variability*, a
term used by cognitive researchers that means that male talent is more
widely distributed—more at the top and the bottom of score distribu-
tions—accounting for more extremely bright men than women.
Benbow's colleague David Lubinsky found that, at the top extreme, the
female advantage in verbal skills disappeared in the top 1 percent.[45]

Sandra Witelson, a behavioral neuroscientist at McMaster University
in Ontario, Canada, thinks that biology plays an obvious role in cognitive sex differences. Conversely, Janet Hyde, a socially oriented
researcher and psychologist at the University of Wisconsin, disagrees.
Hyde and psychologist Marica Linn at the University of California at
Berkeley have found that overall sex differences in verbal ability have
almost disappeared. Using measures of "effect size" (the proportion of
the standard deviation by which the sexes differ), where 0.80 is
regarded as a large effect, they found an effect size of 0.23 in favor of
females in pre-1973 studies, but after that date, it fell to 0.10.

Hyde and University of Wisconsin psychologists Elizabeth Fennama
and Susan Lamon did a companion study of differences in math performance. They found comparable effect sizes in favor of males of 0.31
before 1973 and 0.14 after, showing the gap between males and females
similarly diminishing. Psychologist Dian Halpern of the University of
Southern California challenges the techniques used in these studies, saying that if Hyde and her colleagues had eliminated statistically insignificant results from the verbal study, the women's advantage would have

remained, and if they had not eliminated SAT data from the math study on grounds that the data would overwhelm the other results, the advantage of males that has stood for 23 years would have held.[46] Other scientists maintain that social influences are more important than test results such as these. They say this is because smart boys are encouraged to excel more than smart girls and take more advanced science and math courses in high school. However, with all the disagreement and debate, none of the researchers suggest that this finding should limit the mathematical or scientific aspirations of qualified women.[47]

In her book *The Mismeasure of Woman,* Carol Tavris puts the significance of math test scores into context by noting the observations of respected scientist Robert M. Sapolsky. He contrasted the importance of being classified "treatment" or "nontreatment" in groups of anthrax victims with that of being classified male or female on the math SAT. For the anthrax victims, there was no overlap of the groups when they were represented on a bell-shaped curve—it was a black or white situation. Untreated people died within 48 hours; those treated with antibiotics lived. As for the math SAT, the overlapping outcomes for men and women were almost total; only a small number of males scored outside the female range. Sapolsky concluded that anyone looking at these overlapping curves and claiming to be able to predict anything about how an individual boy or girl would do in math was grinding an ideological ax or "his own ability to reason mathematically is severely impaired."[48]

Significance of Brain Differences. Scientific evidence establishes that men's and women's brains are structurally different in a number of ways. They are different in size, with the male brain the larger of the two. Men's and women's brains have been observed electronically during various kinds of activity, and they often function differently. It is also true that plausible speculation says that male and female brains developed differently in response to different environmental requirements over the period of their evolution. Young men and women test differently, with men excelling in math, but the apparent significance of these results is eroded by the reality that the difference occurs only at the extremes of the bell-shaped curves representing the overlapping male and female populations. The curves overlap one another to such an extent that, for all practical purposes, most men and women have about the same measured abilities on the tests. So it seems almost pointless to argue strenuously that cultural patterns greatly influence the outcomes—there's not enough difference to really matter.

With all the fascinating scientific tidbits that show how the genders differ, none of them seem to have much meaning for the average woman or man doing the typical job in the modern workplace. Granted, the sexes are structured a little differently in their brains as they are in the rest of their anatomies, but none of these differences appear to make much practical impact on their capabilities. Yes, women and men function somewhat differently, using different parts and patterns of their gray matter to perform the same mental tasks, but with no significant difference in the outcomes.

Demonstrated differences between the brain structures and intellectual capabilities of men and women notwithstanding, the vast majority of both sexes fall within the overlapping middle area of their two performance curves, so that they function in essentially the same way. There are measurable differences at the extremes, but in a world where average abilities are quite good enough for most jobs, these differences have virtually no impact. For the relatively few positions that call for exceptional intellect, there are enough people of both genders from which to draw a balanced workforce. And there is always the added consideration that, again with few exceptions, ability in the average range usually combines with other human qualities (for example, ambition, personality, motivation) to produce more exceptional achievers than does intellect alone.

Psychological and Cultural Differences

There appear to be real differences in how men and women behave and show emotions—how they feel about and react to many classic situations in life, love and war among them. These differences, and others that may or may not be real, are used as a justification for typing the genders occupationally. In some instances, jobs have been defined as more suited to one gender or the other, i.e., "women's work" or "men's work." Psychology and culture illustrate the applied side of the physical body and brain differences we have already discussed. It is in the cultural practices of our health care establishment, workplace, educational, and legal systems that we see long-held beliefs about the genders put to everyday use. The topics that follow sample psychological and cultural truisms about gender and ponder the degree to which they are either myth or reality.

Behavioral and Emotional Differences.   The stereotypical male is the aggressive, predatory member of the species. Evolution is credited with giving men and women different reasons for emotions such as jealousy and possessiveness, as well as gender-specific criteria in mate selection. In short, prevailing stereotypes tell us that women and men have different drives that cause them to behave differently, and that some of these traits affect how they act in the workplace.

■ *Men are more aggressive than women.*

Medical biologist Anne Fausto-Sterling says that literature does not offer much concrete support for the conventional wisdom that aggressive behavior is simply due to high levels of male hormones.[49] Some studies show that hormones may be a contributor to aggressive behavior but that the trait is heavily influenced by the differences in how boys and girls are raised—the former to be aggressive, the latter more conciliatory.[50] Betty Yorburg, author of *Sexual Identity: Sex Roles and Social Change,* supports the case for cultural influences being more important than hormones, noting that most societies define aggression as a male characteristic, force women to hide emotions related to hate, and limit men's expression of feelings related to love.[51] In *Sex: Does It Make a Difference?* Grams and Waetjen also argue against physiological differences as the main cause for aggressive behavior: "Sex differences in physique and temperament are so complicated that it is misleading to assert that one sex is stronger or weaker than the other. As old myths and stereotypes fade away, as boys and girls have more equal access to vigorous play, to adventure and excitement, to achievement and prestige, it is likely that there will be an equalizing of the score."[52]

The weight of the evidence is against the myth that men are forever doomed to be more aggressive simply because of their hormones or cultural evolution. It is unfair to stereotype all men as one step up from animals that are controlled by, rather than in control of, their aggressiveness, just as it is simply wrong to use hormones as an excuse for unacceptable behavior. Over time, behavior translates into cultural patterns, and different expectations for boys and girls might well change how they will act and interact as men and women.

Psychologist Carol Tavris makes the point, however, that, regardless of the reasons, certain kinds of aggressive behavior are clearly identified with men in our society. While discounting the hormone theory as a reason why it must always be that way, Tavris realistically observes, "It is absurd to speak of 'sex differences' in rape rates, for instance, as if men are merely somewhat more likely than women to rape; the rate for women is virtually zero." In other words, establishing that aggression may not be a "hard-wired" male trait due to hormones alone doesn't mean that we should ignore the realities of contemporary behavior in our culture.[53]

■ *In mating behavior, men are predatory and women are selective.*

A man has traditionally *sought out* a woman to bear his child; a woman has typically *selected* a man to father her child. "These differences in sexual strategies between males and females spring not from sex role training but from traits and behavior patterns that over millions of years of hunter-gatherer culture proved to have survival value, were favored by natural selection and, as a result, became hard-wired into the expanding human brain....[R]ecent evidence indicates that humans anatomically identical to modern humans were hunting the fields of the Middle East more than 90,000 years ago. So despite the fact that we live in a culture with little resemblance to the...culture in which we evolved, there's no doubt that we are genetically adapted to that environment," according to author Michael Hutchison.[54] He speaks for a school of thought advocated by many cultural anthropologists including Lionel Tiger and Robin Fox, who, in their classic book *The Imperial Animal*, built the logical, if not entirely provable, case that men are men and women are women, behaviorally, because of long years of doing what worked.

- *Men and women feel jealous about different kinds of behavior because of anthropological motivations: women value a reliable partner with whom to rear children, and men prize a sexually faithful one to ensure that their traits are perpetuated.*

In a study conducted by David M. Buss, a psychologist at the University of Michigan at Ann Arbor, "202 men and women [were asked] whether it would upset them more if a sexual partner had sexual intercourse with someone else or if the partner formed a deep emotional attachment to someone of the opposite sex. Nearly two out of three men said sexual infidelity would distress them most, whereas 85 percent of the women deemed emotional infidelity the most upsetting." Laboratory measures of men's and women's heart rate and electrical activity of their skin agreed with the verbal responses.[55] The studies illustrate that both men and women feel jealousy, but for different reasons.

- *Men attach relatively more importance to women's youth and physical attractiveness because of an ancient desire to find the best mates to bear their children; women find men's maturity and material well-being more important because of a drive to provide sustenance and security for their offspring.*

In an article entitled "Darwin's Minds," *Science News* writer Bruce Bower summarized the conventional wisdom: "Males compete for mates by acquiring and displaying signs—such as personal and material resources—of their ability to provide for a family. Females accentuate their fertility by trying to appear youthful and attractive."[56] Some studies over the years have shown this to be true in many cultures, while others have shown that "graceful aging...alters the mating equation. In industrial societies where woman show fewer physical signs of aging, women in their 40s may be more likely to marry younger men. Conversely, ...men in their 30s who marry older women...possess less physical attractiveness than peers who marry women slightly younger than themselves."[57] When the biological imperative to successfully reproduce is no longer the basis for man-woman relationships, evolutionary standards for judging desirability become less important as well.

Significance of Behavioral and Emotional Differences. Male aggressiveness is real, but for most men it does not produce urges beyond the control of their brains, unlike the case with some of the lower species. It is important to realize that aggression isn't simply a given, solely attributable to male body chemistry. Current attitudes, partly arising from the women's movement, suggest that less aggressive roles for men would be appropriate, particularly in the work world, and new standards of behavior for both women and men are replacing those based on the need to reproduce and survive.

Women and men have long histories of different roles and behavior that have promoted the survival of the species. The resulting differences produce partly valid and partly antiquated ways of behaving that need to be modified to fit the roles women and men play in a modern society. It has become much less relevant for men and women to view each other largely from the perspective of long-lived mating rituals; modern culture demands that their relationships have a broader base. But traditional gender roles—roles that have worked for the survival of the species—have been reinforced through countless generations, and they won't fade overnight. This is not to suggest that things shouldn't change; rather, it will take conscious effort to learn new roles and establish new relationships at work and elsewhere in our lives.

Communication Differences.   A best-selling book called *You Just Don't Understand* by sociolinguist Deborah Tannen made it virtually impossible for anyone not to realize that men and women have different styles of communicating. But although most scientists and academics might acknowledge that the genders communicate from different perspectives, they don't agree on why this is so. Here are several points to illustrate the issues.

- *Women and men communicate differently and, as a result, misunderstand each other in both their personal and business lives.*

Tannen and others observe that men and women have different patterns of communication. In *You Just Don't Understand,* she describes her view of the differences: "Men are more often inclined to focus on the jockeying for status in a conversation: Is the other person trying to be one-up or put me down? Is he trying to establish a dominant position by getting me to do his bidding? Women are more often attuned to the negotiation of connections: Is the other person trying to get closer or pull away? Since both elements are always present, it is easy for women and men to focus on different elements in the same conversation."[58] Tannen points out that both sexes are concerned with achieving status and avoiding failure as well as with making connections and avoiding isolation, but that women focus on the latter and men on the former, making their styles of communication different.[59]

Psychologist Carol Tavris likes linguist Robin Lakeof's explanation of the differences between men's and women's communication better than Tannen's. She takes the feminist view that men's language is that of the powerful, and women's is a way to survive in a world in which they are powerless.[60] If you accept her belief, anyone, female or male, develops "women's language" if she or he is in a subordinate position. The subordinate person becomes skilled at anticipating what others want or need ("women's intuition") in order to survive. Some illustrations of groups who use women's language are blacks with whites and prisoners with guards. Because of this, women more than men do what linguists call "code switching"—talking in a man's way when they have to do business, reverting to female way when they don't.[61] In this way of thinking, women's intuition is "subordinate's intuition."[62] For Tavris, the fact that women are outsiders, not that they have some universal conversational style, is what creates communication differences between the sexes.[63] Her view is that while it is true that women and men communicate differently, the difference isn't because of something inherently found in their "nature, or capacity, or personality traits"[64] but because of the way the culture has made them communicate to survive.

- *Women are more empathetic and more intuitive than men, and these qualities show in the way they communicate.*

Tavris believes that alleged sex differences in characteristics like intuition and empathy are merely what people expect and that when behavior is observed, differences based on sex are rare. She takes the view that women have learned to read people better because they must do so in order to survive,[65] writing that "this is not a *female* skill; it is a *self-protective* skill, and the sex gap fades when the men and women in question are equal in power."[66] Tannen puts it differently: "[I]n many ways, differences between women's and men's styles are not symmetrical. When men and women get together in groups, they are likely to talk in ways more familiar and comfortable to the men. And both women's and men's ways of talking are typically judged by the standards of men's styles, which are regarded as the norm."[67] So whether you are more comfortable with the feminist Tavris or the academic Tannen, communication style differences between women and men do exist, and they can be attributed to men's traditionally dominant position.

Significance of Communication Differences. Understanding communication styles is important in evaluating a woman's approach to management or other measures of her competency. Observers of men's and women's communication agree that each gender has its distinctive style. The difference seems to boil down to culturally established ways of behaving that typically have given men the dominant role, leaving women to develop a necessarily more conciliatory style. This has made the male style the standard by which both genders are judged.

The differences appear to be products of the culture and will narrow as the power balance between women and men narrows. As with any established cultural trait, communication style differences will pass gradually and will linger longer in the social arena than in the workplace, where the pressures for change are greater. There is no urgent reason why one or the other style must be adopted for men and women to work successfully together, but understanding the differences between the genders is a basic tool with which to deal with these differences.

The myth is that women have an inherently different and, moreover, inferior communication style that limits them to subordinate roles. The reality is that the communication styles of both women and men are evolving with the culture and will probably end up becoming a blend of the best of both—true to the model of successful adaptation that has perpetuated the species.

Medical and Health Differences. Although the trend is to minimize the significance of most gender differences, medicine is one field in which accurately understanding and correctly acting on those differences is crucial and cannot wait. Acknowledged differences in the physiologies of women and men matter a great deal in delivering health care equitably. Here are some of the the realities of modern medicine and gender:

■ *Women and men do not receive equal levels of medical treatment and services.*

Former director of the National Institutes of Health Bernadine Healy says that women's medical complaints often aren't taken seriously and that women with "men's diseases"—such as coronary heart disease—aren't treated as aggressively as men.[68]

■ *Women's medical treatments are often incorrectly based on research conducted only on male subjects and do not take into consideration the importance of biological differences.*

The 70-kilogram (154-pound) man has long been the human model used for study in medical schools and in determining dosages and prescribing treatments.[69] A report of the Council on Ethical and Judicial Affairs of the American Medical Association put it this way: "One concern is that medical treatments for women are based on a male model, regardless of the fact that women may react differently to treatments than men or that some diseases manifest themselves differently in women than in men."[70] Another example often cited is that women may need variable doses of some medications because of changing body chemistry during the menstrual cycle, whereas the dosage for men should remain constant. Jean Hamilton, a psychiatrist at the University of Texas Southwestern Medical School, says, "If we're going to give women the equivalent medical treatment as men, we'd better find out about sex differences where they exist. Someday men and women may be treated differently for conditions such as Alzheimer's disease and epilepsy, and the treatments will be more effective because they are different."[71]

■ *The diagnosis and medical treatment of women reflect subtle biases regarding the relative worth of women and men in our society.*

In a 1992 article called "How Women Get Bad Medicine," Carol Stevens writes: "Conventional medical wisdom...holds that heart disease is primarily a male disease. Yet for the last two years more American women have died of heart disease than men. The medical community also considers lung cancer a man's health problem. Yet the death rate for lung cancer has increased more than 100 percent in the last twenty years—virtually all due to the growing number of women smoking."[72]

A 1991 *Journal of the American Medical Association* article made these points about the differences in women's and men's medical treatment:

Gender has been found to correlate with the likelihood that a patient with kidney disease will receive a kidney transplant. The discrepancy between sexes was most pronounced in the group 46 to 60 years old, with women having only half the chance of receiving a transplant as men the same age.

In the diagnosis of lung cancer once smoking status and other medical considerations were taken into account, men still had 1.6 times the chance of having a cytologic test done than women did.

In the treatment of coronary heart disease, 40 percent of the male patients were referred for cardiac catheterization, whereas only 4 percent of the female patients were referred for further testing. Even after adjusting for test results, age, symptoms, and previous heart attacks, men were still 6.5 times more likely to be referred for catheterization than women, although men have only three times the likelihood of having coronary heart disease than women.[73]

Subtle attitudes and stereotypes that women's health complaints are more often attributable to emotional rather than physical causes, "over-anxiousness" about their health, and a "general perception that men's social role obligations or of their contributions to society are greater than women's may fuel these disparities. For instance, altering one's work schedule to accommodate health concerns may be viewed as more difficult for men than women. Overall, men's financial contribution to the family may be considered more critical than women's."[74] The American Medical Association did an analysis of gender and treatment and found that women heart patients were twice as likely as men to have the abnormal results of an exercise test blamed on psychiatric or other noncardiac causes. It concluded that physicians are more apt to see an emotional problem as the cause of women's maladies than men's.[75]

■ *The position of women as recipients and providers of health care is changing significantly.*

In 1991 Healy wrote in the *Journal of the American Medical Association* that "women's health, in general—in terms of research, services, and access to care—has come of age and become a priority medically, socially, and politically."[76] She went on to note that the number of women entering medical schools has steadily grown and that women hold two of the highest federal government positions in the Department of Health and Human Services—surgeon general and director of the NIH. Healy mirrors the changing attitude of the medical establishment toward women when she suggests that "we must train *all* medical students, male and female, to understand the biological differences between the sexes, to take the time to listen to their patients, to respect their patients' concerns and anxieties, and, most of all—as so many women have consistently written to me—to take them seriously."[77]

Women currently make up 34 percent of medical school graduates and nearly 17 percent of all practicing physicians. In 1992, for the first time women accounted for more than 54 percent of first-year obstetrics and gynecology residents.[78]

■ *Women use health care services more often than men.*

The 1991 *Journal of the American Medical Association* report on ethics found that "Some evidence indicates that, compared with men, women receive more health care services overall. In general, women have more physician visits per year and receive more services per visit."[79] This is true even for the same illness or complaint, and although the reasons are not clear, "real differences in morbidity and mortality between the sexes..." do not explain it.[80]

■ *Women and men react to pain differently, but both tolerate it equally well.*

Pain researcher Ronald Melzack, of McGill University in Montreal, found no gender differences regarding the raw ability to tolerate pain. However, in terms of expressing their pain, men and women are different, says David Spiegel, "Men are probably more reticent, actually, than women....Women are better than men at accommodating to sick roles—more graceful at allowing themselves to be cared for. Men tend to either be strong and in control of everything or regress and act like two-year olds. On the other hand, men are 'too good sometimes at focusing away and minimizing' [and wrongly ignoring the problem]."[81]

Significance of Medical and Health Differences. It is a myth that men and women receive equal medical treatment. Women receive it more often than men but are taken less seriously, and they rank lower in priority for testing and treatment for some major health problems. Further, their care is administered on the basis of male standards that often are not appropriate for women. These shortcomings are recognized in the medical establishment, and with the dramatic increase in the role of women as primary health care providers and managers, the problems are being addressed. Health care issues, particularly pregnancy and childbirth, are significant because they affect judgments of women's reliability in the workplace, and they have an impact on the cost of providing employee benefits. As society moves toward universal health care, the point of cost becomes moot, since costs will be borne in some form for all citizens. And no evidence exists that women's medical problems are more severe than men's or that their medical problems make them significantly less reliable employees, especially as society gradually restructures to accommodate the bearing and rearing of children with the careers of working women and their spouses.

Occupational Differences. Some employers make subtle distinctions, sometimes based on stereotypes, when they consider the merits of women and men employees. Some of their opinions are founded on myth; some are based on reality. Some of the differences employers think about are leadership style, inherent physiological and psychological limitations, family obligations, the ability to maintain a work schedule, commitment, and the importance of work in an employee's life. What follows is expert opinion on the validity of these issues.

- *Women and men have different leadership styles.*

Judy Rosener, a faculty member at the Graduate School of Management at the University of California at Irvine, claims that men are "transactional" leaders who depend on formal authority and organizational power, whereas women are "transformational" leaders who "encourage participation, share power and information, enhance other people's self-worth, and get others excited about their work."[82] She explains: "Until the 1960s, men and women received different signals about what was expected of them. To summarize a subject that many experts have explored in depth, women have been expected to be wives, mothers, community volunteers, teachers, and nurses. In all these roles, they are supposed to be cooperative, supportive, understanding, gentle, and to provide service to others. They are to derive satisfaction and a sense of self-esteem from helping others, including their spouses. While men have had to appear to be competitive, strong, tough, decisive, and in control, women have been allowed to be cooperative, emotional, supportive, and vulnerable. This may explain why women today are more likely than men to be interactive leaders."[83]

Cynthia Fuchs Epstein, distinguished professor, Graduate Center, City University of New York, responds that Rosener's research was flawed because she asked men and women to describe their own management styles rather than observing them as they worked. When asked about their own behavior, they stereotyped themselves according to culturally accepted ideas of how the genders "should" behave. Epstein used an example from her own research when she cited a woman lawyer who described herself as "caring" but who was characterized as a "barracuda" by a male associate.[84]

Felice Schwartz, founder of the women's interest group Catalyst, says that the command-and-control style of leadership usually identified with males is more suited to a manufacturing economy and that as we change to an information-service economy, the interactive mode will be more effective. She believes that companies need to "find ways in which male and female manager-leaders can work together and learn from each other. Ideally, the amalgam of these styles will be viewed not as gender-related but rather as appropriate for both men and women."[85]

Jane Mansbridge, of the Center for Urban Affairs and Policy Research, Evanston, Illinois, concludes that whatever the sex differences in management style, they are minuscule and insignificant when compared with other differences. "The differences are what most researchers would call 'small' (about one-fifth of a standard deviation). The differences between men and women may be much smaller than the differences between managers of small and larger companies or old and new companies. They may even be smaller than the differences between old and young managers, Eastern and Midwestern managers, or managers with professional parents and managers with working-class parents....Gender differences are sexy, in part because sex is sexy, so we notice them more than other, larger differences....[N]either women nor men should focus on gender differences when they decide whom to hire or what job to take. Gender differences are fascinating, but they don't explain much of the variance between one manager and another."[86]

- *Relatively minor physiological differences between women and men have been used as a basis for justifying major occupational and social inequities.*

In practice, cultural factors outweigh physical differences in determining occupational opportunities and limitations. According to author Betty Yorburg, sex typing is a major factor in American society, contributing to stereotyping, which in turn perpetuates bias: "Sex typing exists in all segments of American society, although it varies somewhat in degree within the different classes and ethnic groups. Conceptions of the ideal female or male are still quite widely held, however, despite the rise of the women's movement, changing economic and political conditions, and the continued spread of modern values, such as individualism and egalitarianism.[87]

Melissa Hines, a neuroscientist who worked with Roger Gorski at UCLA, says: "It's a big step from seeing relatively subtle hormonal contributions to behavior to seeing the average woman make substantially less money than the average man or seeing the vast majority of heads of state and CEOs being male."[88] Feminist psychologist Carol Tavris develops the line of reasoning further:

[T]heories of sex differences in the brain cannot account for the complexities of people's everyday behavior. They cannot explain, for instance, why, if women are better than men in verbal ability, so few women are auctioneers or diplomats, or why, if women have the advantage in making rapid judgments, so few women are air-traffic controllers or umpires. Nor can brain theories explain why abilities and ambitions change when people are given opportunities previously denied to them. Two decades ago, theorists postulated biological limitations that were keeping women out of men's work like medicine and bartending. When the external barriers to these professions fell, the speed with which women entered them was dizzying. Did everybody's brain change? Today we would be amused to think that women have a brain-lateralization deficiency that is keeping them out of law school. But we continue to hear about the biological reasons that keep women out of science, math, and politics. For sex differences in cognitive abilities to wax and wane so rapidly, they must be largely a result of education, motivation, and opportunity, not of innate differences between male and female brains.[89]

- *The burden of a career and a family weighs disproportionately on women.*

During a 1-week period, "The average working mother spends 44 hours at work and 31 hours on family responsibilities; her spouse spends 47 hours at work and 15 hours helping around the house," according to *Management Review*.[90] More women than men report that they have feelings of conflict over family versus work obligations, and they feel a great deal of pressure as they try to balance careers and children. In commenting on the plight of modern women, Patricia Madoo Lengermann and Ruth A. Wallace write in *Gender in America: Social Control and Social Change:* "To the degree that the woman is working in essence at two full-time jobs, salaried worker and mother-housekeeper, she is ultimately finding her most valuable power resource, her own capacities to change her environment by reflection and by work, diminished. She is being denied time to reflect on her situation and on ways to improve it. She is being worked to the point of being chronically tired and hence unable to act effectively on ideas she may have for improving her situation."[91]

And such pressure has unwelcome consequences on both the personal and the professional fronts. "Right now women with MBAs are two to four times as likely to seek psychological counseling as men with MBAs," writes Oren Harari, a professor at the University of San Francisco and consultant with the Tom Peters group.[92] Of course, one factor in this statistic is men's reluctance to seek help in managing their anxiety. Psychologists John Money and Patricia Rucker explain: "After stunting and deforming a man's emotional development, the 'tough' stereotype bars him from seeking professional medical help for emotional disorders. Men are no more immune to depression, for example, than to stomach ulcers, but men who wouldn't hesitate to consult a doctor for a persistent bellyache wouldn't dare to consult a psychiatrist for a persistent depression-ache, and those who have the good sense to do so are constrained to keep it a dark secret."[93]

On the job front, a survey of 4000 of the highest-paid officers and directors of the nation's largest 1000 companies revealed that only 9 were married women with children,[94] a fact partly explained by Felice Schwartz in *Breaking with Tradition: Women and Work, The New Facts of Life:* "For some time women had the illusion they could 'do it all' and 'have it all' because they had the illusion that men 'had it all.' Now that illusion has been cast aside, and women know they have to order priorities and make trade-offs, just as men have always done. If they want high-achieving careers, that probably means they're going to have less time with their children. Conversely, if they want to participate actively, day by day, in their children's lives, they'll probably have to put a ceiling on their career aspirations, at least for a finite period."[95]

■ *Women rely more on flexible work schedules and are absent from work and change jobs more often than men.*

Department of Labor Current Population Survey data for 1989 categorize 4.6 percent of men and 6.1 percent of women as "Persons with a Job but Not at Work." Contrary to what you might expect, more men than women cited "illness" as the reason—24 percent men versus 21 percent women. But the overall group differences are hidden in the "All Other" category, which accounts for 15 percent of the men's and 21 percent of the women's reasons for not being at work; this category is likely to include factors such as caring for sick children.[96] Although myth would have it otherwise, men have more flexible work schedules (12.9 percent) than women (10.6 percent) according to the 1989 Current Population Survey data for "Flexible Work Schedules,"[97] possibly because flexibility is more a privilege of power than a response to need. Job mobility rates were 10.7 percent for women and 9.2 percent for men in 1990, although women's job tenure with one employer actually increased relative to men—3.3 to 3.8 years for women, with men steady at 5.1 years, for the period 1983 to 1991.[98] These data show that women and men are more alike than different in their work habits, and the data fail to support negative stereotypes of women as unreliable workers.

■ *Women's identities are less tied to their work than are men's.*

Psychologists John Money and Patricia Tucker, writing in *Sexual Signatures: On Being a Man or a Woman,* point out: "As the price of intensive procreation men were saddled with the main burden of the family breadwinning. Although this burden has been eased considerably now that wives are gainfully employed in some 40 percent of all U.S. husband-wife households, the stereotype still ties a man's worth to this work, whether it's the family's only economic lifeline or not. He is not allowed to build his gender pride and confidence on what he is, only on what he does, and since past performance is heavily discounted, he must keep doing until he drops."[99]

Carol Tavris says that in the 1970s sociologist Rosabeth Moss Kanter did conclusive studies that explain why women, contrary to men, often value the social aspects of their work more than the work itself. Kanter believed that the "conditions of employment, not qualities of the indi-vidual, determine what most people value about their work. That is, women and men who are in dead-end, low-paying, unstimulating jobs tend to focus on the aspects of the job that are, by default, the most plea-surable: namely, relationships with others."[100] The implication is that, as women assume more challenging and satisfying work, they will identify with it more.

Significance of Occupational Differences. The stereotypical view of women's management style conforms to the cultural role they've had—they are more conciliatory and less aggressive than men. But that opinion is becoming more myth than reality since we have begun to realize that the stereotypical male management style does not apply to all men and also since more women have entered the ranks of management and the two styles have blended. The reality is that different styles of management are equally effective and that the variations in managers' styles are caused by many factors *other than* gender differences. Myths of "women's work" and "men's work" are fading as cultural barriers fall and women enter and excel in fields previously denied to them. Family responsibilities are still disproportionately borne by women, and, although some men have assumed a greater share of the burden, the reality seems to be that wom-en's careers, more than men's, will yield to family obligations. The belief that "women are too different to do the work of men" is not supported by hard data from the Department of Labor on women's reliability and job commitment and appears to be more myth than reality. Differences between women and men in the workplace can be found in everything from management style to family obligations, but they are simply not sig-nificant enough to bar women from the workplace or place limitations on their career potential.

Conclusions

That women and men are different in some important ways is obvious. That the differences matter very much in a modern, technology-based society and workplace is simply untrue. When most woman-man differ-ences are examined objectively, reasonable people usually conclude that:

- Women and men are more alike than different.
- There are more differences *within* the genders than *between* them.
- The differences of "nature" are indisputably true but relatively insignif-icant in the context of modern work, and occupational differences are largely the result of "nurture"—cultural rather than genetic—so that both genders have essentially the same occupational capabilities.

This is true for most of what we know about sex differences, whether they are the measurable differences in the human body and its chemistry or the unmeasurable differences in style between men and women. The differences are there to observe and sometimes marvel at, but when they are used to predict that some people are not capable of doing a job successfully or to hold people back from having a chance, a convincing case cannot be made.

Human relationships are too complicated to be viewed in simple black-and-white terms. In the final analysis, women and men are each other's complements, inseparable if the species is to thrive. Carol Tavris says that we have a perception problem that blurs this reality: "As long as the question is framed this way—'What can we do about *them*, the other, the opposite?'—it can never be answered, no matter which sex is being regarded as 'them.' The question, rather, should be this: 'What shall we do about *us*,' so that our relationships, our work, our children, and our planet will flourish?"[101] She has a point. If the reality of man-woman differences doesn't justify gender separateness in the workplace, we're left with only sexual stereotypes to maintain the myths that keep us apart.

None of this argues that gender differences aren't real. Sandra Witelson, professor of psychiatry at McMaster University, says: "The sexes are different and it does no good to assume they're not. We're not going to help equal opportunity and equal recognition when we assume both are equally good in all aspects, when it may well be that there are certain things each sex is somewhat better at."[102] The operative word is "somewhat," and the overarching point is that the real differences are generally of such a minor significance that they have very little to do with successfully carrying out modern workplace tasks in the vast majority of cases.

In the final analysis it is unlikely that we will be able to definitively categorize the different occupational potentials of women and men. Ruth Hubbard, a retired Harvard biologist and student of women and biology, concludes: "On average, women and men perform differently. But when it comes to trying to assign causes or reasons, that's where [the scientists] get into trouble. In most societies men and women live very different lives, and so we develop very different capabilities. We don't know how to translate anatomical sex differences into behavioral difference."[103] And medical biologist Anne Fausto-Sterling, says: "I do not argue for a program of behavioral research that ignores biology. Instead I put forth a plea to release biology from its sacrosanct status as First Cause and give it a more appropriate place in the network of disciplines that constitute the proper study of humankind."[104]

In looking at the myths and realities surrounding the differences between the sexes, we find that biological data must be tempered with data from other disciplines, among them anthropology, psychology, and linguistics, to arrive at comprehensive explanations about why and how women and men are different and what it all means. It's time to stop splitting the scientific hairs of woman-man differences; gender is rarely an objective reason to deny anyone the opportunity to do the work he or she chooses.

PART 2
Regulating the Interaction of Gender Differences

3
Laws, Regulations, and Gender in the Workforce

Gender issues have dominated the 1980s and 1990s the way racial issues dominated the 1960s and 1970s. The workplace has become a battle-ground where women and men sometimes spend as much time jockeying for position as they do getting the job done. One sex has dominated the other through the ages, and while we can cite isolated examples of prevailing women, like Cleopatra or Margaret Thatcher, the over-whelming pattern is one of men as the dominant gender. In the rela-tively short history of the United States, every law or government initiative on gender, from women's suffrage in 1920s to the glass ceiling initiatives of the 1990s, has been designed to improve the position of women. Even the Equal Employment Opportunity Commission's 1990 *Policy Guidance on Current Issues of Sexual Harassment*, the government's official guideline on defining sexual harassment, reinforces the histori-cal assumption that women need protection from the excesses of men, with the caveat that roles might occasionally be reversed:

> To avoid cumbersome use of both masculine and feminine pro-nouns, this document will refer to harassers as males and victims as females. The Commission recognizes, however, that men may also be victims and women may also be harassers.[1]

In most discussions of laws, regulations, and court cases on issues of gender, it is the female victim versus the male oppressor. Now and then we read or hear about cases in which, for example, a man charges discrimination because an employer preferred a woman for a particular job, but these situations are few and far between. Interestingly, Michael Crichton's novel *Disclosure*, a fictional account of a man on the receiving end of sexual harassment, found a receptive audience in 1994 and rose to the best-seller list.

Men and women are slowly working toward a more equitable power balance in their individual relationships. This is partly because of education and enlightenment, but it results primarily from the prevalence of dual-income families, which has made working women omnipresent, though not always willingly accepted, as peers. The largely male workforce has been forced to acknowledge not only their presence but their capabilities.

With a few major exceptions, such as the abortion issue, government has not ventured deeply into the private lives of women and men. However, in recent years, it has entered the arena of workplace gender issues with a vengeance. Whether we see this as positive and necessary may well depend on our position in the established order as well as on how we view the role of government in our society. Regardless of your personal feelings, if you have management responsibilities or work in a mixed-gender organization, you need to understand the dynamics of the movement. To keep your organization productive, you, as a manager, have to know the rules of engagement if battles erupt along gender lines in your area of responsibility. Even more important, if you have learned the lessons as well as the rules of recent history, you can promote working relationships within your company that prevent unresolvable conflicts from arising in the first place.

The Hill-Thomas hearings brought sexual harassment out of the closet. They exposed a fault line running between the genders that will become permanent unless men and women can understand each other well enough to agree upon rules for interacting in the workplace that are accepted by both sexes. Most women and men manage to distinguish between behavior that is appropriate in a social setting but not in a work environment, and they do so with acceptable grace; but some people do it poorly—so badly, in fact, that laws are needed to prevent abuse.

One caution, and a note of irony—no one is immune from potential sexual harassment problems. The authorizing signature on the last page of the 1988 edition of the EEOC publication quoted above was that of Clarence Thomas, Chairman. The document he signed consists of 30 detailed pages describing what constitutes sexual harassment and how the agency he led would deal with those who perpetrate it on others.[2] The guilt or innocence of Justice Thomas notwithstanding, the contrast between the testimony at his confirmation hearings and the policy guidance he issued a few years earlier starkly illustrates the complexity of mixed-gender working relationships *and* how limited presumed immunities can be. Who would have imagined that the nation's chief enforcer of equal employment opportunity law would be accused of sexual harassment?

In the struggle to maintain productive working relationships, everyone has interests to protect:

- The woman trying to pursue her career, deal with capable, perhaps powerful men, and not become a casualty of a system that blocks her opportunities for advancement at a certain point on the career ladder because of her gender.

- The man trying to pursue his career, deal with capable, perhaps attractive women, and not become a casualty because of rules that improve women's opportunities and sometimes limit his, just because of his gender.

- The senior manager trying to run his or her enterprise efficiently, profitably, and in the best interests of its owners, employees, the public—and himself or herself—without becoming a casualty by breaking laws or applying them unfairly.

Although antidiscrimination laws are written to provide equal rights and opportunities for women, they have an impact on all the people mentioned above. The task of making the rules work for those they are intended to help without adversely affecting others falls upon the manager. Implementing women's rights is another turn in the endless cycle of broad ideals whose complexity becomes more apparent as they approach the point of application.

Therefore, hands-on managers need to have a basic knowledge of the most important points made in the courtrooms of the land. This chapter is designed to help them gain this knowledge. After summarizing the landmark statutes, from early constitutional amendments to modern executive orders and legislation, we provide a sampling of cases that give the law context and practical meaning for managers.

The Law and Managing Gender Issues at Work

For nearly 125 years, Americans have established rules so that women and men, who often have different interests and priorities, can live and work together. These rules have ranged from the general to the specific. As much as we would like to say that the movement for gender equality in the workplace came from some innate sense of justice as women moved into the workforce, in reality it took the force of law to move in that direction. The benchmark events that have given women and men equal status under the law in American society and its places of work are:

- 1868—Equal Protection Amendment
- 1920—Voting Rights Amendment
- 1963—Equal Pay Act
- 1964—Civil Rights Act of 1964
- 1968—Executive Order 11246 as amended by Executive Order 11375
- 1972—Equal Employment Opportunity Act
- 1978—Pregnancy Discrimination Act
- 1980—Sexual Harassment Guidelines
- 1991—Civil Rights Act of 1991

More follows about each milestone and what it means for the men and women sharing today's workplace.

1868—Equal Protection Amendment

The Fourteenth Amendment, Article XIV of the Constitution, became law on July 28, 1868, and says in part:

> No State shall make or enforce any law which shall abridge the privileges or immunities of citizens of the United States; nor shall any State deprive any person of life, liberty, or property, without the due process of law; nor deny to any person within its jurisdiction the equal protection of the laws.

This provides the constitutional basis for complaints by U.S. citizens that they are being treated unfairly or unequally. The Fourteenth Amendment allows the federal government to correct wrongs not adequately remedied by the individual states. As women demonstrated that they were not being treated the same as men in various segments of society, including the workplace, they sought the remedies provided by the federal system. The response was a series of national laws addressing women's issues.

1920—Voting Rights Amendment

The Nineteenth Amendment, Article XIX of the Constitution, became law on August 26, 1920, and says in part:

The right of citizens of the United States to vote shall not be denied or abridged by the United States or by any State on account of sex.

With the right to vote came the practical political clout needed to advance issues of interest to women. Coincidentally, Congress established the Women's Bureau in the Department of Labor the same year.

1963—Equal Pay Act

The Equal Pay Act of 1963, an amendment to the Fair Labor Standards Act of 1938, and the first federal sex discrimination law, was enacted in 1963 and implemented in 1964. It prohibits wage discrimination based on gender. Women and men with similar skills doing essentially the same work under comparable conditions with virtually the same responsibilities must be paid equally. "Title 29...proscribes sex-based discrimination in compensation for the same or substantially the same work except when the differential is the result of '(i) a seniority system; (ii) a merit system; (iii) a system which measures earnings by quantity or quality of production; or (iv) a differential based on any other factor other than sex.'"[3]

The act gave teeth to the concept of equal pay for equal work. It did not address a woman's right to hold any job for which she is qualified; it established that she must be paid the same as a man doing the same job. As an aside, Betty Friedan's *The Feminine Mystique,* a landmark popular book examining the causes and effects of the underemployment of educated American women, was published the same year.

1964—Civil Rights Act of 1964

Title VII of the Civil Rights Act of 1964 became effective in 1965, prohibiting discriminatory employment practices based on sex, as well as race, color, religion, and national origin. It was amended in 1972 to cover federal workers, and in 1978 to give enforcement authority to the Equal Employment Opportunity Commission. The act made the following actions unlawful if done on the basis of sex, race, color, religion, or national origin:

- For an employer to discriminate in hiring, promoting, firing, wages, conditions, and privileges of employment

- For an employer to segregate, limit, or classify employees in any way that would deprive them of opportunities on the job or otherwise adversely affect their employee status

- For a labor union to refuse membership, refuse to refer for employment, expel from its membership, classify membership applicants, or make referrals for employment

- For an employment agency to classify employees or refuse to refer them for employment

- For an employer, a labor organization, or a joint labor-management committee to use an employment practice that has an adverse impact unless a business necessity can be established—and even that is not a valid defense against intentional discrimination

- For an employer, a labor organization, or a joint labor-management committee to use different tests, alter or adjust test scores, use different cutoff scores when selecting, promoting, or referring applicants for employment

- For an employer, a labor union, or a joint labor-management committee to refuse to admit employees or applicants to training or apprenticeship programs

- For an employer, a labor union, or a joint labor-management committee to discriminate against employees because they have made charges, participated in an investigation, testified, or participated in a hearing under Title VII.[4]

Title VII is the statutory backbone of the civil rights movement, including the rights of women at work. It is the most frequently cited statute in equal employment opportunity law. According to this act, when a woman is harassed or paid unfairly, her civil rights are violated. This constitutes a violation of federal law, and responsibility for the advocacy of her rights is elevated from the state or local level to the national level. Among the more sensational outcomes in the enforcement of the law have been a $300 million class-action settlement against State Farm Insurance and $40 million judgments against General Motors and USX Corporation. But even the less impressive average cost of $75,000 to a company facing a discrimination case illustrates the power of the legislation as an instrument of social change.[5]

1968—Executive Order 11246 as Amended by Executive Order 11375

In 1965 President Lyndon Johnson issued Executive Order 11246, requiring that government contracts of $10,000 or more contain provisions against employment discrimination because of race, religion, color, or national origin. Executive Order 11375 added gender to the list of prohibited discrimination criteria and required that employers file affirmative-action programs. Enforcement responsibility rests with the Office of Federal Contract Compliance Programs (OFCCP) in the U.S. Department of Labor.[6] As an impressively large purchaser of goods and services, with this executive order the federal government put the power of the national purse behind the Civil Rights Act of 1964.

1972—Equal Employment Opportunity Act

When Congress passed the Equal Employment Opportunity Act, it provided detailed guidelines for employers in a document entitled *Guidelines on Discrimination because of Sex*. This document established the "thou shalt nots" of sex discrimination in employment. It brought such terms as *bona fide occupational qualification* and *sexual harassment* into the national vocabulary and spelled out what could and could not be asked on job applications and in interviews.

1978—Pregnancy Discrimination Act

The Pregnancy Discrimination Act of 1978 amended Title VII to specifically prohibit discrimination on the basis of pregnancy, childbirth, or related medical conditions. The act made the following actions illegal:

- Refusing to hire or promote women because of pregnancy

- Terminating the employment of women because of pregnancy

- Arbitrarily establishing a leave policy for pregnancy that is not based on the ability of the pregnant woman to continue working

- Penalizing women returning to work after childbirth in areas such as credit for previous service, accrued retirement benefits, and accumulated seniority

- Firing or refusing to hire women for exercising their right to have abortions[7]

This legislation removed the uniquely female function of childbearing as a justification for different treatment at work, reducing the aura surrounding pregnancy and limiting its impact on women's careers to something more comparable to an ordinary and necessary medical procedure or a temporary disability.

1980—Sexual Harassment Guidelines

The Equal Employment Opportunity Commission's 1972 document *Guidelines on Discrimination because of Sex* was amended to reaffirm that sexual harassment is an unlawful employment practice under Title VII and to clarify what constitutes sexual harassment and an employer's responsibilities to prevent it. The definition says that:

> Unwelcome sexual advances, requests for sexual favors, and other verbal or physical conduct of a sexual nature constitute sexual harassment when: (1) submission to such conduct is made either explicitly or implicitly a term or condition of an individual's employment, (2) submission to or rejection of such conduct by an individual is used as the basis for employment decisions affecting such individual, or (3) such conduct has the purpose or effect of unreasonably interfering with an individual's work performance or creating an intimidating, hostile, or offensive working environment.[8]

The *Guidelines* made employers responsible for preventing sexual harassment, including the acts of its agents and supervisory employees, whether or not the employer knows about, authorizes, or even forbids the offending actions. Responsibility for harassment in the workplace extends to fellow employees, and even nonemployees, if the employer or its agents or supervisors know or should know of the conduct and do not take immediate and appropriate corrective action.[9]

The first two conditions in the definition of sexual harassment are known as *quid pro quo* ("this for that") *harassment*, which occurs when sex is expected in exchange for favorable employment decisions or treatment. The third is called *hostile environment harassment*, which occurs when an atmosphere is created on the job that interferes with an employee's right to work without intimidation or disruption from unwelcome sexual behavior.[10] The EEOC *Guidelines* were unanimously affirmed by the Supreme Court in its 1986 decision in *Meritor Savings Bank v. Vinson*, and they are widely relied upon as guidance for the courts.

1991—Civil Rights Act of 1991

According to the Bureau of National Affairs, an organization that monitors and reports on legislation, the Civil Rights Act of 1991 was a congressional effort to overturn a series of Supreme Court decisions and inform the "conservative-dominated court that its overall judicial attitude on...civil rights is not what Congress has in mind."[11] Key provisions regarding sex discrimination include:

- In 1989, the Supreme Court in *Wards Cove Packing Co. v. Atonio* made it easier for an employer to defend against disparate impact charges.* The 1991 act restored balance by requiring the employer to show job relatedness and business necessity for an employment practice being challenged. It also said that disparate impact is established if the employer fails to adopt an available, less discriminatory alternative and that business necessity is not a valid defense for intentional discrimination.[12]

- The Supreme Court ruled in *Price Waterhouse v. Hopkins,* referred to as a *mixed-motive case,* that if a discriminatory employment decision would have been made for another, nondiscriminatory reason anyway, the employer would not be liable for intentional discrimination. The 1991 act says that discrimination is illegal even if other, lawful factors were partial motives for the action.[13]

- By extending the 1866 Civil Rights Act, the 1991 act allows recovery of compensatory and punitive damages, as well as attorneys' fees, by victims of intentional sex discrimination; previously these damages and fees were limited to cases of racial and ethnic bias. Most compensatory damage awards and all punitive damage awards are limited by employer size. Any party to such an action can now demand a jury trial.[14]

- The 1991 act prohibits adjusting employment test scores, using different cutoff scores, or changing the results of tests on the basis of sex or other protected criteria; actual scores must be reported.

- Title II of the act, called the *Glass Ceiling Act of 1991,* sets up a commission to study artificial barriers to the advancement of women and minorities at work and to recommend ways for overcoming them.[15]

The main thrust of the Civil Rights Act of 1991 was reaffirmation of congressional interest in civil rights in general and sex discrimination in particular. In effect, the new Civil Rights Act recalibrates the courts, removing ambiguities and making clearer Congress's intention that the broad principles of civil rights not be lost in the fine points of judicial and legislative phrasing. Similarly, the Glass Ceiling Act sets the tone

---

Disparate impact occurs when an employee is adversely affected by practices that appear to be gender-neutral but are in fact discriminatory.

for the future by focusing on the removal of poorly defined barriers to women at work.

Applying the Law to Gender Issues at Work

Legal challenges to employers on gender issues fall into two major areas: (1) violation of the equal pay statutes as they apply to sex and (2) discrimination against someone under the civil rights laws because of her or his sex. The former is limited to disputes involving pay, but the latter can range from equal opportunity to compensation to sexual harassment.

This section describes real-world situations in which employers have found themselves in court defending themselves against employees' charges that they were wronged because of their sex. These cases, on equal pay and sexual harassment, provide "thinking points" for managers as they go about their daily business with a workforce composed almost equally of men and women:

- What makes employees believe that management has done them wrong?

- How do employees' grievances find the basis for a court hearing under the equal pay and civil rights laws?

- What are an employer's greatest vulnerabilities?

- What are an employer's most likely defenses?

- How have the courts reasoned on the basic issues?

Six cases are described within each of two sections, equal pay and sexual harassment. From these cases and others like them we have listed summary points for managers under each heading. The summary points may trigger memories about your own working experiences that make the case histories, which may be the kinds of situations you face as a manager, valuable in handling gender issues in your own company.

The discussions on the six cases in each category cover the issues surrounding the suit, the points the courts deemed critical in their resolution, linkage between the cases, and the overall significance of the cases to managers who want to avoid becoming a party to similar challenges. Each group of six cases is presented in chronological order, from the earliest to the most current. The choice of cases is not exhaustive; some are well-known classics, and others are more obscure building block cases that simply demonstrate how the law operates in different circumstances. Not every case we mention in the book is among the dozen we've chosen to develop at some length. But in most instances, all the cases we cite illustrate similar issues in similar ways.

The law is constantly unfolding. In the fall of 1994, the Supreme Court ruled that a woman need not prove psychological injury to establish that she suffered sexual harassment in the form of a hostile work environment (*Harris v. Forklift*). And another refinement of the law occurred in New York, where the U.S. Court of Appeals for the Second Circuit reversed a lower court decision and concluded that a woman who had reluctantly acceded to a sexual relationship with her boss could sue under federal civil rights law—the focus properly being on the prohibited conduct, not the victim's response (*Kariban v. Columbia University*).

Case law tends to evolve until it yields certain points of relative clarity that become precedents for future rulings and, eventually, such well-known guidelines in our society that we follow them without being ordered by a court. Some of what you will read may sound familiar because the cases made the popular or professional news; other aspects may surprise and inform you. In either instance, the value of the cases lies in making you an informed manager who can avoid sexual harassment and equal pay conflicts before a costly hearing becomes the only way to resolve the issue—whether you are a principal in the case or a third-party manager just trying to run an organization in the midst of such a challenge.

Read the cases not as an aspiring corporate counsel but as a manager looking for commonsense lessons without getting bogged down with legalese. In general, ignore whether the employer is in the private or the public sector or the particular industry used in the example. Instead, identify parallels with your own situation, and consider how you might handle the same issues in your own work environment. As you review the lessons for managers following the cases, think about the contested issues with which you can identify, the people involved in them (most probably women and men not unlike you and the people you manage), and the "there but for the grace of the gods go I" aspects you'll recognize in many of the cases.

Six Court Cases on Equal Pay

In modern case law, the oldest category of federal antidiscrimination protection for women at work is equal pay. It began with the Fair Labor Standards Act of 1938 and evolved into the Equal Pay Act of 1963. The former didn't specifically address gender but gave both sexes the beginnings of fair treatment on issues of pay. The 1963 amendment addressed sex discrimination directly, proposed equal pay for equal work, and prohibited separate standards of compensation based on sex, with a few exceptions like merit pay and seniority.

When the Civil Rights Act became law in 1964, and the Equal Pay Act was implemented the same year, both pieces of legislation came to be used as legal bases to resolve pay disputes when gender was at issue. The equal pay cases that follow also contain references to civil rights law, since the two often overlap.

Case 1

Christensen v. The State of Iowa[16]

Issues

- If women hold jobs that are of "equal value" to their employer as those held by men, are they being discriminated against if they don't receive equal pay, even though their jobs do not constitute "equal work" and they have "equal access" to either kind of job?
- What is more important in determining whether discrimination has occurred—"equal worth" or "labor market value"?

Summary of the Case

In 1977 a group of women representing the exclusively female clerical workers of the University of Northern Iowa contended that the practice of paying the mostly male physical plant workers higher wages amounted to illegal sex-based pay discrimination because the jobs were of equal value to their employer. They initially made claims under the Equal Pay Act that were abandoned, in part because of their inability to prove that they were being denied equal pay for equal work. Instead, they proceeded under Title VII of the Civil Rights Act.

The university's defense was that it had implemented a personnel evaluation scheme known as the *Hayes system* to objectively evaluate each job based on its relative worth to the employer and that any remaining pay differences were justified by the local labor market. The women clerical employees claimed the university's approach merely perpetuated a discriminatory system in violation of Title VII and that they should be paid the same as men working in the physical plant because their effort was worth as much as the men's to the university. The court disagreed, saying that the purpose of Title VII is to provide equal opportunity, not to correct inequities based on supply and demand or other economic factors that determine wage rates for various kinds of work. It said that equality of opportunity was not at issue in this situation and that the women were seeking "an invalid construction of Title VII that may establish a prima facie (legally sufficient to establish a fact or case unless disproved) violation of that act whenever employees of different sexes receive disparate compensation for work of differing skills that may, subjectively, be of equal value to the employer, but does not command an equal price in the labor market. Appellants' theory ignores economic realities. The value of the job to the employer represents but one factor affecting wages. Other factors may include the supply of workers willing to do the job and the ability of the workers to band together to bargain collectively for higher wages."[17]

The trial court made these findings, which were not questioned on appeal:

- Plaintiffs made no showing that the work of clerical employees was substantially equal to that of physical plant employees.
- Nonfaculty job openings at the university were posted and circulated in an open manner that did not favor men over women.
- Plaintiffs were not locked into clerical positions by any university policy or practice.[18]

The courts found that the women clerical employees "failed to prove by a preponderance of evidence that they have been discriminated against in terms of compensation because of sex."[19]

Conclusions

Establishing a case for sex-based wage discrimination requires more than showing differently compensated women and men separated into categories of work that appear, subjectively, to be of comparable worth. The laws are limited to settling questions of equal pay for equal work (the Equal Pay Act) and outright discrimination in which one class is paid less solely because of gender and not other economic factors (Title VII of the Civil Rights Act).

Case 2

Lemons v. City and County of Denver[20]

Issues

Were nurses being discriminated against when they were not paid the same as higher-paid but differently classified workers who the nurses felt better represented their "worth" to the city and community than did other nurses, even though the work was not "equal"?

Summary of the Case

In 1980 nurses working for the city of Denver sued their employer, claiming sex discrimination under the Civil Rights Act and the Fourteenth Amendment. They contended that nurses are predominantly women, historically underpaid, and worth as much as other, higher-paid work classifications in the city's personnel system. They maintained that basing their pay on that of other nurses in the labor market amounted to sex-based discrimination. The trial court found, and the appeals court affirmed, that it had no authority to order a remedy under the Civil Rights Act or the Fourteenth Amendment:

> The plaintiffs did not show that the work in the classification they sought was equal to that in which they found themselves. The only showing was that the City's system of pay and classification provided equal pay for equal work. The proof demonstrated that the City provided equal opportunities for women including plaintiffs and the class. The parity plaintiffs seek is not a remedy which the courts can now provide.[21]

The opinion drew parallels to *Christensen v. The State of Iowa* (Case 1), in which a broader class of employees, clerical workers, failed in a similar suit.

Conclusions

For the nurses to have brought a case they could win, they would have needed to prove, for example, that women and men nurses were being paid differently for the same work, something they were not even attempting to show. Another approach might have been to show studies that found them comparable in value to other classes of workers who were paid more simply because they were men. To argue only that the work of nurses was worth the pay of workers in other classifications receiving higher wages, whether or not the work was equal to that in their own classification, was to beg the logic of the labor market that had decided, fairly or not, what the job of nursing was worth relative to other kinds of work.

Case 3

International Union of Electrical, Radio and Machine Workers, AFL-CIO-CLC v. Westinghouse Electric Corporation[22]

Issues

If Title VII of the Civil Rights Act says that it is illegal to pay employees different wages on the basis of race, religion, or national origin, can employers use the Bennett Amendment to the Civil Rights Act* as a defense against discrimination charges when they pay women and men different wages due to their gender?

Summary of the Case

In 1980 workers for Westinghouse claimed that the company deliberately set the wages lower for jobs done predominantly by women and that the practice violated the Civil Rights Act of 1964 even though the jobs did not necessarily involve equal or substantially equal work. It was shown that Westinghouse established a job classification structure in the 1930s that set lower wage rates for classifications that were predominantly female. In 1965, when the company removed the sex distinction, it retained the practice of paying women less.

Westinghouse knew that under Title VII it could not make wage distinctions based on race, religion, or national origin (for example, Protestant welders could not be paid differently than Catholic plumbers if the reason was their religion), but the company contended that the Bennett Amendment specifically allowed the sex distinction.The trial court held that the plaintiffs had no case under Title VII since the Bennett Amendment made it necessary for them to show that they did equal work. Because the question was thought to be one that would likely recur, the appeals court addressed the meaning of the Bennett Amendment and concluded that it was not the intention of Congress in passing the amendment to prohibit bringing an action under Title VII. It remanded the case for further proceedings, saying:

> We make no judgment as to whether, on the merits, the plaintiffs will be able to sustain their burden of proof. We rule merely that they must be given the opportunity to present the case to a fact-finder to evaluate their evidence.[24]

The court also said that if the plaintiffs could show that Westinghouse deliberately set lower wage classifications for jobs primarily filled by women, they would prove that a violation of Title VII had occurred.

A dissent to the court decision was filed; it maintained that "read together, Title VII and the Equal Pay Act provide a balanced approach to resolving sex-based wage discrimination claims. Title VII guarantees that qualified female employees will have access to

---

*The Bennett Amendment to the Civil Rights Act says that employers may make a distinction on the basis of sex in determining compensation if the difference in wages is authorized by the provisions of section 206(d) of the Equal Pay Act. Equal pay for equal work is required except when pay differs on the basis of a seniority system, a merit system, wages that result from a quality- or quantity-based production system, or any factor other than sex.[23]

all jobs, and the Equal Pay Act assures that men and women performing the same work will be paid equally....This approach [assures] that the courts and federal agencies will not become entangled in adjudicating the wage rates to be paid for dissimilar jobs—a process in which they have little expertise."[25]

The result of the appeal was to counter the trial court's ruling that, on the grounds of the Bennett Amendment alone, action under Title VII could not proceed. The case was returned to the lower court for trial on its merits.

Conclusions

The Westinghouse case began to establish sex-based pay discrimination as something to be considered under broader provisions than merely the Equal Pay Act. The appeals court said that the Bennett Amendment could not be used to short-circuit the protection of the Civil Rights Act by requiring that people claiming sex discrimination fulfill a provision not required of people seeking to remedy race or religious discrimination, for example.

Case 4

County of Washington v. Gunther[26]

Issues

Is an employer protected from action under Title VII of the Civil Rights Act if deliberate sex-based wage discrimination is proved, even if equal pay for equal work is not at issue?

Summary of the Case

Washington County, Oregon, had a prison system with separate facilities and guards for women and men inmates. The women guards were paid substantially less than their male counterparts and in 1981 sought relief under Title VII on the grounds that the county was intentionally discriminating against them because of their sex. They claimed that they were paid lower wages for substantially the same work done by the male guards, basing their assertion on the fact that the county set a lower wage rate for female guards than warranted by its own labor market survey.

The trial court ruled against the plaintiffs on the basis that their claim could not be raised under Title VII unless the equal work test of the Bennett Amendment was satisfied, and it was not. "The appeals court reversed, holding that persons alleging sex discrimination 'are not precluded from suing under Title VII to protest...discriminatory compensation practices' merely because their jobs were not equal to higher paying jobs held by members of the opposite sex."[27]

The plaintiffs claimed that the employer had evaluated the jobs of the men and the women, determined that the women should properly be paid about 95 percent as much as the men but actually paid the women only 70 percent as much as the men—and that the difference was due to intentional sex discrimination.[28] The Supreme Court affirmed the judgment of the Court of Appeals that the principle of equal pay for equal work was not a precondition for hearing a sex-based wage discrimination case under Title VII.

Conclusions

The Supreme Court's ruling in *Gunther* ended employer use of the Bennett Amendment as a means for circumventing the sex discrimination provision of the Civil Rights Act where equal pay for equal work is not a factor.

Case 5

Plemer v. Parsons-Gilbane[29]

Issues

Is demonstrating that a woman and a man were paid differently for the same job enough to prove that the woman was discriminated against?

Summary of the Case

In 1983 Christine Plemer was working for Parsons-Gilbane as a personnel assistant and was promoted to equal employment opportunity representative, the company's sole full-time EEO person, reporting to the part-time EEO officer. When the company decided to hire a full-time EEO officer, Plemer applied for the position, was unsuccessful, and resigned, claiming sex discrimination and constructive discharge (that is, that what the company did amounted to firing her). The company gave Plemer a 5 percent retroactive raise and then hired a man for her vacant position at a salary 6.8 percent higher than the one to which she was raised upon her resignation. When the man hired to replace Plemer resigned, he was replaced by a female employee from within the company, who was paid a salary 8.8 percent less than the vacating male's starting salary.

Plemer cited the Equal Pay Act to claim that she was paid less for equal work, and Title VII to show that she was intentionally discriminated against because she was a woman. The court viewed the situation differently then in the Gunther case (Case 4) and determined that Plemer had no convincing proof that her company knew she was worth more and deliberately paid her less:

> Plemer asks too much. She would have the courts make an essentially subjective assessment of the value of the differing duties and responsibilities of the positions…and then determine whether Plemer was paid less than the value of her position because she was female. If Plemer had shown that the company had placed those values on her and Willis' respective duties and responsibilities and were paying Willis the full value while paying Plemer less than her evaluated worth, her claims could be considered. It is not the province of the courts, however, to value the relative worth of Plemer's and Willis' differing duties and responsibilities.[30]

Since Plemer claimed that her employer discriminated against her individually (disparate treatment) and not that she was adversely affected by practices that appeared to be gender-neutral but were in fact discriminatory (disparate impact), she needed to prove intent, which she could not do.

The appeals court agreed with the trial court that Plemer had not made a sufficient case for losing the promotion because of sex discrimination, or that she had been constructively discharged, or that she had proved that the employer knew her pay should be more and deliberately paid her less because she was a woman. However, the lower court had refused to consider the statistical evidence Plemer had brought to court to rebut her employer's evidence to the contrary. In the opinion of the appeals court, her statistics were relevant to her ability to make a prima facie case under the Equal Pay Act and Title VII by showing that she was paid less than her male successor for the same work; further, although her statistics were possibly inadequate by themselves, they should have been considered at the lower court level as part of that case. The appeals court then ruled that Plemer deserved a hearing on her equal pay claim and that her statistics should be considered. It also reversed the award of attorneys' fees against her, disagreeing that her claim had been frivolous.

Conclusions

Plemer's claim that being passed over for a promotion and doing what she viewed as the same work as a higher-paid man did not necessarily constitute sex or pay discrimination in the opinion of the courts. The court distanced itself from being the arbiter of what the efforts of individual workers might be worth in the labor market, limiting its role to deciding whether, as in *Gunther* (Case 4), after worth had been established, discrimination occurred. The appeals court protected the employee's right to raise such issues and present statistical evidence as proof without the threat of the cases being ruled frivolous.

Case 6
American Federation of State, County, and Municipal Employees, v. State of Washington[31]

Issues

Do employers discriminate when they establish systems that effectively create male job classifications and female job classifications that require the same or equal skill but pay those working in the "women's jobs" less?

Summary of the Case

In 1983 the state of Washington was accused of sex discrimination because it paid many of its women employees less than men for comparable work. The state had studied the matter a decade earlier, confirmed the problem, admitted it was discriminatory, and did nothing to remedy it.

About 15,500 of the state's 45,000 classified employees fell into job categories in which at least 70 percent of the workers were women. Studies showed that there was a 20 percent disparity between the salaries of those workers and men in positions that "required an equivalent or lesser composite of skill, effort, responsibility, and working conditions as reflected by an equal number of job evaluation points."[32] A "1974 report also found that the degree of discrimination increased as the job value increased. For jobs evaluated at 100 points, men's pay was 125 percent of women's pay. For jobs evaluated at 450 points, men's pay was 135 percent of women's pay."[33]

A class action suit was filed by the unions on behalf of the workers; sex-based wage discrimination based on the theory of comparable worth (equal pay for equal work) was alleged. Title VII of the Civil Rights Act prohibits disparate treatment and disparate impact. Employers can act in such a way only if they can demonstrate legitimate and overriding business necessity.

The court noted the history of the defendant: knowingly discriminating on the basis of sex, running separate help-wanted ads for male and female jobs, and ignoring studies that confirmed the existence of a segregated workforce. It found that the defendant failed to demonstrate a legitimate and overriding business justification for the discrimination. Discriminatory intent was established on the basis of the perpetuation of the disparity in salaries and by showing inverse correlations between the percentage of women in a job category and its salary. The defendant failed to establish any of the defenses to disparate treatment claims (merit pay, seniority, and so forth).

A Title VII case boils down to determining "whether the employer is treating some people less favorably than others because of their race, color, religion, sex, or national origin."[34] More than 200 exhibits comprising several thousand pages made it clear that the state of Washington had acted in a discriminatory way.

The court ruled:

> After careful review of the record herein, this Court cannot reach any conclusion other than the State of Washington has, and is continuing to maintain a compensation system which discriminates on the basis of sex. The State of Washington, has failed to rectify an acknowledged discriminatory disparity in compensation. The State has, and is continuing to treat some employees less favorably than others because of their sex, and this treatment is intentional.[35]

The court ordered injunctive relief from the discriminatory practices, back pay, and "any other relief that may be just and equitable."[36] It set aside claims by the defendant that states' rights amendments to the Constitution protect it from the court's action and that the cost and disruption of the settlement would be intolerable. The court appointed "a Master to assist the Court in the implementation of this decree" and retained jurisdiction in the case to implement the decree.[37]

Conclusions

State of Washington established that no matter how large or ingrained the pattern of discrimination, if it is blatant, demonstrable, ongoing, and rooted in long-standing studies that prove its existence, the courts have no choice but to correct it under law. No relief is available to the offending institution on the basis of states' rights or the burden of the remedy.

The Equal Pay Cases—Lessons for Managers. Workers and managers alike are subjective in how they assess the contributions of their associates. They see each other as more or less valuable members of the team for reasons that run the gamut from personalities and energy levels to the nature of the group of which they are a part. Being a woman or a man was, for a long time, a starting point for determining how much a person would be paid or what kind of job he or she might hold. Such thinking passes slowly.

The law does not allow today's manager the luxury of such prejudices. In the workplace arena, where the rules are constantly changing, managers and the people they supervise need the discipline of the kind of thinking that keeps them out of legal trouble and the type of judgment that helps them respond appropriately when confronted with a gender conflict on the job. What we've learned in recent years is reflected in rulings by the courts on the cases brought before them. The following list has been drawn from the six decisions we just reviewed and is provided here to help you deal with compensation issues in the 1990s:

- Civil rights and equal pay legislation is not intended to address economic questions such as subjective worth or supply and demand; rather, it addresses equal opportunity, equal pay for equal work, and outright sex-based discrimination.

- "Equal pay for equal work" is an unambiguous concept. If a woman and a man do essentially the same work, and you pay one of them lower wages for reasons other than those allowed in the Equal Pay Act (seniority, merit, and so forth), you will probably not be able to defend your actions in court. The equal pay for equal work provisions of the Equal Pay Act do not insulate employers from the sex discrimination protections of the Civil Rights Act; attempts by employers to use the Bennett Amendment to make equal pay a prerequisite to equal rights in gender cases have been unsuccessful in the courts.

- "Comparable worth" is a more ambiguous concept. Unless a study has been done or statistics exist to establish comparability, you stand a good chance of successfully attributing pay differences between workers to their labor market value. However, when job evaluations establish the comparable worth of positions held predominantly by men and those held predominantly by women, and those standards are ignored by employers, the courts may conclude that the reason for the differences is sex-based discrimination unless a convincing argument for another reason is produced.

- If you are faced with defending yourself against a discrimination charge based on unequal compensation, having made a good faith effort to achieve fairness in your workforce will help your case. Using an objective job evaluation system, posting job notices openly, encouraging both genders to apply for all vacancies, and filling vacancies based on merit will help show that the labor market, and not historically discriminatory practices, can be a legitimate reason for a pay differential.

- "Sex-based discrimination" is presumed when you pay a woman a lower wage than a man and cannot demonstrate a labor market value difference or show an allowable reason for the discrepancy such as seniority, merit, or a quantity or quality of production differential. You cannot pay a man more for the same work that a woman does, nor can you pay him more simply because he is a man. However, you *can* pay him more if the labor market indicates that what he does is of greater value to you than what his female counterpart does.

- To justify receiving higher pay, it is not enough for women to demonstrate that they are in a predominantly female class of employment that is being paid less than other groups that are mostly male. They have to show that the work is equal or that they are being discriminated against because of their sex, and not just because of the kind of work they do. However, when you, as employer or manager, establish the labor market value of your employees and then apply that knowledge unevenly to different groups, you are probably discriminating because of some group characteristic such as gender.

- An established company's history in dealing with wage structure issues can come back to haunt it. Westinghouse's well-documented 1930s sex-based personnel policies laid the basis for successful arguments that the "changes" it made in the 1960s simply perpetuated what had gone before. By knowingly maintaining a personnel system that discriminates on the basis of sex and not acting in good faith to correct it, a company invites judgment against itself.

- Corrective actions that change the appearance, but not the effect, of company policies can be challenged successfully if the effect is still discriminatory.

- Wise employers take a broad view of regulations and direct their compliance efforts according to the intent of the rules rather than looking for shelter in a narrow construction of the law that will give way to the broader principle as challenges are brought before the courts. For example, employers attempting to use the Bennett Amendment to the Civil Rights Act to say an equal pay claim is a prerequisite to righting sex discrimination wrongs under Title VII proved to be unsuccessful as a defense.

- In hiring and promoting you need to show that you have objective reasons for your selections and for the pay relative to other workers— particularly if a rejected candidate or a worker receiving lower pay is a member of a protected class under the Civil Rights Act. Be alert to hiring or promoting in ways that will help you avoid being charged with disparate treatment of an individual or with an even broader pattern of discrimination in which your overall actions have a disparate impact on a whole class of employees.

- It is unlikely that the courts will find any reasonably plausible case frivolous and thus award the employer damages.

These points are our commonsense conclusions drawn from the cases summarized earlier in the chapter. We believe that they represent accurate and useful guidance, but of course, they should not be substituted for the professional advice of legal counsel.

Six Court Cases on Sexual Harassment

The first modern federal legislation to help women gain fair treatment at work was the Equal Pay Act, but the most dramatic impact on the uneasy truce between the sexes in the workplace has come from enforcement of the sexual harassment guidelines of the Civil Rights Act. Sexual harassment law goes beyond mere equality and to the heart of the established cultural prerogatives of the sexes. The federal government has declared the workplace a sanctuary in which the traditionally predatory ways of men are forbidden if they infringe on a woman's right to work in a nonthreatening environment. Thus, an entire society has begun the process of dichotomizing man-woman behavior between what is appropriate to the social arena and what is both appropriate and legal at work. As is often the case with sweeping reforms, the judges of the land have been the referees and the decisions flowing from their chambers have defined new rules of behavior.

The following six case summaries describe some of the conflicts that have occurred in the mixed-gender workplace and the reasoning that has been used by the courts to resolve them. The section ends with points that distill the wisdom of these cases and others into a primer for managers trying to operate successfully in a complex work environment.

Case 7
Katz v. Dole[38]

Issues

Can a valid complaint based on sexual harassment be brought under Title VII even though a woman fails to prove that personnel actions taken by her employer were a result of different treatment due to her gender?

Summary of the Case

Deborah Katz was trained as an air traffic controller for the Federal Aviation Administration in Washington, D.C. In 1983 she claimed that she was subjected to frequent verbal abuse of a sexual nature by male controllers. When she complained to her supervisor, who, along with other supervisory personnel, had participated in harassing her, he suggested that she solve her problem by submitting to the sexual advances of the person about whom she was complaining. Although the trial court ruled against her, the appeals court found that she had made a case for her sexual harassment under the hostile environment category of Title VII and could have established it under the quid pro quo category since submitting sexually was suggested as a condition for improving her job situation. Katz also showed that the employer not only had been informed of the problem but had participated in the wrongful behavior. The appeals court reversed the trial court's decision that there had been no sexual harassment and remanded the case for remedies, but it affirmed the lower court decision that Katz had not been the subject of disparate treatment because of her sex. In each of the incidents, the defendant was able to show that the reasons for treating her differently were the result of misunderstandings or had other plausible causes not related to the sexual harassment.

Conclusions

The *Katz v. Dole* decision sent an emphatic message that blatant sexual harassment is indefensible. When the facts of the case, including testimony of the defense witnesses, confirmed harassment, the prima facie case for discrimination was made and the burden shifted to the employer. It was shown that the work environment was "poisoned"; that is, hostile environment harassment had occurred, and that an exchange of sexual favors was made a condition for favorable work decisions (quid pro quo harassment), all with supervisory knowledge and participation. Disparate treatment, denial of favorable schedules, and so forth, were not established, however, because the employer showed that such decisions were made for reasons other than the plaintiff's sex.

Case 8

Meritor Savings Bank, FSB v. Vinson[39]

Issues

- Do unwelcome sexual advances that create a hostile working environment constitute discrimination on the basis of sex?

- Can a Title VII violation be proved when the district court finds that the sexual relationship between the plaintiff and her supervisor was voluntary?
- Is an employer strictly liable for a hostile working environment created by a supervisor's sexual advances whether or not the employer knows or should have known of the supervisor's misconduct?

Summary of the Case

In 1986 plaintiff Mechelle Vinson alleged that her supervisor constantly subjected her to sexual harassment, during and after business hours, in and out of the workplace. She contended that he coerced her to have sex with him on many occasions, fondled her in front of other employees, and raped her on several occasions, and that she submitted for fear of jeopardizing her employment. The offensive conduct stopped a year before Vinson filed charges. Both supervisor and employer denied all allegations, claiming that the charges were fabricated in response to a work dispute.

The trial court found no discrimination, that the relationship had been voluntary, and that the employer was not liable because it had in place a policy against discrimination and a grievance procedure that the plaintiff did not use. The appeals court ruled that the lower court's concentration on the voluntary nature of the sexual relationship was immaterial if Vinson had tolerated the relationship as a condition of continued employment. It held the employer absolutely liable for its supervisor's actions. The Supreme Court upheld remanding to the lower court on hostile environment grounds and held that a proper inquiry should focus on the unwelcomeness of the conduct, not on its voluntariness—voluntary participation is not a valid defense. On the employer liability question, the Supreme Court affirmed EEOC guidelines that *common-law agency principles* (employers are responsible for the actions of their managers, who are their agents) be used in deciding individual cases, rejecting both the idea of automatic liability and the position that notice is always required.

Conclusions

Meritor v. Vinson established that unwelcome sexual behavior can indeed create a hostile working environment that constitutes discrimination on the basis of sex under Title VII. It further established that the correct inquiry for the courts is not whether the victim submits voluntarily but whether the sexual relationship is an unwelcome one linked to conditions of employment. Employer liability remained a matter of judgment in individual cases. It is not to be automatically assumed; nor is it easily dismissed merely because the employer has a policy against harassment and a grievance policy. For such policies to be effective, the employer cannot overlook harassment it reasonably should have seen and corrected; and notice is not always required, since intimidation might make it an unreasonable expectation. Other details of *Vinson*, such as the role of the plaintiff's previous behavior and dress, are discussed in the lessons for managers points at the end of this section.

Case 9

Broderick v. Ruder[40]

Issues

- Do pervasive, unwelcome sexual advances, requests for sexual favors, and other verbal or physical conduct of a sexual nature create a hostile or offensive work environment actionable under Title VII?
- Does affording preferential treatment to female employees who submit to sexual advances or other conduct of a sexual nature violate the rights of others under Title VII?
- Is information about the general work atmosphere, including treatment of other employees, relevant to a plaintiff's claim of hostile environment harassment?
- Can diminished performance that is the result of the discriminatory behavior and retaliation due to an employee's complaint be used as a basis for removing the complaining employee?

Summary of the Case

Catherine Broderick worked as a staff attorney for the Securities and Exchange Commission (SEC) in suburban Washington, D.C. In 1988 she claimed that her employer was responsible for creating and failing to remedy a sexually hostile work environment and that her supervisors retaliated against her for opposing it. She worked for the SEC for more than eight years and received only one promotion. Her supervisors maintained that this was because she did substandard work and did not take criticism well. Broderick charged that she was being retaliated against for not taking part in, and in fact opposing, practices at the office that created a hostile work environment. Male supervisors openly had affairs with female subordinates, who received favorable treatment. Unwelcome sexual advances and demands for sexual favors were common. Broderick established a prima facie case for her harassment and showed that she was reprimanded and threatened with termination when her complaints persisted—and that her complaints and the threats were linked. The employer claimed that Broderick was the subject of only isolated instances of quid pro quo harassment, but the court found that she had in fact suffered from broader hostile environment harassment created and allowed by the employer, who, under common-law agency principles, was responsible for the high-ranking supervisors who perpetrated it.

Conclusions

An atmosphere in the workplace that includes pervasive sexually offensive behavior, even though much of it is not directed at the plaintiff, can affect her work and violate her rights. The supervisors violated her rights, and those of others, by showing preferential promotion and other favorable treatment for women who cooperated sexually. Diminished performance is not a legitimate basis for removal when it is an outgrowth of an employer's discriminatory behavior. Retaliation against women exercising their rights under Title VII is, in itself, illegal.

Case 10

Waltman v. International Paper Company[41]

Issues

Must a plaintiff prove that her harassers engaged in a conspiracy, that the employer had a policy of discrimination, that she was harassed by the same people over a period of time, and that there were no gaps in harassment incidents (permitting her to establish a claim of continuing violation of her civil rights and thus overcoming the 180-day limit for filing an EEOC complaint)?

Summary of the Case

Susan Waltman worked as a power plant employee for the International Paper Company in Louisiana. In 1989 she alleged that she was physically and verbally harassed by about 80 percent of her male coworkers and a contractor's employees. She also claimed that she was denied promotion because of her sex. In dismissing most of her complaint, the district court held that her claims went beyond the 180-day filing limit and were otherwise unfounded. The appeals court disagreed, reversing and remanding for a full trial on the merits. It found that Waltman had sufficiently established her case for continuous discrimination, with incidents ranging from lewd graffiti, gestures, and comments to physical touching and attacks over a period of years. Supervisors responded to her complaints by stopping certain offensive actions, but they did not reprimand the offending employees or correct the overall hostile environment. Waltman was denied promotion, in part as a result of opinions of coworkers who harassed her. She eventually took extended sick leave that was an outgrowth of the harassment and quit soon after returning to work.

Conclusions

An employer is not immune from sexual harassment charges because of technicalities like 180-day filing limitations, if the violation was continuous and even one incident occurred during the period. The plaintiff bears no obligation to prove conspiracy, a company policy of discrimination, or the seamless character of the harassment to establish a continuing violation. Employer actions that include moving an employee to another shift, reading its antidiscrimination policy aloud to its employees, and so forth, are not sufficient to satisfy its obligation to provide a workplace free of harassment that substantially and negatively affects women workers. Subjective promotion criteria and promotion policies that include input from offending employees imply discrimination and warrant a hearing.

Case 11

Andrews v. City of Philadelphia[42]

Issues

- What is the relative importance of jury findings and a judge's separate ruling?
- What is the relative importance of an overall situation versus individual incidents in establishing hostile environment sexual harassment?
- To what extent does qualified immunity protect public officials from liability when they should have known the legal standard?
- How immune are jurisdictions (in this case, a city) and their officials from liability for the discriminatory acts of their supervisors and employees?
- Is sexual harassment enough of an outrage to constitute the intentional infliction of emotional distress?

Summary of the Case

In 1989 two female Philadelphia police officers alleged that both their rights to equal protection and their civil rights were violated by coworkers who harassed them because they were women. The women, who worked in the accident investigation unit, also charged intentional infliction of emotional distress. The appeals court described their situation like this:

> The evidence in this case includes not only name calling, pornography, displaying sexual objects on desks, but also the recurrent disappearance of plaintiffs' case files and work product, anonymous phone calls, and destruction of other property. The court should review this evidence in its totality...and then reach a determination.[43]

Although the case was legally complex, it boiled down to a trial in which the jury delivered a verdict for the female police officers based on their claims that they received unequal protection, were discriminated against because they were women, and were the victims of intentionally inflicted emotional distress. In a separate action before the bench (not the jury trial), the court found for the defendants on the Title VII claims that the women's civil rights had been violated.

An immediate motion by the plaintiffs to the court to make its judgment consistent with the jury's verdict was denied. A simultaneous motion by the defense to ignore the jury's verdict and find for the defendants partly succeeded in that it removed the intentional infliction of emotional distress claims against the supervisors and the city and removed the unequal protection claims against the city. The female officers appealed, arguing that there was enough evidence to support the jury verdicts and that the trial judge had misapplied the law and failed to reconcile his Title VII findings with those of the jury.

The appeals court ruled that the essential conditions of a Title VII claim existed, the jury findings were improperly ignored, and common-law agency principles had not been properly considered in weighing the city's responsibility for the actions of its supervisors. In the absence of retaliatory behavior, it ruled that the emotional distress charge failed to rise to the required level of outrageousness. The appeals court also affirmed the trial court's decision that the city was not liable for unequal treatment claims, since the evidence presented failed to show that it authorized or acquiesced in the discriminatory conduct of its supervisors. The appeal resulted in a new trial on the merits for the hostile environment sexual harassment claim under Title VII.

Conclusions

Although the law provides for independent judgment, a jury finding of discriminatory behavior cannot be ignored by the court. According to this appeals court, the lower court bears a responsibility to rebut, not just disagree with, the jury finding. The trial court in this case erred in focusing on the individual incidents and not the overall pattern of sexual harassment that denied these women what Title VII promises: a workplace where sexual harassment will not adversely alter their ability to perform. Public officials have no immunity from laws they reasonably should be aware of, like antidiscrimination. A city, or any employer, bears a heavy burden under common-law agency principles for the actions of people to whom it grants authority. When that authority is misused to discriminate, the employer may be found liable. Finally, sexual harassment alone generally does not rise to the level of outrageousness necessary to substantiate a case for intentional infliction of emotional distress. Retaliation for turning down sexual propositions is usually required.

Case 12

Ellison v. Brady[44]

Issues

- What tests should be applied to determine whether conduct is sufficiently severe or pervasive to alter the conditions of employment and create a hostile working environment?
- What remedial actions can employers take to shield themselves from liability for sexual harassment by employees?

Summary of the Case

Kerry Ellison and Sterling Gray met while training to be Internal Revenue Service agents in San Mateo, California. The class went to lunch in groups, and Ellison once went with Gray alone. He began to show unwelcome interest in her, and she tried to avoid him. Gray wrote Ellison what she described as a "bizarre" note which she showed to her supervisor, who said that it constituted sexual harassment. Ellison said that she would initially like to try and handle the situation herself and asked a male coworker to tell Gray to leave her alone.

However, Gray then wrote Ellison a lengthy letter expressing continuing interest in her, mailing it to St. Louis, where she had gone for training. After receiving the letter, Ellison immediately telephoned her supervisor and asked for a transfer or the transfer of Gray. The IRS moved Gray to San Francisco and told him not to contact Ellison. Gray filed a union grievance and returned to San Mateo after six months. When he returned, Ellison asked for a temporary reassignment and filed a formal sexual harassment complaint. Gray wrote Ellison a third letter, still maintaining that they had some sort of relationship. Although the IRS investigator of

Ellison' s complaint agreed that Gray's behavior constituted sexual harassment, the Treasury Department (IRS is under Treasury) denied Ellison's complaint on the grounds that it did not describe a continuing pattern of sexual harassment covered by EEOC regulations. On appeal, the EEOC concluded that the IRS had taken adequate action to prevent repetition of the problem. In 1990 Ellison filed a complaint in federal district court, which found that she had failed to state a prima facie case of hostile working environment sexual harassment.

Ellison appealed, and the appeals court examined relevant case law and determined that "Gray's conduct falls somewhere between [the extremes of] forcible rape and the mere utterance of an epithet."[45] It emphasized the perspective of the victim and stated that "Title VII's protection...comes into play long before the point where victims...require psychiatric assistance."[46] The court went on to say that because women are most often the victims of rape and assault, they may reasonably worry that harassing behavior may escalate to violence. Therefore, the court determined that a reasonable woman or reasonable victim standard should apply when judging whether or not sexual actions are threatening enough to create an abusive working environment. "To avoid liability, employers may have to educate and sensitize their workforce to eliminate conduct which a reasonable victim would consider unlawful sexual harassment."[47] The appeals court further found that the employer's action against Gray was inadequate in that it did not reprimand him, put him on probation, or inform him that repeated harassment would result in suspension or termination. The expectation that the victim should move to a less desirable location to avoid her harasser was also unacceptable. The appeals court reversed the trial court's decision that Ellison did not make a prima facie case of hostile environment sexual harassment and remanded the case for further proceedings under the finding that she had.

Conclusions

The test of whether certain behaviors are severe or pervasive enough to constitute harassment should be the judgment of a reasonable woman or victim. To shield itself from liability, an employer must take actions reasonably calculated to end the harassment.

The Sexual Harassment Cases—Lessons for Managers. The EEOC publishes periodic notices that give policy guidance on defining and handling sexual harassment. These notices are based on case law and precedents that are constantly evolving in the light of new decisions by the courts. The points that follow draw heavily not only on the six cases summarized above but on many others used by the EEOC to establish its operational guidelines for investigating complaints. The information that follows gives a commonsense understanding but certainly not definitive guidance on sexual harassment law. Although some overlapping is inevitable, the points are grouped under four topics: (1) kinds of harassment, (2) when behaviors become harassment, (3) the reasonable person standard, and (4) employer liability. Even this general guidance will put you in a better position to avoid the many pitfalls to be found in managing a mixed-gender workforce.

Kinds of Harassment

- *Quid pro quo* sexual harassment occurs when submitting to or rejecting sexual advances becomes the basis for favorable or unfavorable employment decisions affecting the person being propositioned.[48]

- *Hostile environment sexual harassment* occurs when unwelcome sexual conduct unreasonably interferes with a person's job performance or creates an intimidating, hostile, or offensive working environment, even if it does not result in tangible or economic job consequences.[49]
  Note that quid pro quo and hostile environment harassment often operate in the same situation. For example, making the work environment so unpleasant that the person quits will, in some instances, amount to forcing the person to barter sexual favors for peace on the job or for the job itself.[50]

- *Continuing-violation sexual harassment* takes place when the offending behavior occurs over time and not as a series of discrete acts. As long as the violation occurs at least once during the 180 days preceding the filing of a charge, earlier actions can become part of the suit as well. There is precedent (*Meritor v. Vinson*) for ignoring the 180-day rule entirely; therefore the rule should not be relied upon as a defense.[51]

When Workplace Behavior Becomes Sexual Harassment

- Title VII does not prohibit all conduct of a sexual nature in the workplace, only advances that are unwelcome and constitute a term or condition of employment. Or sexual conduct has to be "sufficiently severe or pervasive 'to alter the conditions of [the victim's] employment and create an abusive working environment.'"[52]

- Sexual attraction is a recognized part of the normal social exchange between employees, so it is important to distinguish between "invited," "uninvited-but-welcome," "offensive-but-tolerated," and "flatly rejected" sexual advances. *Unwelcome conduct* is that which the employee does not solicit or incite and, in addition, regards as undesirable or offensive. Although the victim is expected to communicate that the harasser's conduct is unwelcome and is encouraged to file a complaint, these expectations are not uniformly enforced, since the courts have recognized that fear of retaliation can silence a victim. The victim's conduct should consistently demonstrate that the harasser's behavior is unwelcome, and the credibility of both parties is a valid consideration during investigation of complaints.[53]

- A single incident or statement does not normally constitute harassment. A sustained pattern of offensive conduct usually needs to be proved unless a single incident was severe or physical.[54] Unwelcome, intentional touching of intimate body areas is of sufficient gravity to violate Title VII. In such cases, the employer bears the burden of demonstrating that the conduct did not create a hostile work environment.[55]

- A voluntary sexual relationship that is still an unwelcome one constitutes sexual harassment. Voluntariness is not a defense; the focus, according to the Supreme Court, should be on the unwelcomeness, not on whether the victim was a voluntary participant.[56]

- When an employee at first welcomes a sexual relationship or the kind of behavior that creates a working environment she later finds hostile, to prevail in a complaint she bears the burden of making it clear to the offending party that the sexual relationship is no longer welcome. If she is then denied an employment benefit because of her announced change of attitude, the action constitutes quid pro quo harassment.[57]

- Several requests over a period of months by a coworker to have a sexual affair, followed by coolness but no coercion, pressure, or abuse, do not in themselves constitute hostile environment sexual harassment.[58]

- The courts have ruled that a plaintiff's previous behavior can be a factor in the disposition of a complaint, especially in hostile environment harassment cases, where the victim regularly participated in the kinds of behavior she now complains about. However, this is not a valid defense against quid pro quo harassment or justification for more extreme, abusive, or persistent comments or a physical assault. Provocative dress, speech, and behavior are admissible in a sexual harassment case, but their relevance is carefully weighed against the potential for unfair prejudice.[59]

Reasonable Person Standard
- Deciding whether harassment is severe or pervasive enough to create a hostile environment is a matter for the objective judgment of a reasonable person. Title VII was not designed for the purpose of "vindicating the petty slights suffered by the hypersensitive." So sexual flirtation or innuendo, even vulgar language that is trivial or only annoying, might not be judged as making the workplace a hostile

environment. Behavior has to substantially adversely affect the work environment in the judgment of a reasonable person.[60]

- The reasonable person standard is also used to determine whether challenged conduct is sexual in nature or is a normal social exchange between the sexes. For example, was the remark an invitation or a proposition? how long should it take to accept no as an answer?[61]

- Reasonable person judgments cannot be made in a vacuum but should consider the context in which particular behaviors occur and the perspective of the victim. Gender or sexual slurs, displays of "girlie" pictures, and so forth, can constitute a hostile work environment even if segments of the workforce think that they are harmless or insignificant.[62]

- A woman does not forfeit her right to be free from sexual harassment by accepting employment in an atmosphere that traditionally has included vulgar, antifemale language and behavior. The fact that it existed before she came, and that she entered the job environment voluntarily, does not alter Title VII's mandate prohibiting such behavior and attitudes from poisoning the work environment for those the law was designed to protect.[63]

- The courts have recognized that women are more threatened by sexual advances than men and have established the reasonable person standard to emphasize the perspective of the victim, referring to it as the *reasonable woman* or *reasonable victim standard.*[64]

Employer Liability

- An employer can be liable under Title VII if the offensive conduct is directed toward a person because of gender, even though sexual activity or language is not involved, and Title VII can be used to establish the existence of discriminatory terms and conditions of employment.[65]

- There is no definitive rule on employer liability in hostile environment sexual harassment; common-law agency principles are used to establish employer liability. If the offending person is shown to be acting as an agent of the employer or with the authority of the employer, it is difficult for the employer to escape liability.[66]

- According to the Supreme Court, an employer is neither automatically liable, nor freed from liability by not being informed of the problem. An employer is certainly liable if it "knew, or upon reasonably diligent inquiry should have known," of the harassment. If it is common knowledge in the workplace, the employer is presumed to have known as well.[67]

- Having a policy against harassment is not enough to relieve an employer of liability if the policy is not an effective one or if it is not rigorously enforced. If the employer knows about harassment by supervisors or other employees and does not make vigorous efforts to stop it, the employer becomes liable for the employees' actions. In the absence of a strong, consistently applied and effective policy against harassment, employees can reasonably assume that harassing behavior by supervisors, who are given "apparent authority" by the employer, will be ignored, tolerated, or even condoned by the employer. (*Apparent authority* is the power given to supervisors to make employment decisions such as hiring, firing, and promoting affecting those who work for them—the greater the apparent authority, the more power to impose an unwelcome sexual liaison or make the working environment a hostile one.) The employer can divest its supervisors of this type of apparent authority by implementing a strong policy against sexual harassment and maintaining an effective complaint procedure.[68]

- Title VII imposes on employers a duty to provide their employees with a workplace free of sexual harassment. The responsibility associated with that duty cannot be delegated to anyone else.

- The employer is liable for *constructive discharge* (when an employee is effectively dismissed because the working conditions are so objectionable that the employee feels compelled to quit). An important factor to consider, however, is whether an effective internal grievance procedure exists. An employee who quits without giving the employer a fair opportunity to remedy the situation may have difficulty proving a constructive discharge complaint.[69]

- The employer might be liable for discrimination against qualified employees if it denies them job opportunities that have been granted to employees who have submitted to sexual advances.[70]

- An employer cannot remove an employee because of diminished job performance that is a result of the employer's discriminatory behavior.[71]

- Although the EEOC's guidelines are not controlling on the courts, they represent a body of experience and informed judgment that is frequently used by the courts and the litigants in cases of sexual harassment.[72]

These points are offered as reasonable representations of the law and should be taken as general advice believed by the authors to be valid. However, they are no substitute for legal counsel and are not intended to take the place of professional advice in the constantly evolving area of employment law.

How a Charge Is Filed

If a sexual harassment problem cannot be resolved within the place of employment, employees who believe that they have been discriminated against may file a complaint with the EEOC. However, even if an internal grievance has not been filed, employees may choose this course of action rather than using a company procedure, and they can file before or after an internal grievance has been registered with their employer. Both courses of action are sometimes taken simultaneously because an internal grievance does not prevent the Title VII charge-filing time period from expiring. It is important to note that filing of an EEOC charge does not allow an employer to stop action on an internal complaint, to ignore evidence of ongoing harassment, or to not take prompt remedial action. In fact, immediate and appropriate action by the employer will often administratively close a case before the EEOC.[73] In any event, manager and employee alike should be aware of the filing procedures:

Title VII Charges*

- Charges may be filed in person, by mail or by telephone by contacting the nearest EEOC office or calling 800-669-4000. The EEOC has 23 district, 1 field, 17 area, and 9 local offices.

- Title VII charges must be filed with the EEOC within 180 days of the alleged discrimination. In states or localities where there is an antidiscrimination law and agency authorized to handle complaints, a charge must be presented there first. In such instances, the EEOC charge must be made within 300 days of the incident or 30 days after receiving notice that the agency has terminated its processing of the charge, whichever is earlier.

- The EEOC may file a lawsuit if it finds reasonable cause to believe that discrimination occurred and conciliation efforts fail. An individual may file a private suit within 90 days of receiving a notice of right-to-sue from EEOC.

---

*Information from this point to the Conclusions section of this chapter has been taken from the EEOC brochure *Information for the Private Sector and State and Local Governments.*

Equal Pay Act Complaints

- Individuals are not required to file an EPA charge with EEOC before filing a private lawsuit. However, some cases of wage discrimination may also be violations of Title VII. Charges may be filed concurrently under both laws under the procedures used for Title VII.

- An EPA lawsuit must be filed within two years (three if for willful violations) of the discriminatory act, which is usually paying a discriminatory lower wage. Filing with the EEOC will not stop the passing of these time limits.

- The EEOC may find reasonable cause to believe discrimination occurred and file a lawsuit on behalf of the victim, if so a private lawsuit may not be filed.

General Procedures

- The EEOC interviews the potential charging party to obtain as much information as possible about the alleged discrimination. If all legal jurisdictional requirements are met, a charge is properly drafted and the investigative procedure is explained to the charging party.

- EEOC notifies the employer about the charge. In investigating the charge to determine if discrimination occurred, EEOC requests information from the employer that addresses the issues directly affecting the charging party as well as other potentially aggrieved persons. Any witnesses who have direct knowledge of the alleged discriminatory act will be interviewed. If the evidence shows there is no reasonable cause to believe discrimination occurred, the charging party and the employer will be notified. The charging party may exercise the right to bring private court action.

- If the evidence shows there is reasonable cause to believe discrimination occurred, EEOC conciliates or attempts to persuade the employer to voluntarily eliminate and remedy the discrimination, following the standards of EEOC's Policy on Remedies and Relief for Individual Cases of Unlawful Discrimination. Remedies may include reinstatement of an aggrieved person to the job he or she would have had but for the discrimination, back pay, restoration of lost benefits and damages to compensate for actual monetary loss. Limited monetary damages may also be available to compensate for future monetary loss, mental anguish or pain and suffering, and to penalize a respondent who acted with malice or reckless indifference. The employer may also be required to post a notice in the workplace advising employees that it has complied with orders to remedy the discrimination.

- EEOC considers the case for litigation if conciliation fails. If litigation is approved by the Commission, EEOC will file a lawsuit in federal district court on behalf of the charging party(ies). Charging parties may initiate private civil action on their own in lieu of EEOC litigation.

EEOC's Statement of Enforcement Policy commits the agency to consider for litigation each case in which reasonable cause has been found and conciliation has failed. If EEOC decides not to litigate a case, a notice of right to sue is issued, permitting the charging party to take the case to court if he or she chooses. Most charges are conciliated or settled, making a court trial unnecessary.

Conclusions

Laws, regulations, and gender mix with interesting consequences at all levels in the workforce. In the cases reviewed, everyone from government lawyers to mill workers, bank employees to IRS agents, nurses to industrial electrical workers, and college clerical staff to prison guards found reason to seek the judgment of the courts on whether their rights had been violated.

Those who sit in high places have not been spared the expectations of the law. High-ranking officials such as Supreme Court Justice Clarence Thomas, once head of the EEOC, have become entangled in this relatively new form of social regulation. So has Senator Robert Packwood of Oregon, a vocal advocate of women's rights, who ran afoul of the spirit, if not the letter, of sexual harassment law. As his case illustrates, you might pay a tremendous price for being out of touch with today's standards of appropriate behavior.

Times have changed, and managers must understand how to operate intelligently and sensitively as they both work and manage in a workplace where a 50:50 mix of women and men interacts on a daily basis. The ultimate arbiter of whether they succeed is the courts. But the starting point for establishing—and maintaining—productive working relationships between the sexes is knowing the difference between workplace and social etiquette. Knowing how to distinguish between social behavior and professional behavior can be the key to succeeding as a member of the mixed-gender workforce, and this is what we discuss in the next chapter.

PART 3

Working with Gender Differences

4
Workplace Etiquette for Men and Women

The social climate of the workplace has changed dramatically with the burgeoning numbers of women in positions of responsibility in a traditionally male domain. With the complexities of this new work environment comes a need for "rules of the road"—a practical and applied kind of etiquette for colleagues. And this is what we provide in this chapter—a code of conduct for working men and women fashioned from the findings of the first three chapters of this book, which established that:

- Women and men develop differently but have essentially the same abilities

- Woman-man differences are real but not great enough to sustain occupational segregation along gender lines—the introduction of women to the combat arms is a recent example

- The trend toward women becoming the working peers of men will continue

- Woman-man sharing of the workplace can be awkward and uncomfortable—some men resist the change, some women expect the needed changes to occur instantly, and some men *and* women fail to distinguish between appropriate social and professional behavior

- Laws are on the books to make working together in an atmosphere of equal opportunity the rule rather than the exception

So men and women are left with the practical reality of getting their work done together in an atmosphere that successfully distinguishes between "different but equal"—the acceptable reality of our times—and "different but unequal" or "separate but equal"—the failed approaches of the past. As we mentioned earlier, a large part of the problem is separating social and workplace behavior, distinguishing between actions that might be acceptable socially but repugnant and even illegal in an occupational setting.

Unlearning the Stereotypes of Gender

Solving the problems of gender fairness doesn't mean creating an androgynous workforce in which women are indistinguishable from men; it means establishing working conditions in which managers and coworkers relate on the job in ways that accentuate the work being done and the occupational attributes of the people doing it and do *not* accentuate the male-female aspects of their interactions.

Reasonable people acknowledge that some women and men will develop mutually satisfying personal relationships at work—many find love there. What needs to end is men's preoccupation with the narrow sexual dimension of working women—a preoccupation that makes women's pursuit of careers unnecessarily difficult. The modern career woman has many professional contributions to make; to emphasize her sexuality is absurd. On the job, women should be able to receive compliments or accept a lunch invitation from a male colleague or client without needing to be concerned that these actions are linked to career-altering expectations or assumptions that attractiveness cannot coexist with brains. These stereotypical views have understandable biological and cultural roots, but the conscious management of behavior can change them. The caveman's defense "nature made me do it!" won't work anymore. Part of managing our behavior is, of course, etiquette—rules and protocols that govern how we interact.

The modern workplace should be somewhere women can dress and act like women, and men can react to them normally but within the bounds of behavior appropriate to a professional working environment. These new perspectives should become the norm for colleague relationships: (1) Women are the workplace peers of men, and (2) both sexes are at work primarily to get a job done, not to dwell on their sexual identities. Men and women who work together can be expected to distance themselves from both the awkward extremes of nineteenth-century chivalry and sexually aggressive or demeaning behavior that is discriminatory or harassing. In other words, conspicuously and systematically treating each other differently than other coworkers because of gender is not the thing to do, whether it is well-intended or mean-spirited.

Social relationships outside the office among coworkers become a problem mainly when they are based on unbalanced attraction. So the assumption must be that, unless a traditional man-woman relationship is accepted willingly by both parties, neither will be too persistent in attempting to cultivate one. They will, to the contrary, treat each other as the working peers their employer hired them to be and as holders of rights the courts have established to protect them from being exploited because of their sex.

When all is said and done, the workplace is a microcosm of our society. No matter what the setting, women will always attract the interest of men and be viewed by them as desirable, different, and, in some cases, worth pursuing. At the same time, in the modern workplace, men need to respect women's right to function fully as professionals, pursuing their career goals free from unwelcome sexual advances.

Before proceeding, let us acknowledge that, in these liberated and changing times, there are exceptions when roles are reversed and men are the objects of unwelcome attention by predatory women. *Time* reported a survey in 1992 showing that 15 percent of men said they had been sexually harassed.[1] With all due respect to such surveys, and although there is a measure of comfort in that the tables have sometimes turned, such stories have a "man bites dog" ring to them—the kinds of abuses suffered by women are rarely experienced by men. For now and the foreseeable future, it is men's behavior toward women at work that needs the most adjusting, so this chapter on workplace etiquette will portray the roles accordingly. In doing so, we try to avoid demonizing men or being naive about the fundamental attraction between the sexes, while making the necessary points about behavior that needs to change.

Why Working Relationships Are Different

Coercive sexual relationships occur in the social arena, but the odds are that power will play the major role in tilting the sexual tables at work. When colleagues, regardless of gender, interact in the workplace, relative power is always playing in the background. Make the coworkers men and women, and the power factor not only doesn't go away, its significance is amplified by an equally pervasive underlying force: sexual attraction.

Interacting at work should be, by definition, substantially different from interacting socially, gender notwithstanding. For women and men the impact is double: they deal not only with the phenomenon of their relative power but with the force of attraction—shared or otherwise.

Most women and men have a fairly realistic view of whether a member of the opposite sex would plausibly be interested in having a relationship with them. This self-moderating factor usually protects us from having to fend off across-the-board sexual advances at work. Since most of us recognize when an attraction is not mutual, we usually know when not to "try it on."

Svengalis, attractive or not, are mentors to and users of their attractive associates, and dirty old men (and women) broker power for company, but they are exceptions to the rules that typically govern the pairing of women and men. Some members of either sex will opt for differentially attractive partners for reasons ranging from placing a lower priority on traditional attractiveness to intellectual compatibility, shared interests, and so on. Still others are willing to be exploited in return for the benefits received, financial or otherwise. In spite of these exceptions, natural selection, plus the fact that many workers are already committed to previously chosen mates, reduces the likelihood of predatory behavior at work.

With the field narrowed and workplace etiquette made easier by the fact that not every gender-mixed pair of colleagues feels the chemistry of sexual attraction, problems still occur. If you get unwelcome signals that a coworker is attracted to you or has unrealistic expectations about a personal relationship with you, begin correcting the misperception by rationally and sensitively (at first) communicating the obvious: "I am not interested in a relationship." If the necessary changes in behavior do not follow, protect yourself accordingly and escalate the bluntness of your responses, up to and including the full exercise of your legal rights.

For mutually attracted coworkers, the process can be more difficult, but the choice to say no is still yours. Friendship or even sexual attraction does not automatically translate to willingness to move on to a sexual relationship, so you must make your position unambiguous when the situation demands it.

Making the exercise of such choices polite, relationship-preserving practices in the workplace environment of power, rewards, and punishment is what on-the-job etiquette is all about. As we develop the protocols in this chapter, remember the realities of the context in which they must be applied:

- Working relationships are relative power relationships, whether they are between superiors and subordinates or between peers who are in fact always jockeying for position.

- Mixing genders at work inevitably spawns a certain number of sexual attractions that vary in intensity and mutual acceptability. Mismatched expectations have to be resolved without destroying working relationships, putting either party at a professional disadvantage, or ending up in court.

Workplace etiquette embodies these points and gives you guidelines that can help keep you out of trouble. It enables you to communicate the necessary messages, save face, and minimize the likelihood of disruption in that most essential of all relationships between working men and women—the one within which they accomplish their professional goals.

On-the-Job Etiquette for the Sexes

Any kind of communication takes two people to make it work. In the vast majority of contemporary cases, this means that women need to get their personal and professional act together enough to assert their desires with neither whining nor apology. And men must be sufficiently attuned to the changed work environment to hear what women are saying and react rationally, without being wounded or vengeful, as though spurned in some now defunct (at work, at least) mating ritual, or off-put to the extent of dismantling otherwise productive professional relationships. This is the stuff of the new business etiquette—nitty-gritty and personal, on the job where women and men live and die professionally by how well they continue to relate after sorting out the gender relationship basics. Etiquette: It isn't just RSVPs and the selection of the appropriate fork anymore; it's the daily life of men and women, together at work.

This book is a hands-on manual for managers and men and women who work together. Just exactly how hands-on it is depends on individual situations and the people who are trying keep a working relationship in balance. This chapter is a codification of common sense that colleagues sometimes need to break the ice on sensitive subjects that are keeping them from getting their work done.

In cases when you believe that your problem is discussable, you might look for a private moment together, get out this book, open it to the relevant page, and say; "See this? It might not be exactly what's going on between us, but it's close enough to recognize some parallels. Read it and let's correct our problem. We work well together, and solving this will help us do so even better." In less comfortable cases, when discussion isn't possible and confrontation isn't desirable, the examples in this chapter that support our code of workplace etiquette can provide you with a starting point for understanding and disarming potentially destructive situations less directly.

In other cases, when management intervention is necessary, this chapter can help managers become aware of man-woman workplace relationship dynamics they might not have previously appreciated.

Armed with this knowledge, managers can better judge when to act, leave things alone, suggest remedies, or quietly adjust the environment, including their own behavior, to achieve the kind of "work around" (or solution) that preserves viable gender-mixed working relationships.

No book alone is a substitute for authoritative help when the circumstances demand it, but many workplace relationship problems are first encountered at a point at which the people involved can arrive at a satisfactory solution—by themselves or with the help of a perceptive manager—without involving legal counsel. If that sounds like your situation, whether you are the manager or an employee, try understanding and then influencing the troubling situation before offense is taken, power is exercised inappropriately, and the whole matter deteriorates into bad feelings or a sexual harassment case. Gender problems in the workplace vary in seriousness from simple misunderstandings that can be easily resolved to discrimination or harassment that requires official remedies. Certainly don't put anyone at risk by not invoking the full protection of your company policies or the law, but consider the possibility of a less formal solution if the problem warrants less drastic action.

The topics that follow bracket 14 categories of workplace etiquette and suggest protocols for the working man, woman, and manager. A single situation may illustrate a theme, but the lessons apply more broadly to areas such as gender-mixed office teams, job interviews, or mandatory after-hours business socializing or travel. Each topic includes advice on how to behave reasonably while respecting the rights of both women and men as they pursue their careers together.

Topic 1 "Anthropology, Biology, and Colleague Relationships" Etiquette

High on the list of workplace etiquette problems is dealing with the "boys will be boys" syndrome. Whether they are welders in the Jacksonville Shipyard or surgeons at the Stanford University medical school, the problem is much the same. Some men have an ingrained expectation that they can comment rudely on the sexuality of women and even take the prerogative of touching them as though they were interacting in caves thousands of years B.C. instead of in a twentieth-century place of work.

"What do they expect?" "It's the natural thing to do!" "That's how we perpetuate the species," say the offenders. Right! And we still wear loin cloths and eat what we can hunt and cook over an open fire. No, today's standards are different, and reverting to primitive relationship building is something best left to our private lives, though many people would argue that it no longer has a place there either. Organized society, through its legislative bodies and courts, has declared that the workplace shall be free of sexual bias and coercion. Women have the right to do their jobs free from crude expressions either of lust or attempts to preserve male sanctuaries that are now open to women. Although both lust and resistance to change can be understood, it is reasonable to expect that inappropriate behavior will be curbed. We may not be able to control how we feel, but we *can* control how we act—"irresistible impulse" is not a valid excuse.

Etiquette for the Working Man.   Suppose you're a man smitten by the way your colleague fills out a sweater, a medical smock, or a uniform. Or maybe it's the way she arranges herself as she leans over a computer table, a medical laboratory exhibit, or a welding generator. It turns you on—fine. You've had a perfectly normal reaction to an attractive female. Then comes the involuntary and unspoken "Here we go again," as you acknowledge to yourself that you're interested in something more than routine coworker interaction. That's OK too, depending on what you do next.

At this point, social and working protocols diverge. Reactions to the call of a sexy woman, deliberately sent or otherwise, might include an open compliment followed by a suggestion that the two of you get together for lunch, dinner, whatever. Off the job, this is a normal way to open the door to the possibility of a personal relationship. If you make an approach and she is agreeable, fine, but she might make a polite excuse or simply say no if she's not interested. If you're still interested or not sure what her message really is, you can press your point a bit more strongly and ask again, and again. In an off-the-job social situation, that is OK. It is different at work.

On the job you're out of line unless you stop either at your self-acknowledgment of the attraction and decide for whatever reason not to pursue her or after she lets you know, subtly or not, that she isn't interested. Unless there is unambiguous encouragement, let things go at that, or you're asking for trouble.

Applying the "normal" social follow-through is inappropriate at work because your coworker can't escape—she has to confront you every day. In the worst case, you might have power over the progress of her career or even whether she continues to have a job. Within the workplace she has a right to expect you to "give it a rest" and let her function as a colleague without the intrusion of gender issues. Reason, backed up by the law, says that this is the way things must be if females are ever to succeed as something other than "full-time women," never to become competent and respected professionals but forever limited by their sexuality.

Unless a woman invites you to be a more intimate part of her life, during working hours you and your female coworkers operate under limitations that don't exist outside working relationships. Accept them. It is hoped that you understand why it is this way, but even if you don't, recognize the rules and realize that you can get burned if you don't make the essential distinction between your workplace and social prerogatives with women.

Etiquette for the Working Woman. Suppose that you are the woman in the scenario just described. Like it or not, because of your sexual identity, you will never be one of the guys. Make them understand from the beginning what your boundaries are, that you are a professional with knowledge and skill—a coworker—and that you expect to be treated with the same respect they treat their male colleagues. You have the power to make a lot of trouble and greater ability to prevent a problem than you might think you have. By reacting correctly, you can stop a reasonable man, who might be *slightly* out of line, in his tracks. If the guy turns out to be a jerk, the boundaries you set give you the basis to enforce your rights with the help of others, including the courts, if necessary.

Just like the men, you really can't play the traditional woman-man game on the job, so resist that temptation. No, you're not being told you "asked for it" just because you are sexually attractive. No woman does that when her final word is no. But you don't serve your interests by encouraging what you ultimately don't want. Forgo the ego trip you'd experience from eliciting a bigger compliment than might come naturally from the guy's first reaction to you. Unless you want to work out a more intimate and complex relationship with him, nip it in the bud now. You won't have to be rude to most men to accomplish your purpose. Just say no and mean it, and keep meaning it, unequivocally—not yes today and no tomorrow or an excuse that seems to mean maybe. You can telegraph the message, and a reasonable man can read it. If you don't want to go to the next plateau of interest exploration, stop the process now. If he persists after your instincts tell you that he should have gotten the message, go to the next stage of directness by saying that you have no interest in pursuing a social relationship and want his initiatives to stop immediately. If that doesn't do it, get help. You be the judge of whether a friend or coworker should try to convey what you have been unsuccessful in doing yourself or whether the problem needs to start its way up the management ladder. If it's your boss, remember that every boss has a boss. Go where you need to go; do what you need to do. There is no reason in this day and age to endure sexual harassment.

Etiquette for the Manager. Managing a "boys will be boys" breach of working etiquette demands the same kind of resoluteness and unambiguous behavior suggested for the woman on the receiving end of inappropriate sexual advances. A manager has to grapple personally with his or her own values and reach either (1) a heartfelt conviction that the behavior is unacceptable or (2) a pragmatic recognition that it is ethically or legally unacceptable. The next step is to take whatever measures are necessary to eliminate the problem and to do so with the same vigor demanded for other objectionable tasks such as implementing reductions in force. However, don't think that we are making a comparison between enforcing the reasonable rights of women and the bitter pill of layoffs; the analogy is aimed at those in management who harbor reservations and hang back from doing what they must. If only "true believers" can be relied on to enforce the rules, the necessary changes will be slower in coming. The suggestions that follow will result in the desired outcome regardless of a manager's personal feelings.

Managers' etiquette for ending "boys will be boys" problems requires that:

- Managers do not participate in the same kinds of behavior
- Managers do not encourage the behavior either directly or by silent acquiescence
- Managers communicate clearly that they will not revisit the same problem—stop means stop *now*
- Managers demonstrate a willingness to punish the offender if the offending behavior continues

Topic 2 "Assuming You Know" Etiquette

Although few among us would admit to having our behavior unduly influenced by stereotypes, most of us would, in private moments at least, assert that we "know" a few things about members of the opposite gender. As a group, "they" have certain characteristics about which we can safely generalize. "They" come to their problems, careers, and relationships at work with certain axes to grind. And "we" can predict what "they" are going to do in certain situations! Otherwise you are stereotype free! Right? Wrong! Both women and men stereotype their gender opposites, but because women are currently the most disadvantaged in terms of workplace opportunity (for example, the glass ceiling), stereotypes about their abilities, competence, what they want, why they think what they think, what professions are appropriate for them, and so forth, have an unduly negative impact on them as a group.

Etiquette for the Working Man. Suppose that you are in charge of planning the expansion of your company's operations into a new territory. Lots of travel will be required from a team of people with a variety of professional expertise. How do you choose them? The rules are obvious: Your selections should be based on ability to do the job—period. Still, you find yourself trying to make accommodations based on what you *think* are people's personal situations, for example, "Maybe it would be better to assign Jack to this one since his wife doesn't work." You also find that you have even more concerns and envision more limitations when women are considered, for example, "Linda just got married, and her husband might be upset if she's on the road a lot. I know I would be." Or "Julie is awfully pretty, and I don't know about sending her out with all these guys."

You say that this is only natural. No, it is only habit! Under the new social contract giving women equal status with men at work, expectations that the rules should be different for women because of their obligations to home and family have gone by the board. It isn't that no accommodation will ever be necessary—women have babies, men don't—but limitations are often self-imposed (for example, the voluntary choice of the mommy track) and none of your business as a man. They *are* your business as a manager—make your objective business decisions and let her alter her career commitments if she so chooses and pay the consequences, if there are to be any. Otherwise, gender is not your concern either in making work assignments or in being part of a mixed-gender work team.

Your proper role is to be objective, to avoid the stereotypes of gender, and to let the occupational choice chips fall where they may. The chips will land where they do because of the different lifestyle choices women and men make, but it is not your job to encourage or impose sex-linked career limitations on your associates. Don't do it materially by your actions or subtly by your underlying thoughts or values or your assumptions about what is either "right" for the society, their families, and so forth, or what is the unarticulated "preference" of the woman you are, however benevolently, trying to "take care of."

Etiquette for the Working Woman. You are an ambitious woman, committed to a long-term career. You also have a husband and children. Your professional talents make you an obvious choice for the business team being assembled in the above scenario. But you are absolutely sure that the man putting the team together will exclude you because (you think) he thinks that you shouldn't spend long periods of time away from your family. What should you do? Ideally of course, you should have to do nothing; you can assume that you'd be chosen because you're the best person for the job. But we're not yet at the point where what "ought to happen" always does.

A good opportunity is at hand. Tell the team leader that you want to be part of the project. It certainly is your right to have a full-throttle career, but you may have to communicate your position to project yourself beyond limitations that might wrongly be imposed on you. Do it purposefully, not stridently (unless you meet serious objections), and in harmony with the needs of your organization, and you can do a lot on your own behalf.

Exceptions to the fully committed career are possible. While the mommy and daddy tracks are anathema to the more extremely positioned managers and rights advocates, the reality is that they offer a viable alternative for some workers and companies—as long as they are chosen voluntarily and not imposed by the organization. If you opt for a personal life that demands limitations at work, don't be unrealistic and deny not being as across-the board committed as others with whom you might be competing for advancement. Life is filled with choices; some of them impose limitations and lend truth to stereotypes in individual situations. In fact, you might choose to be the stereotypical supermom with a demanding career that requires long hours and lots of travel, while you still manage to join the PTA, be a den mother, and be a Brownie troop leader. Or you may opt for something less hectic. The choice is yours to make, and it is for you, not your coworkers, your manager, your company, your mother, or anyone else to place a value on the label you choose to wear.

Etiquette for the Manager. Managing a mixed-gender workforce imposes obligations on the one who does the managing not to bring his or her own stereotypes to the process or to let others whom he or she supervises do so as they work alongside their opposite-gender peers. As a manager, you must force yourself to recognize and abandon culturally ingrained expectations of limitations on what people, be they women or men, are capable of or willing to do. The new ethic of the workplace lets the individual make her or his own lifestyle choices, which, of course, have an impact on careers. Managers should judge only competencies and offer opportunities. If limitations are to follow that accrue to gender, let the individuals involved impose the limitations upon themselves. Managers are cautioned not to let the breadth of choices be unfairly different for one gender or the other. It is inappropriate to approach women or men with choices not available to both—special treatment is still different treatment.

Managers' etiquette for ending "assuming you know" problems requires:

- Self-monitoring to avoid the use of stereotypes in your personal management actions

- If you are a woman, not selectively perpetrating stereotypes that are to your advantage

- Making decisions based on competencies, not gender stereotypes that preclude opportunities because the manager perceives that he or she knows what is best for employees

- Allowing the managed to deal with the personal consequences of their career choices and work assignments

Topic 3 "Closed-Door and Locker-Room" Etiquette

There are two levels of behavior in our working lives: (1) that which is openly expressed and (2) what comes out behind closed doors. We understand that building special relationships—sometimes open, at other times private or even clandestine—is an accepted, if not always attractive, route to serving self-interest in the job world. That will never change. What we can change is the reception given to closed-door commentary that violates the rights of others. Sexism, racism, unequal treatment do not become "right" behind closed doors. There is usually a friendly audience behind a closed door, and those who express their bigotry in private seldom have to defend their opinions.

Merely feeling indignant or repulsed will not accomplish the needed changes, but the firm exercise of your convictions can. This area of workplace etiquette asks that you set a positive personal standard for what you encourage or tolerate in your private interactions with others. While self-righteously flailing at windmills is rarely productive in the modern place of business, you can politely but directly discourage the surreptitious expression of values that are unacceptable when displayed openly. This has special relevance for workers trying to emerge from the stereotypes of sex discrimination.

Etiquette for the Working Man. Which of the following has more relevance in a closed-door discussion of a woman's qualifications for being hired, promoted, or assigned to a particular job?

- The size of her bra
- Her likely sexual prowess
- Who she's living with
- None of the above

In front of a camera, there are few men living who wouldn't answer "None of the above." But in the privacy of the locker room or executive suite, the other answers are likely to be heard. We all know it's just good, healthy "guy talk" that means no harm, but if we don't appraise the career prospects of a man this way, why do we do it with women?

Why women? Because it's macho; because it's a habit; because it draws a favorable response from our audience—another man or men. Does it hurt the woman? Probably, but even if it doesn't, it perpetuates the "us and them" divisions along gender lines that we are obligated to dismantle.

This doesn't call for a moral stand on the soapbox, just a commitment to avoid the practice when tempted personally and to cultivate the habit of not cheering on others who do it. The problem isn't limited to flip comments about the female anatomy; it might just as well be the prospect of a pregnancy, commitment to career versus family, willingness to travel with male colleagues, or any of a host of residual concerns men have about working women.

The solution is not found in secretly fuming about such things behind closed doors but in determining what concerns are legitimate and addressing them. Translate the hidden agenda question "Will she be able to accompany me on quarterly visits around the territory without raising eyebrows?" into "Can she do what needs to be done, some of which includes visiting field operations and making a good impression?" Or change "Two ambitious women will never be able to collaborate on a project like this!" to "Can Sandra and Carolyn work together well enough to accomplish the goals we have in mind?" Remember, this could just as easily be, "Can Bill and Larry...or Marilyn and Joe...?" It takes conscious effort, but we can rise above interjecting sexual elements into issues that have nothing to do with sex.

Etiquette for the Working Woman. The challenge for the working woman who gains access to the inner circle is not to become part of the problem. It isn't easy to join the club and not perpetuate its sins in the name of strengthening one's position. As women move into the ranks of the decision makers, they must not become self-serving echoes of behavior they loathed when they were on the other side of the closed door.

Every time you smile with pained tolerance at an off-color remark or make the extra effort to repair a colleague's sexist gaffe so that you can somehow accept being in the same room with it, you give the offender a new lease on life. In his eyes, if you find his company and way of doing business off the record OK, how far out of line can he really be? You're a good egg and a woman and you always find a way not to be offended. Everyone should. Obviously, you think it's OK, so it must be OK.

As with men, no theatrical protests are called for. Just stick to what you believe and don't tolerate verbally or physically offensive behavior. Take every chance you get to ratchet up your standards and those of your coworkers, including those of your mentor, who may be a regular offender behind closed doors. Don't give a bigot the comfort of even reluctant approval. Find your own safe and comfortable method of chipping away at inappropriate comments, but don't be oversensitive and make a big deal over every remark or look that doesn't please you.

Etiquette for the Manager.   In every manager resides authority and with it the potential for being a bully. It takes special vigilance to balance the two, especially in matters of group values. As a manager, you are expected to set a moral tone for your operations and you can demand standards of behavior. The standards you set must be ones you yourself follow if you expect your employees to do the same. You can't forbid sexist language if you close the door and tell jokes about women to some of your colleagues. Depending on the scope of your responsibilities and the size of your organization, your obligations extend to people you supervise who might act the same way with their subordinates. Changing the values of a society through the roles of men and women at work requires moral leadership from managers who have the courage to recognize the possibility that their own metamorphosis may be incomplete.

Managers' etiquette for ending "closed-door and locker-room" problems requires:

- Being open to the possibility that your own candid comments are being tolerated rather than respected

- Making a conscious effort to address substantive matters in a consistent manner, whether the audience is public or private, resisting the flip, superficial, or sexist, and making it clear that you expect the same from your subordinates

- Using your authority to accomplish the goals of your organization, not to perpetuate your own biases

- Reading between the lines for indications that your subordinates haven't been comfortable enough to mention that they find some of your behavior objectionable

Topic 4 "Competition Mentality" Etiquette

Few differences are more clearly drawn in nature than those between women and men, but most of them are insignificant when it comes to doing modern work. However, when human beings discover differences between groups of people, they tend to join one side or the other and turn dissimilarity into competition, rather than viewing differences as positive or complementary. "Us versus them" thinking is all around us, and it is reinforced every time men and women look at one another, communicate, or ponder what their gender opposites want. Like so many characteristics that define the sexes, the "usness" and "themness" of being women and men won't go away. Making the mixing of genders work in the business world cannot rely on "us" ever becoming the same as "them." Instead, employees and managers alike need to retool their thinking and move away from the view that to be different (from "us") is to be inferior or threatening.

Women and men need to develop fresh attitudes toward special rules that separate work from social behavior. Love, sexual attraction, deference toward romantically special people in our lives—even competition for and with them—won't be altered simply because men and women are working together on a daily basis. But it's necessary, and it's time, to separate social instincts and predatory sexual behavior from workplace interaction between the sexes. At the same time, we must not move too far in the other direction and revert to a natural tendency to cluster monolithically by gender at work, where our task should be collaboration, not competition.

Etiquette for the Working Man. Suppose that you are a man assigned to complete a product research study with a woman coworker. The starting point is to define the task and divide up the work. She begins with suggestions, and you have some ideas of your own. The two of you have known each other superficially in the department but have never shared an assignment. So, as with most beginning colleague teams, you go through a period of sizing each other up, politely setting boundaries, and establishing informal authority relationships.

On the sizing-up dimension, all is well. She is prepared to do this job—that became obvious in your early conversations. Next are the boundaries. No problem there—neither of you threatens to complicate the working relationship with personal problems or social expectations that don't fit. But to your surprise, you have a problem with the last one—the authority relationship. Sure, you know that equal opportunity plays here—she's your peer and as apt to want to (and be able to) offer leadership and decision making to the effort as you are. Still, it's hard to let it go at that. She is, after all, new to authority and leadership—there's not a lot of precedent in the company for people like "her" doing things like "this."

In other words, in your mind if not in fact, you find yourself stereotyping, lowering her potential and lessening her professional prerogatives because she is a woman and you're a man. You actually experience twinges of competitive thinking that are clearly sexist at their roots. You, a man, are the more "natural" leader and decision maker, and you find yourself competing to remain so. It's partly just professional ambition, but there is an undeniable sex bias component in your reactions as you negotiate your partnership with a coworker who, in addition to being competition on your career ladder, represents a whole new *class* of competitors—women.

The proper etiquette is to acknowledge the problem to yourself. You probably don't need to discuss it with her unless you've *acted* on your feelings. At the same time, you have to admit the potential for those feelings to color your judgment and limit your ability to contribute successfully to this assignment. You have to manage your behavior. Test and challenge your own thinking when it threatens to detract from the kind of relationship you would build with a man doing the same job. Consciously factor out the "I've got to hold my own against this woman!" thinking and replace it with a more rational judgment of her contributions, not her gender. The solution is to realize that you are competing with her in part because she's a woman and, over time, eliminate that irrational element from what can properly remain the comfortable combination of collaboration and competition that drives most effective professional teams.

Etiquette for the Working Woman.   As the woman in the above example, you might sense that you are sparking more competition than is healthy for getting the job done, and you might feel that it is largely due to the gender difference. You have a balancing act to perform. Your first obligation is to persist and not acquiesce to either a hidden or an overt expectation that you will assume a secondary role. But, equally as important, if you want positive results, try first to make your point skillfully with the strength of your talents and not the soapbox of your cause. At times with some people, the diplomatic approach will not work, and you must never stand for abusive behavior that threatens you. Such situations may have to be resolved with confrontation or even legal means. But try it the other way first. Make a distinction between the guy who is a sexist jerk and the one who, like many, is making the awkward transition from "hearing" the new rules of the workplace to "living" them.

Reasonable men and women must together make the effort to build working relationships with one another. Once you've done the obvious and presented yourself in a manner that stresses your desire to be a professional and not a personal associate, you will need some patience as your male peer sorts out the reality that you want to take responsibility, make decisions, risk failure, and share the glory or the embarrassment of the project's outcome. Try not to enter into the relationship with a chip on your shoulder that says, "Move over Jack, I've got a right to run this thing and I'm gonna do it." Be the partner you'd like to have—offer leadership, accept his contributions, and generally set the tone of a sharing business relationship in which neither member has to be subordinated to go forward. If he shows indications of a male-superior competition mentality, counter his behavior objectively and with the offer of face-saving—the first few times, at least. He might say, "Here Jane, let me have the phone—I can straighten this out!" You might counter firmly but collegially (covering the mouthpiece of the phone with your hand), "Thanks, Tom, I can handle it." Run these scenarios a few dozen times, and a reasonable man will see that he has a capable peer for a partner and will drop behavior that is condescending or protective. If he doesn't, he will show himself clearly as a "problem" you'll need to deal with less collegially or, in some cases, get some help with from management.

Etiquette for the Manager.   One of a manager's greatest gifts to an organization is team building—it's your job to get people to work together effectively. Now you have the added challenge of doing this with gender opposites who sometimes find reasons to balk at the very cooperation you are trying to establish. Do not focus unduly on gender as the reason two people fail to work productively together, but on the other hand do not be naive about the possibility that gender might play a part in the problem. Use objective judgment; assign the proper weights to the possible causes, but don't overlook the possibility that the male team member is hung up on sharing what he sees as his turf with a woman. He says he's working with her, but he brings conditions, limitations, even reluctance to the effort, weighing it down unnecessarily and most likely impeding productivity. Confront a situation like this directly but be low-key at the outset—broach the subject and see what reaction you get. Give some specific examples of behavior that your see as problematic and illustrate them (use something like the "Let me take care of that" example from above). Sometimes your job as manager is to open people's eyes to the consequences of their own behavior. Act as a facilitator when you can; be more forceful when you must. Unless you see a major problem that requires strong intervention, be a patient teacher, help your employees save face, make change easy for both male and female, and help your charges recognize and fix their own problems whenever possible. This is especially important when egos and long-standing identities are involved.

Managers' etiquette for easing "competition mentality" problems requires:

- Structuring teams based on the competencies of the members, not on the basis of their genders, knowing that the new challenges presented by mixed teams may require special management skills

- Looking for root causes when mixed-gender teams malfunction; one possibility to consider is the competition mentality

- Being prepared to help the adjusting team members save face but never being ambiguous or apologetic regarding the need to stop unreasonable competition based on gender

- Being open to the possibility of an overly ambitious woman injecting an unproductive amount of gender-based competition into a working relationship

Topic 5 "Giving and Taking Our Lumps" Etiquette

If women and men are to work together and equitably share in the benefits of the workplace, they have to bear an equal share of unpleasant tasks as well. Unequal treatment based on dated stereotypical behavior of being "easier" on the women, "harder" on the men, or other such expectations that might "naturally" pop into our minds have no place in the modern workplace.

Not only is special treatment based on gender passé, it is a deterrent to women's prospects for establishing themselves as respected equal partners. The same goes for giving the medicine as taking it. It doesn't fall only to the male manager to cope with the "hard" cases, be they discipline, promotion, compensation, or dismissal. The new ethic is that the prerogatives of a position should be gender-blind. If a stern rebuke is in order, it doesn't matter whether a woman or a man is on the receiving end—and the same goes for the person delivering it. The leveling effect of equal treatment in professional communications should actually bring added civility to the workplace. The objective is rational business communication, stern and change-inducing if that's what the situation demands. This means that communication shall not be deliberately tempered according to the gender of the person being addressed, that is, the traditional and sometimes crude man-to-man communication or the sugar-coated man-to-woman communication.

If firmness is required, be equally firm with both genders, not unduly kind to a woman or extra harsh with a man. Effective business communication should result in getting the job done efficiently, and if this means dealing with problems along the way, use strictly business language and whatever supporting action is called for by the situation, gender notwithstanding.

Etiquette for the Working Man. You are a man running an administrative organization of several dozen employees in an urban environment with a mixture of genders and races. A problem has developed with the use of office telephones for personal reasons. You've tried circulating a memorandum suggesting that personal business on company phones should be limited in both frequency and time spent. You've asked your administrative assistant to enforce the solution without confronting anyone directly—they know who they are, and reasonable people should get the point. You've even mentioned it in staff meetings, but the problem persists and it is clear that it really stems from only two staff members, one a woman and the other a man. You are the only person who can solve the problem.

You hate dealing with things like this. You experience a complex set of feelings ranging from the fact that you view yourself as an executive who shouldn't have to handle such mundane matters to the universal desire to be liked. And then there's the big reason—you are especially reluctant to use the force necessary to impress the woman with the seriousness of her problem.

Things deteriorate to the extent that you call the male offender into your office and make your point about telephone use and abuse. Once the conversation begins, it isn't hard to treat him like any other man you've confronted. You present your expectations and describe the consequences if they aren't met. He reacts the way you've seen other men react and says, "OK Boss, no problem," and it's done. You feel that you've been effective. He took it like a man!

After some hesitation, you decide to do the same with the woman. You start out the same way, but then your mind fills with thoughts such as it is more "natural" for women to gossip on the phone, to have family members call, and to take longer to get something said. This is not the objective face-off you had with the man. You make excuses for her, trying to explain and justify the obvious; you ask for her cooperation instead of demanding it. You've been far less effective in solving the problem with her because you let yourself be drawn into gender-stereotyped thinking instead of using objective business communication. You put on the velvet gloves because you were talking to a woman, even though the merits of the case clearly justified otherwise. And the results could have been predicted—the man stopped abusing the phone; the woman backed off for a short time and then continued to behave as she always had.

The answer is simple: Treat people as the employees they are, with the fairness and courtesy they deserve but not with a double standard based on sexual stereotypes. Your popularity is not increased by giving women special treatment. On the contrary, the practice is generally resented by both genders—even though a person is not apt to ask for more objective treatment when getting off more lightly in a disciplinary situation. You bear the obligation to sort out the merits of your management problems objectively and to implement your strategies for change without consideration for the gender of the person being addressed.

Etiquette for the Working Woman.   You have an obligation in situations like the one described not to cultivate an aura of privilege—even a subtle one—based on being a woman. And if you are a woman manager, you must be especially cognizant of the necessity to treat your charges equally—no overempathizing because you "understand" the kinds of problems women have (as the male manager in the above situation did). As in many examples of workplace etiquette, you can't have it both ways. If you want equal treatment across the board when it comes to opportunity, you have to expect and be receptive to both dishing it out and taking it in the less pleasant aspects of your work.

Everyone needs to make a personal effort to increase sensitivity to what constitutes reasonable standards of behavior in a place of business. Many problems like the telephone example would not occur if we consciously managed our behavior to separate social habits from working ones. There is a common perception that women spend more time on the telephone socially than men. Whether research would confirm that or not, if it is true in your case, make changing the habit at work a conscious effort.

You can also be receptive to giving and taking criticism when you know it is reasonable. In this case, although it would be unrealistic for the female telephone abuser to emphasize her guilt and invite stronger punishment, she could have made it easier for the manager. As an employee, if you sense sexist compensation coming into the conversation, even when it helps you in the short term, confront it pleasantly if you can. For example, if you were the woman in the above scenario, when the manager said, "Connie, I know women have to stay in touch with their kids during the day, but in your case it's creating problems for us," you might have responded, "I guess that's a problem for anyone with responsibilities off the job. But now that you mention it, I see where I need to limit my phone time with the kids and I'll take care of it." In not letting the manager twist in the wind while trying to give you an out, you can acknowledge a legitimate problem and volunteer to fix it. In doing so, you establish yourself as someone capable of recognizing your own shortcomings and correcting them. Your image as a worthy member of the team, free of the need for special considerations, has been enhanced. This is a far better option than letting your manager be the loser, frustrated over a failure to effectively resolve the problem, with his (or her) sexist approach uncorrected, and the possibility that you'll "pay" in some less direct way later.

Etiquette for the Manager. Being in charge means having to deal with unpleasant situations as well as bask in the glory of a job well done. Managing a mixed-gender workforce means learning to impose your professional judgment on women and men equally. In doing so, you may sometimes notice a difference in your own approach that you can trace back to your beliefs about how women "should" be treated and, perhaps, how women "are." To command the respect of the men and women who work for you, you have to get beyond having two sets of standards for how women and men should give and take their lumps at work. The tendency toward special treatment has to be replaced by an emphasis on developing a firm but fair approach you can apply without gender as a consideration. For example, in the case above, instead of, "Connie, I know *women* have to stay in touch...," try "Connie, I know *parents* have to stay in touch..." and take it from there, making clear that excessive personal phone calls won't be tolerated for anyone in the company, parenthood notwithstanding.

Managers' etiquette for easing "giving and taking our lumps" problems requires:

- Sensitivity to the possibility that you are intimidated by the prospect of disciplining or being professionally firm with colleagues of the opposite sex because you view them as different in their capacity to take it, because women "ought" to be treated in a certain way, or because you overempathize with someone of your own sex

- Awareness that overcompensation can become the problem that leads you to what you seek to avoid—unequal treatment based on gender

- Developing objective management techniques that lessen the possibility that you will treat women and men differently when firmness is required

- Erasing stereotypes and replacing them with rational perceptions of your employees that help solve problems without introducing gender into the picture

Topic 6 "Sexual Stereotype" Etiquette

We already have mentioned sexual stereotyping as at least a partial reason for gender-related problems in the workplace. Still, it is necessary to isolate stereotyping as the root cause of most generalizations that divide women and men and provide both the quiet, unspoken bases for their prejudices as well as the most frequently verbalized complaints about gender opposites.

Many otherwise sophisticated professionals still harbor stereotypes of gender that limit their ability to get the most from their relationships in today's working environment. Men and women present polite exteriors to each other, but they retain internal resentments that automatically cause them to typecast others simply because they belong to the opposite sex.

Gender stereotyping creates serious problems for both sexes. At the extremes, women view all men as sexist pigs, and men see women primarily as the objects of their lust. Even if we back off from these extremes, we find a workplace filled with polite coworkers who tolerate each other but who have overarching resentments that limit their ability to function fully together. Problem attitudes based on stereotypes affect not only how we see ourselves but create irrational premonitions about colleagues of the opposite gender. By seeing their opposites as bundles of stereotyped expectations that are not in sync with their own, they expect the worst of one another and unnecessarily limit their relationships.

Etiquette that will alleviate the problem of stereotyped identity and role expectations requires attitude changes by both genders. Learning to see the promise and not the threat of gender opposites takes effort and increased awareness of the difficulties ingrained expectations can cause on the job.

Etiquette for the Working Man. You are a man interviewing for a new position. As you meet the staff after your initial conversation with the hiring official, you are on your best behavior. But you sense tension between you and the woman who manages the division with which you'll be having frequent and important interactions. You can't put your finger on it, but the chemistry isn't right. It is as though the two of you resent one another; yet you've barely met. Hostile sparks fly back and forth between you even though the conversation is polite and your ideas about business and how to do it are similar. If *she* were a *he*, you'd be looking forward to the prospect of working together on a daily basis.

In talking it over with your best friend on the golf course the next weekend, you find yourself making more references to her being a woman than as a potential professional peer. If you didn't know better, if it wasn't *you* under the microscope of your own criticism, you'd swear that gender was the dominating factor in your judgment of her! Could an enlightened guy like you have this kind of problem? You bet!

Contrary to popular myth, a man's lustful thoughts about a woman are not always first and primary. Reaction to a person of either gender depends on where you are and what the circumstances are. In this job interview situation, power ranked highest in your personal hierarchy and you resented her authority. What is a *woman* doing already occupying a position like the one to which you are only aspiring?

The key for you in this problem involves raising your overall comfort level with women in positions of authority. As long as you have the attitude that, because a peer or superior at work is a woman, she is somehow less deserving of business success than you or another man, you will react to her negatively and most likely draw a similar response from her. Put the two responses together and it is difficult for either of you to act collegially and treat each other fairly. Like an animal sensing danger, she reads your resentment and discomfort with her. As the job seeker, you may well be the loser.

Etiquette for the Working Woman.   The woman bears part of the blame for this less than successful job interview. Assuming there were no other causes for the bad chemistry—that it resulted from his resentment and her reacting to it—she did little to turn the situation in a positive direction. Instinctively, men and women tend to give what they think they are getting in a confrontation that comes about because of irrational stereotyping. Masking bad feelings instead of disarming them is a common approach. Why should you, a professional woman in a position of power, feel any obligation to pull the fat out of the fire for some male chauvinist? He's the one with the problem! The answer: because it is more important for women and men to build successful working relationships than to get even with someone they don't even know! Dismantling the confrontation mentality has to start somewhere. Men need to learn new ways of dealing with women peers, and you, as well as your male counterpart, bear an obligation to work at breaking down the walls that divide you on the job.

There has to be a stacking of arms as the war between the sexes draws to a close. As the woman in the kind of interview described above, at least try to determine whether a positive gesture on your part might help keep another man-woman working relationship from failing before it can even get started. If he still responds inappropriately, back off and cast your blackball when the hiring decision is made. But first, do your part to avoid a gender confrontation based on traditional prejudices and resentments.

Etiquette for the Manager. Since you come prewired with one set of prejudices or the other, refereeing your own kind when managing gender-opposite problems can be awkward. Once you become aware of what your biases are and can control your own behavior, you need to help your staff dismantle their automatic predisposition to see one another through gender-colored glasses. Sexual stereotyping is a two-edged sword in working relationships, and there are times when it can harm the person initiating the problem (such as the interviewee in the example above) more than the recipient. Women, men, and the businesses that employ them gain by putting sexually stereotyped working relationships behind them, and you, as a manager, have to make this clear to those who work for you.

Managers' etiquette for easing "sexual stereotype" problems requires:

- Assessing your own attitudes and developing the ability to deal with gender opposites without irrational bias based on a person's sex
- Identifying potential relationship issues among your workers that appear to have no objective basis except for gender stereotypes and trying to resolve them before they become major problems that interfere with getting the job done
- Structuring your introductions of gender opposites so that you emphasize their objective professional characteristics without regard to gender
- Confronting directly and neutralizing the impact of sexual stereotyping when it comes to your attention

Topic 7 "Invitations, Approaches, and Propositions" Etiquette

When men and women occupy the same space, social interactions of various kinds are inevitable. Most of them will be collegial and nothing more. Others will be passionate and resolve themselves awkwardly or artfully, depending on the people involved. As long as the process of relationship building between women and men doesn't interfere with job function and productivity, it is their business and no one else's.

Although this is a perfectly rational approach in theory, on a practical level it takes effort to keep relationships from interfering with work. Sustaining man-woman colleague relationships can be difficult. Cliques based on race, religion, and so forth, affect overall workforce morale. Interject the man-woman element, and the complexity of interactions increases even more. The introduction of gender to workplace groupings opens up issues such as jealousy, triangles, favoritism, territoriality, mismatched attraction, exploitation, and awkward breakups. On the other hand, the odds of finding true love in a place—the workplace—where people of similar backgrounds and interests come together, have never been greater. And most of us, despite all the potential problems, would not preclude personal relationships between men and women at work even if we harbored the unrealistic notion that we could.

Women and men need ways to cope with social approaches in the work environment that lead somewhere other than to happy romantic endings. Job etiquette is not closed to the possibility of workplace personal relationships, and even romance, but sustaining relationships that are both personal and professional calls for expert behavior management. Know what you're getting into and set your boundaries. Men and women should give as much as they choose and no more, and balancing their expectations takes discipline and mutual understanding. Don't automatically overlook the possibility that workplace mixed-gender relationships can be managed, limited undertakings that go beyond the merely collegial but fall short of the romantic. This is not the traditional approach, but as our book *More than Friends, Less than Lovers: Managing Sexual Attraction in Working Relationships* explains, it can be done.

Workplace etiquette calls for preserving the right to terminate without prejudice a relationship—either proposed or actually begun—that one party doesn't want to continue or to refuse to begin a relationship in the first place. At work it isn't as simple as saying no and walking away never to see the person again. People earn their livings and build careers there. They return day after day, see one another with the same frequency, and, possibly, begin and observe the development of relationships with others.

Etiquette for communication between working men and women can help. Although either gender can be the object of unwanted attention, it is more common for women to have to say no to men; therefore, the following example illustrates an unwanted male-initiated advance.

Etiquette for the Working Man. You are working closely with a woman colleague and find her attractive. Lunch has been a part of your routine for some time, so you decide to try to escalate the relationship. She's friendly, and she obviously enjoys your company, so you're surprised when she repeatedly dodges your after-hours invitations to get together. What began as a simple next step in your mind becomes a challenge. You wonder what's wrong. Why can't this work? It's not a problem you're used to having. In your experience with women, reluctant reaction always means that you need to try harder. Right? Probably not.

Workplace etiquette demands that you adapt your normal social behavior to the job setting and take a more restrained approach. Be more aware that you are being told no, however subtly. She will probably be less direct and more polite than she would be if you were in a dating situation. Think about it—you're a great working team and your careers are advancing because of what you do together professionally. The last thing she wants is to alienate you and end that. But she simply may not want an expanded social relationship with you—other interests, not mixing work and pleasure, you're not her type, or whatever. It's her call—the reason doesn't matter. Ask again if you feel so inclined, but be prepared to back off without offense or awkward persistence when she discourages you. Don't push to a point that you force her to tell you no in a way that will embarrass both of you and make your working relationship uncomfortable and, therefore, less productive, maybe even for the indefinite future.

Etiquette for the Working Woman. In this situation the woman is obligated to make up her mind and communicate her desires clearly. Assuming that you are in a position to become romantically involved, and company policy doesn't put the two of you on the chopping block for doing so, you may decide to accept his invitation to move the relationship forward. If a more intimate relationship is *not* what you want, make your boundaries known early and firmly. Since you will continue to meet and work together, look ahead to the consequences of encouraging any behavior that might end in a damaged working relationship. Otherwise, you will be forced to be less and less polite if he continues to pursue you socially. Or worse, you could wind up in a relationship you don't want, one that might end in traumatic personal and business consequences.

Job etiquette for the working woman boils down to being aware that most men are predisposed to escalating their relationship with you if they find you attractive. Some of them will not act on their instincts; others will. When they do, you need to make your signals unambiguous and yet face-saving for the coworker you are rejecting. This is one way to successfully apply business etiquette to an environment in which social behavior inevitably intrudes.

Your rights are only as good as your skills in not surrendering them prematurely in a man-woman relationship you really don't want. Reclaiming what you give away—willingly or under pressure—can require the painful legal enforcement of prerogatives you can often preserve from the outset with applied business etiquette. If you mean no, say no. If you begin a relationship and decide it's not working, exit it promptly, as politely as possible, but unequivocally. If you have a relationship, both sides must preserve an attitude that separates work from pleasure; that is, you must exercise different prerogatives when the man or woman in your relationship is also a business associate. It may be difficult, but conscious management of your behavior is required. Be sure that you both have the same understanding of the rules before you enter into a personal relationship, reinforce them as it progresses, and implement the rules in a businesslike way if the personal relationship ends before your working one does.

Etiquette for the Manager.   "No fraternization" rules remain on the books of many companies, but expecting easy compliance is unrealistic. If you are in a position to enforce the rules, do what you must, but offer your people more than a denial of human nature as a means of getting through awkward relationship moments on the job.

Managers' etiquette for easing "invitations, approaches, propositions" problems requires:

- A conviction that man-woman relationships in the workplace are fundamentally different and an expectation that behavior on the job will be different from behavior in a purely social setting
- That you unambiguously support a woman's right to say no to unwanted advances
- That you leave the management of mutually accepted relationships to the individuals involved *as long as they don't interfere with work*
- That you be sensitive to how the exercise of power, including your own, can result in unwanted relationships, even "voluntary" ones

Topic 8 "Attractiveness and Power Relationship Management" Etiquette

An attractive woman in a world of men has a balancing act to perform. She may be a target for abuse, but she can also be the object of favorable treatment that is hard to resist and can be damaging to her career and to the business as a whole. (The same can be said for an attractive man in a world of influential women, but this situation is fairly rare.)

The etiquette involved here is a variation of that described already in Topics 1 through 7. Without belaboring the points, let us just say that the woman must understand that some of the short-term advantages her attractiveness might give her can also make establishing her long-term professional credibility more difficult. The men involved need to make a conscious effort to behave toward attractive women as professional colleagues rather than as sex objects. This is true not only where sexual harassment or exploitation is involved. Lower-threshold preferential treatment that unfairly dominates a woman's professional time and impinges on her identity as an independent professional is also damaging.

Etiquette for the Working Man.   You are a middle-aged manager smitten by an attractive and younger associate of the opposite sex. She makes you feel good. You've never had much attention from women, and you feel as if this is your chance to experience it. You married early, and your relationship with your spouse is routine, though generally pleasant. In fact, you would say that you have a happy marriage. You have nothing improper in mind with your lovely female subordinate—no affair—so here is your chance to feel the high and pay no price. Right?

Wrong. You are mixing personal pleasure with workplace responsibilities and power relationships. Even if you mean no harm, the truth is you are giving your young, attractive colleague little choice but to be attentive to you simply because of your position. This isn't healthy for you, the woman, your other employees, or your business. Power is a relative thing, and you may not believe that you have much power compared with others in the company. But anyone who works for you, especially a woman whose career you influence, is going to find it hard to treat you objectively. When you impose your sense of values or humor, or merely dominate her time when she would more naturally be doing other things professionally, you foster an unnatural relationship that damages her occupational prospects.

Etiquette for the man in this situation suggests that you separate your appeal as a man from the power of your position and let the women who do business with you function without the burden of a "special" relationship. Whether the women want it or not, tolerate it well, or openly resent it, you are at fault for trading power for their attention. This is but another version of the overarching theme of separating social and professional transactions.

Etiquette for the Working Woman.   Your reaction to a situation like the one above depends largely on your sense of professional security and momentum. If you are on an upward career path, you will be wise to disengage and keep moving if you find yourself in a position where you are expected to be an ego-stroking aide of a male mentor. You have more to gain by pursuing your objectives with the assistance of advocates who will not demand your attention in such a way that your image as an independent person and competent professional is damaged. If your advancement options are more limited, you may feel that your ability to sidestep this kind of patronizing behavior is also limited. You must decide whether to tolerate it while you do your best to accentuate professional opportunities and minimize being exploited as the business hours companion you'd rather not be. Another option is to have a frank discussion with your mentor; this may or may not result in the desired behavior changes. In all cases, of course, you always have the option to look for another job.

Etiquette for the Manager. Those who have fallen from power often say, in retrospect, how naive they were to assume that the attention they received was based on their personal appeal rather than on their positions of power. On a smaller scale, all managers face the same situation. Whether it is you or those who share power under your supervision, note this lesson before exercising, or being manipulated by, relationship influence that has no place in the contemporary man-woman working equation.

Managers' etiquette for easing "attractiveness and power relationship management" problems requires:

- Awareness that working relationships are power relationships and that the attention you receive from subordinates of the opposite sex is, by definition, colored by that reality

- That you monitor your own behavior and your subordinates' behavior to avoid relationships that squander professional time pursuing largely personal satisfaction from opposite-sex colleagues

- Recognition that the inappropriate exercise of power can damage your professional reputation as well as that of the "favored" subordinate—remember: there are others with even more power than you

- Encouraging those under your supervision to continue to grow professionally rather than tethering them for your personal satisfaction

Topic 9 "Male Standard" Etiquette

Whether we are discussing the "70-kilogram man" medical standard or the way we evaluate management styles, the default value is usually male. But women are increasingly setting standards in the world, and the once universal male models are changing to incorporate female elements.

For business etiquette this means being less myopic when judging the worth of a management style or the approach taken in solving a problem. Like other areas of etiquette we've discussed, this one applies to both genders, but the preponderance of change is needed among men. The type of male thinking that only recently "allowed" consideration for the views of women can no longer be supported—women have earned rights and influence, and standards tempered by their thoughts and actions are justified. We are not suggesting that male standards be replaced with female ones; rather, we propose an amalgam that consists of the contributions of both genders.

When realities change, so do accepted behaviors. The new business etiquette rejects the male standard for the broader-based standards that have evolved—or should have evolved.

Etiquette for the Working Man. You are the male, sexagenarian head of a national association of colleges working with your planning committee on the program for the upcoming annual meeting. Junior staff members suggest that the traditional tours of the city and other amusement-oriented activities that have been the focus for the spouses attending the convention might no longer be appropriate since many of the spouses are working professionals with substantive knowledge in areas relevant to the association's interests. You are appalled. This is the way it's always been, and your wife has a highly visible role in carrying on the tradition.

But you listen to your employees, and what they are telling you makes sense. What used to be a group of nonworking women serving as campus "first ladies" when you entered the business some years ago has evolved into a mixture of husbands and wives, careerists and otherwise, whose interests are diverse. Your standard and the etiquette it imposes on your business in this case need to change to meet new realities. You break with the old and offer a new program with choices that include seminars, panel discussions, and other meaningful activities for people who accompany their spouses to your association's annual meeting.

Etiquette for the Working Woman. For the most part, women no longer need to charge the barricades to make their voices heard; they now work in almost equal numbers with their male counterparts as peers. As a member of the gender whose viewpoint has recently been given the consideration and respect it deserves, you have an obligation to suggest modifications to outmoded practices that prevent the traditional male-dominated workplace from coming into sync with current business realities. Part of your role is to be a literate, well-reasoned catalyst for change from the inside since you now are present when plans that change, implement, and perpetuate standards are created.

Etiquette for the Manager. Male standards are falling from grace, and you have the chance to be an enlightened manager who sees trends and is conscious of changes in society that portend a new business etiquette respectful of the growing presence of women in, and their contributions to, the workplace.

Managers' etiquette for easing "male standard" problems requires:

- Understanding that change is inevitable and that men must share, not merely dispense, power and standards with women

- Putting aside traditional ways of doing and judging things in favor of new ideas more in line with the realities of a mixed-gender job environment

- Demonstrating a willingness to modify standards you've come to accept as timeless

- Setting an example by encouraging needed changes at levels you influence both directly and indirectly

Topic 10 "Meeting People" Etiquette

Most aspects of workplace etiquette are dual-edged, and so is "meeting people." Women can come on as strident, man-hating ultrafeminists who make a collegial relationship with their opposite sex counterparts difficult if not impossible. In most cases, however, men have the greater potential for doing damage. The initial approach by a man can set the stage for a productive man-woman working relationship or can create problems that foretell an EEO case. Objectionable behavior by either gender includes almost anything other than treating a colleague as a peer in whom you expect to find competence and the stuff of a productive teammate. To get off to a bad start if you are a man, try asking "What's a pretty woman like you doing in a place like this?" or put out signals that she has an uphill battle establishing herself with you as a serious businessperson. If you are a woman, see how he reacts when, even before you say hello you make it clear that you know he'd rather be working with a man, sees all women as sex objects, and is just waiting for you to make a mistake.

These are obviously extremes, but milder versions of these kinds of behavior often get business relationships between mixed-gender peers off on a bad footing from which recovery is difficult. The secret to a good beginning is the simple, but often ignored act of treating an associate of the opposite gender just the way you would treat someone of your own gender occupying the same job. This is what coworkers should want and expect from each other. As a man, avoid the common approach to nearly any relationship with a woman in which you default to the "first-date" mode. As a woman, avoid the knee-jerk tendency to take offense at advances that haven't even been made. To corrupt the legendary Clinton campaign message: "It's business, stupid!" Tack those words to your mental bulletin board and save yourself some "meeting people" etiquette grief.

Etiquette for the Working Man. You are the male member of a two-person team assigned to audit the books of an out-of-town subsidiary. This morning you meet Joanna, the other half of the team. Although you've seen each other at monthly reviews, you've never really had a conversation. You decide that a good icebreaker would be to ask what her husband does and, early in your conversation, to ask whether he objects to her going on trips like these.

This is precisely the wrong way to begin. Joanna would probably be more comfortable with an out-of-the-gate discussion of business like: "You've evaluated the recommendations from their internal audit. How do you think we should proceed?" Avoid family matters. Comments that imply that she's subordinate to her husband are particularly out of place. Save the personal stuff for dinner some evening after you've established trust on the business level and gotten to know each other. For openers you are better off conveying that you see her as a business partner first, a woman second, and someone with personal relationships that might affect business in some way a distant third. Don't say it in words, necessarily, but let her know that you see this relationship as predominantly professional, and that social asides will be voluntary and at your mutual discretion. Assume that she isn't looking for another friend at the moment, and certainly not an escort. Don't burden the beginning of a new mixed-gender working relationship with anything more than a professional, cordial commencement of the business at hand.

Etiquette for the working man when first meeting a woman colleague calls for setting gender aside, approaching her in a friendly but businesslike manner, just as you would a male coworker, and putting ingrained man-woman social instincts on hold. You don't accomplish this merely by not making a pass or by not lapsing into sexist conversation. Rather, deliberately focusing on business and steering clear of anything that portrays her as requiring special consideration because she's a woman is the kind of behavior you should have in mind. If you were to ask a woman in business today what her one wish might be, it would probably be that she begin and end her professional dealings as a gender-neutral member of the team. Extend that courtesy, and you have discovered the essence of the new etiquette for successfully initiating and sustaining man-woman business relationships.

Etiquette for the Working Woman.   As the woman in the situation just described, don't start out by sending sexist signals of your own. Politely, but firmly, radiate "business" and do not feel compelled to demonstrate that you can be one of the guys or hint that you need special treatment.

With all of that established, deal with what your male colleague delivers. Although you may be legally entitled to pounce at his first misstep, don't instantly assume that he is hostile or sexist. If his faults are not threatening, in the interests of business help him off the hook a few times. For example, turn a spouse and children question around by answering, "I have no problems meeting my travel obligations. Do you have difficulties of your own along those lines?" Unless he is a dunce, he'll probably get the idea.

On the other hand, you may draw a partner who really doesn't "get it," and articulating your position makes not a dent in his sexist armor. Try candidly stating that you are in this situation for professional reasons only and you want to do your job just as he does. Tell him that you expect to be treated with the respect you deserve and will not tolerate having an important professional opportunity diluted with personal matters that are not relevant to the assignment. Communicate that you want to be pleasant but don't intend to be distracted by having to fend off improper advances or inquiries that would be irrelevant if you were a man. Of course, there are legal remedies if he persists.

Etiquette for the Manager.   As a manager, you are responsible for easing the acceptance of women into the modern mixed-gender workforce by setting an example as well as making it clear that they will be treated no differently than their male counterparts. "Meeting people" etiquette is literally the starting point for mixed-gender team building, and the right behavior by the manager sets the parameters that can help make it work.

Managers' etiquette for facilitating the solution of "meeting people" problems requires:

- Setting expectations that first meetings of mixed-gender teams will not focus on gender-laden issues like clarifying family responsibilities or exploring the possibility of a personal relationship

- Emphasizing building professional rather than personal team values where skills and problem solving, not personal matters, constitute the core interests of the woman and man working together

- Acting as a facilitator to assist in righting a relationship that gets off to the wrong start

- Rewarding those who succeed at working successfully through the "meeting people" phase of mixed-gender working relationship building by extending maximum opportunities for them to excel as a team

Topic 11 "Required Socializing" Etiquette

The emphasis on separating social and workplace behavior in mixed-gender working environments can present challenges when the job requires socializing. Office parties, receptions, the after hours of business travel, and dinner meetings all place women and men in social situations within the context of business.

A special kind of business etiquette is called for in these hybrid situations where employees are expected to be cordial and social and yet maintain the necessary professional distance to preserve relationships they will have to continue when the work-social event ends and they go back to business as usual. The challenge for women and men in business is to relax and enjoy each other's company without saying or doing anything that makes returning to a peer or subordinate-supervisor relationship at work awkward. And sexual attraction can make such situations even more difficult to manage.

Personal mixed-gender relationships can blossom at a business function, but the participants have to be realistic about how their relationship might affect them on the job. As mentioned previously, all working relationships involve power, and adding a personal element will necessarily make separating business and pleasure more difficult. In the workplace power can operate to the detriment of either party, whether the relationship is between subordinate and supervisor or between two peers competing for promotion and advancement. In either case, the consequences reach beyond the usual social ones and can adversely affect careers.

Correct business etiquette for "required socializing" centers around the need to keep the relative power of the professional setting in balance at the social function. Men and women who are mixed-gender peers can interact more comfortably than can men and women of different ranks because the use of power—to the advantage or disadvantage of either person—is less likely to occur. Of course, even peers competing for favor, accolades, promotions, or other things of value at work can have serious problems. When a business-social relationship moves from required to personal, the people involved need to remain aware of the downside of even the appearance of improper advantage that might be seen by others as altering formal power relationships that affect their own positions within the business. If people do not understand this, and office morale is adversely affected, management might discreetly caution the senior person and suggest greater sensitivity regarding private social interests pursued in the business setting.

Those unwilling to become involved socially must always have a comfortable way out of the relationship regardless of the balance of power. Management should be alert to seemingly unwanted, one-sided social initiatives at work that threaten productive business relationships. There is a fine line between correctly intervening and interfering with personal matters that are none of management's business. Discreet observation, along with a subtle inquiry that might make a cry for help easier, is the best initial approach when business socializing appears to be leading to a problem the principals don't seem to be dealing with successfully themselves.

Etiquette for the Working Man.   You have the afternoon free while participating as a senior presenter at a conference being held in a resort area. A woman counterpart at the host company has been asked to show you the local operation.

After the morning sessions, the two of you have lunch with the group and then head for the plant together. You both enjoy the business and personal aspects of your day together, and when it becomes apparent that you both have the next afternoon free, she offers to show you the local attractions in the community. You agree and spend the hours pleasantly, looking at snow-capped mountains, walking through the streets of a quaint city, and generally enjoying each other's company.

You leave with mixed emotions about what actually happened. On the return flight, you keep imagining more than reality supports about your new relationship, but your thoughts are so pleasant that you can't get them out of your mind. Back at the office you tell one of your colleagues how much you enjoyed the afternoon spent sightseeing and are just a bit embarrassed when she teases you, saying that you sound slightly enchanted with your female host. Still, you consider calling your new friend to say thanks and test the waters about whether she might have feelings similar to yours, but you think better of it, opting instead for a small, appropriately impersonal gift that includes a card of thanks.

You used proper business etiquette when you resisted the temptation to escalate an enjoyable professional interaction that struck a spark of attraction and let it remain uncomplicated. Although it is conceivable that a pleasant business-social encounter might develop into a sustained personal relationship, the normal presumption should be otherwise. A man (or woman) should not automatically see romantic possibilities simply because a colleague of the opposite sex extends a social invitation that came about simply because of business.

Etiquette for the Working Woman.   For the woman in this situation, the challenge is little different from what usually arises in workplace relationships with male colleagues. You bear the responsibility of setting boundaries appropriately and maintaining them. Although your job may require you to extend social courtesies to male coworkers, remember that you are most apt to be the primary regulator of the direction in which those relationships develop. The signals you send by the warmth extended and the prerogatives granted will chart the course of what follows in the relationship.

"Required socializing" etiquette need not be overly defensive or rigid, but you must evaluate the power relationship and act in the interest of what you can sustain not just in the business-social setting but at the office day after day. Distill the personal from the professional and cultivate only that which is in your best personal and career interests. Do you want your association to be primarily professional? Increasingly social? Can you balance the two? When in doubt, keep business business, even when it wears a social face. Project the personal warmth that you need to build collegial business relationships but decisively withdraw when indications show that your warmth is being interpreted as offering more than you intend.

Etiquette for the Manager.   General advice for managers is to stay out of the social life of an employee unless it has a direct impact on his or her work. However, the opposite situation can be a problem: The required social aspects of the job can negatively affect the private lives and work of the employees. In such situations you have a role in setting standards and expectations. You are a model for correct social interaction at business functions, and your behavior should reflect the realities of balancing personal and professional interests.

Managers' etiquette for easing "required socializing" problems requires:

- Personally recognizing and drawing the necessary distinctions between business and private socializing
- Setting boundaries in business socializing that maintain the professional distance needed to return to official status comfortably

- Lending your influence to preempt authority or socialization abuses when it is apparent that your discreet intervention would be welcomed by one party
- Sensitivity to company practices that create excessive social pressures not warranted by legitimate business considerations

Topic 12 "Saying and Doing" Etiquette

Of the many enjoyable exchanges that ease our way through the stresses of working together, those between women and men are among the most satisfying and necessary. They need to be tempered but preserved. After the Hill-Thomas hearings, many colleagues became paranoid about the possibility of offending gender opposites and suffering negative consequences.

Proper business etiquette for "saying and doing" stems from the old axioms "It's not only what you say, it's how you say it" and "It's not only what you do, it's how you do it." There can be no hard-and-fast rules for spelling out acceptable and unacceptable behavior at work, beyond a ban on openly crude behavior. When it comes to extending a courtesy or compliment, the manner of doing it counts as much as the deed itself. Time and place are critical. What might be an appropriate topic for discussion in a private office may be entirely wrong in a conference room full of people. For example, a "nice dress, it's a good color for you" compliment might be fine in one of your offices, but in a group it's not.

Nuance also is critical. Are the persons delivering and receiving the message likely to hear the same thing, or are they on separate wavelengths and, therefore, not the right people to be kidding with each other? Is the remark or gesture appropriate to the real, not an imagined perception (by one party) of the relationship existing between the two people? Or is someone presuming what doesn't exist and in need of hearing reality? Has the sender been insensitive to the impact of his message on earlier occasions—has he been told no and not heard? Everyone needs to be alert to these kinds of possibilities for miscommunication if the necessary light exchanges between associates, especially women and men, are to play their useful role without offense.

Etiquette for the Working Man. You work with a group of women and find yourself growing close to some and keeping your distance from others, just as you have in the past with male colleagues. Surprisingly, unlike the situation with the guys, the close relationships with female peers cause you some problems in your overall professional role. Sooner or later you end up feeling the need to defend close relationships with women. When you focus your attention on one woman, you are seen as either dominating her too much or overdoing the chivalry bit—doing her favors to the point of awkwardness. What's the problem? Doesn't company policy demand that you welcome women to the team? Isn't that what you're doing?

Not quite. Business etiquette for a man calls for distinguishing between what he does and how he does it. Back to the "nice dress" example. "Nice dress" is OK; "nice legs" is not. And "nice dress" with a smile is fine; but "nice dress" with a wink is not. Another secret to successfully interacting with members of the opposite sex at work is avoiding focus—having the ability to extend a compliment, make a courteous gesture, or offer a kidding rejoinder without imparting a special meaning that comes with saying them too often or too deliberately to one person. If you find yourself reserving certain kinds of workplace comments for a certain person—not the kind of thing you'd say to anyone else under the circumstances—take an objective look at your behavior. If anyone is uncomfortable with what you are doing and how you are doing it, especially the recipient of the attention, you may be failing a crucial test of "saying and doing" etiquette.

Etiquette for the Working Woman.   You are a woman in the above situation and must strike a balance between being gracious in accepting compliments, kidding, or whatever, and maintaining the ability to break it off or reduce it if the attention is inappropriate. You have to decide how much is too much and begin discouraging anything that causes him to continue or identifies you with a male associate in a way you don't want to be perceived. Women in the contemporary workplace often guard against alliances with males that typecast them as part of a pair, romantic or otherwise, restrict their overall professional interactions with others, or otherwise adversely color their perception by others.

The challenge for you as a modern woman is to be a comfortable, interactive associate in your professional group, receptive to legitimate communication from male colleagues, but able to radiate without offense what is welcome and what isn't, when enough is enough. Traps exist for you at either end of the spectrum: (1) Trying to be one of the guys is usually not a successful strategy because, in fact, you are not, and (2) reacting negatively to the normal run of colleague banter and kidding will make you an outsider no matter what the gender mix. Balance is everything, and maintaining the ability to be a part of business communications, informal and formal, is essential to your success—but so is regulating how much and what kind of informal communication comes your way.

Etiquette for the Manager. Managers set the tone for office banter by what they do by personal example and what they tolerate in others. You as a manager enter a delicate area when you intervene in on-the-job communication between coworkers, but on occasion you must. The key to successful intervention is carefully choosing to referee only those interactions that cause business problems.

Managers' etiquette for facilitating the resolution of "saying and doing" problems requires:

- Not placing subordinates, particularly of the opposite gender, in the awkward position of tolerating "compliments" from you that they would reject from others—it is your obligation to be a standard setter

- Maintaining the quality of informal staff exchanges at a level at which they can be enjoyed by the full spectrum of personalities on your staff

- Intervening when informal communications become offensive and are not corrected in the normal process of staff feedback

- Discouraging cliques, nonessential closed-door communications, and an atmosphere that erodes staff faith in the reliability of open, informal exchanges

Topic 13 "Saying it Right" Etiquette

Certain messages must be sent in the mixed-gender workforce that relate to the man-woman equation, and communicating correctly will avoid both misunderstandings and breaking the law. What we say comes back to haunt us in high-tech workplaces. "Paper trails" of correspondence or bookkeeping records once revealed things we thought were long forgotten. Now "electronic trails" in computer memories preserve things we might carelessly communicate by, say, electronic mail in a moment of absolute candor or pique. Witness *Today* host Bryant Gumbel's "private and confidential" memorandum to his boss, made public when it was retrieved from his computer. His relationships with colleagues (for example, weatherman Willard Scott, of whom he had been particularly critical) were damaged at least for a time, if not permanently. Major lawsuits have hinged on the work of electronic investigators whose specialty is searching computer records for incriminating evidence like early drafts filled with more candid information than the final copy.[1]

Rather than having to cover your electronic tracks later, try to say it right in the first place. Think before you speak or write, and you won't have to worry about destroying or defending your improprieties. "Saying it right" business etiquette helps you develop a natural sensitivity and avoid being on record as saying things that offend associates of the other gender.

This is not a matter of being "politically correct." You are not just learning a code and avoiding certain words. Instead, you are consciously managing your speech and actions—you do not display bigotry in any form, not even privately on your own computer in documents intended for your eyes only. The etiquette of "saying it right" boils down to not saying in private what you would not say in public about a woman associate—or a man, if the roles were reversed. You never know when the microphone might be open, or the computer system accessible. You must put stereotyped, hurtful expressions aside, and if you criticize, be sure that you articulate valid reasons for your criticism. Reconsider putting your thoughts into words if they lack rational underpinnings, are essentially sexist, and are not good enough to sustain a complaint in the modern business world. "Saying it right" etiquette helps you to think before you speak or write so that you do not embarrass yourself or, worse, end up in court.

Etiquette for the Working Man.   You are a delightful man in public and would be the last person to utter an unkind word to a woman. But behind closed doors, you lapse into vindictive language about women almost by reflex. As one who manages a diverse work group, you have legitimate cause to be critical of women rather often—it's your job to correct your employees' performance problems. Your inner circle consists mostly of men and a woman or two conditioned to react to you the way the men do. You are not above telling off-color stories in their presence. In fact, it is an informal test you have for "your" women to validate their acceptability as team players. You treat them well and expect their tolerance when you want to vent your spleen against anyone, using any language you find expressive. After all, it is largely for effect. No harm is done. You never would say such things for attribution.

Suddenly the unthinkable happens. One of "your" women decides to leave the fold. Even worse, she is trying to establish the case for a pervasive atmosphere of sexism in the company—environmental sexual harassment. You are part of the universe of managers her attorney identifies as being essential to her credibility. In sworn depositions you find yourself clumsily acknowledging that, yes, you said those things, but anyone who knows you knows they don't reflect your true feelings about women! In short, you discover that you were merely being tolerated by a woman you thought was under your thumb. But over the years, she's become more and more angry, and now information she is providing is damaging you in judgments and decisions you could objectively defend on the merits, had you not clouded them with sexist bile that has become an issue unto itself.

"Saying it right" etiquette for a man means deliberately backing away from old patterns of expression that serve neither gender. Today's high drama behind closed doors may not be worth tomorrow's price paid defending language that paints you as sexually biased in the extreme. Bigotry is not only unnecessary but wrong; other words can accomplish your purposes. Learn to use those words. Don't rely on the grudging tolerance of closed-door associates who may someday decide that the greater good is in a candid revelation of what you say about women.

Etiquette for the Working Woman. As a woman in the above situation, you must balance acceptance and loyalty to your employer against fidelity to your own fundamental values. Concerns about job security make pragmatism understandable, but you do have an obligation to try to change things for the better. You might do this by exerting pressure on those whose respect you command to reduce their reliance on unacceptable language directed toward women. It is likely that you can accomplish at least some degree of this kind of change without becoming a martyr. Judge what you can do in your particular circumstances and begin showing disapproval of what a reasonable person would find objectionable. Don't pretend that inappropriate remarks are cute or OK when that is not what you believe. If you don't think that words will make your point, walk away or otherwise use body language to show your disapproval. If asked, be honest and explain that you find what is being said offensive and unnecessary. Lead the discussion of the business issues before you toward the objective high ground and illustrate by example that opposite-gender criticism can be expressed without offensive language.

"Saying it right" etiquette for a woman means not excusing the man who says it wrong. It also means avoiding compensating by coming up with the female equivalent of his sexist invective. Women in business have the advantage of being without a tradition of sexist misspeaking; don't create an unnecessary burden by assuming one now that a practice which is wrong is also out of vogue.

Etiquette for the Manager. Managers ought to lead change. As a manager, begin with your own behavior and extend your example to others in the form of the expectations and standards you set. The terms you use and find acceptable in your area of responsibility should be on the correct side of sexist language practices.

Managers' etiquette for fixing "saying it right" problems requires:

- Altering company policies that permit expressions that were once tolerated but have no place in the new mixed-gender workplace

- Playing your respective role as an influential member of your workforce in either modifying your own language or leading others to alter theirs when it is inconsistent with everyone's best interests

- Insisting that complaints about people's performance and behavior have substance and that they be articulated in objective terms instead of sexist hyperbole

- Intervening when "saying it wrong" is a regular form of communication in your workplace

Topic 14 "Sharing" Etiquette

Getting the job done requires sharing—men and women doing what is necessary to allocate fairly the space, resources, power, solutions to problems, travel, opportunities, and everything else they need to function successfully in the enterprises that employ them. The etiquette for sharing comes from understanding how gender affects people doing business—how identities and power relationships are linked with gender. This kind of etiquette fails when attitudes, expectations, and preconceived notions justify not sharing career building blocks because an associate is of the other gender. It succeeds when people erase the mental limitations that make them view women and men differently as professionals, and when they declare that gender is no excuse for not sharing the challenges and rewards of full careers.

Etiquette for the Working Man.   You are in a position to influence assignments that affect people's careers. The organization you work for is diverse, with lots of women in professional positions. Since you've come up through the ranks and have spent years interacting with customers, you have a sense of who will be well received on various kinds of assignments, and your judgment is highly respected by management. Plenty of women draw field assignments, but you quietly recommend men when you "know" the person they'll be calling on is Mr. X, whom you just can't imagine receiving a woman favorably.

You justify your actions with the many token assignment recommendations you make for women every month and the belief that you're doing what must be done to get the sale, but nonetheless, you fail the test of sharing. When it comes to the tough calls, you pull down the glass ceiling and discourage the equitable sharing of career opportunities in the form of important assignments. Subtle, real reasons for the selection reside only in your head, even though you amply justify your evaluations. The result is an unfair pattern of assignments, and women who deserve a shot at the tough, potentially rewarding accounts don't get them because of you.

"Sharing" business etiquette for the working man means not just minimizing considerations based on gender but eliminating them. If assignments flow from professional credentials, experience, and position in a rotation of who's up next in a group of peers, don't attempt to alter the pattern because you fear that a woman can't handle this particular set of circumstances. If the job requires an MBA and the woman next in line doesn't have one but the next man does, you have justification. If she lacks experience with the pigments to be discussed with a major paint manufacturer, the man should get the assignment. If the only reason for not sharing the opportunity is some premonition that "she" won't be well-received, recommend her for the job—sex discrimination due to your intuition is not justified. The business etiquette of sharing demands objective, rational reasons for denying opportunities that may truncate the careers of women.

Etiquette for the Working Woman. As a woman in the situation just described, you have to thoroughly prepare professionally to avoid being screened out of assignments on rational competitive grounds. Next, you can take the added step of communicating your desire to take on assignments and perhaps risks. Finally, you should be judicious in choosing your battles, but you must be prepared to strongly challenge denied assignments on the merits, letting it be known that you are paying attention and won't passively stand aside if you are held back from desirable assignments because of your gender.

Depending on the organization and people involved, making your case for sharing assignments fairly may be as easy as honestly communicating with men who previously didn't understand or with women who wrongly assume that your career goals are the same as theirs. Or you may have to deal with tradition-bound men and women who are determined to preserve the status quo. There are no easy answers when you face intransigence, and you are left with options that might include acquiescing and waiting for things to improve where you are, seeking employment where opportunities are more open, confronting the offenders directly, or, if change still doesn't occur, taking offenders to court. What you do is a judgment call depending on your circumstances.

Etiquette for the Manager.   Managers have an obligation not to be a part of this kind of problem. On one side of the issue, you should avoid being perceived as the type of person others are afraid to send a woman on a tough assignment. Within your own company, you should make an extra effort to remove gender from assignment decisions.

Managers' etiquette for facilitating "sharing" problems requires:

- Supporting objective standards that judge women on merit and not gender

- Receptivity, not resistance, to seeing women in business situations they may not have occupied until recent years

- Letting your coworkers know that you will assign any capable person, regardless of gender to any position for which she or he qualifies

- Interacting comfortably with opposite-gender colleagues in positions of responsibility both within and outside your company

Conclusions

The degree to which gender consciously affects human interaction no doubt varies, but in a time of sea changes in how women and men share the tasks and opportunities of the workplace, our society has chosen its course. The path declared as appropriate, first by Congress and later by the courts, leads to equal opportunity for both sexes in their pursuit of careers.

This leaves each of us with the highly pragmatic task of changing human behavior cast into patterns over generations that have looked at the respective positions of men and women differently, and this is perhaps most dramatically demonstrated in the modern workplace. The sweeping changes decided on in the institutions of our land require everyday adjustments by working women and men to make opportunity available to women in a culture in which males have long been dominant. This is not a totally natural change. It requires new ways of interacting and different approaches to thinking about and dealing with the opposite sex. Rules, codes of behavior, and standards are changing even as you read.

What we now recognize as civilized people have moved from the crude social orders of their early history to the complex society of today by using rules of etiquette to point the way, to separate practical rights from wrongs, and to teach their members acceptable ways of interacting. Today the discipline of a new business etiquette is being imposed, this time to alter culturally ingrained roles at work. Men and women are learning new rules for effecting changes in workplace behavior that allow them to be "different but equal" as they move forward along the thousands of career paths that weave the web of a great economy from millions of individual aspirations.

5
Managing
Women and Men

Change your perspective from that of an *individual manager* trying to personally effect changes in the mixed-gender work environment to that of *management* as an influential group struggling with institutional obligations to make social change fit productively into a business enterprise. Almost 60 specific recommendations for individual managers were made in the previous chapter on etiquette, each aimed at helping a manager play a personal role making gender fairness a reality in his or her working relationships. This chapter moves mixed-gender problem solving from the day-to-day performance of the individual manager and focuses instead on the *group*—management—that runs the company.

Management should have the highest motivation to be in the vanguard for changes that will benefit the entire corporate culture by (1) developing a workforce that reaches its highest potential because its attention is on getting the job done rather than on gender-related problems that prevent people from focusing on business practices that make their companies successful and (2) satisfying stockholders who want the profits and a winning public image that flow from a productive workforce unencumbered by grievances and legal problems. Management wants to keep both the workforce and the stockholders happy, and people problems are a major obstacle to doing that. Solving people problems in the 1990s means successfully managing diversity, a large component of which is a mixed-gender workforce. To truly succeed in today's business environment, management needs to consider diversity, including gender diversity, as a positive workplace phenomenon and to establish policies and practices that are consistent with this philosophy. To begin the process, management should:

- Accept gender issues as legitimate concerns of management
- Decide what steps the company must take to eliminate sexual harassment and establish, publicize, and enforce policies to accomplish the elimination of sexual harassment with neither prejudice nor favoritism
- Make a commitment to solving the glass ceiling problem
- Determine how the company will balance the needs of the business and those of its employees who increasingly are parents in two-income households

This chapter explores these points more fully as issues that weave a complex overlay limiting the effectiveness of traditional management practices. In much the same way that holistic medicine treats the whole patient, modern management has to be at least cognizant of the whole employee. If not adequately addressed, each of these four areas of concern can limit productivity, and in pairs or as a group, they may actually destroy it.

A Credible Management Problem

Social challenges such as integrating women into the workforce sometimes strike managers as ideals that can be put aside, "quota" problems that can be relegated to the human resources department or, when things go wrong, turned over to the corporate counsel for legal resolution. These options might have worked in the past, but not anymore. The consequences of not satisfactorily dealing with mixed-gender workforce issues have a practical impact that warrants the undivided attention of management.

For example, it is not unusual for an award of punitive damages to accompany the winning claims of individual workers in sexual harassment cases. Even with the monetary caps imposed by the Civil Rights Act of 1991, damages can reach $300,000 per case, depending on the size of the company. While this is not an overwhelming figure for a large corporation, even if Congress does not lift the $300,000 cap as expected, some experts see corporate America facing potential damages of $1 billion over the next five years.[1]

The federal courts are not a company's only exposure. In a 1992 speech, Jane Walstedt of the Department of Labor's Women's Bureau revealed that: "Top monetary awards imposed on harassers and/or their companies in the past five years under State laws ranged from $900,000 to $3,100,000...[and that] sexual harassment costs a typical Fortune 500 company with 23,750 employees $6.7 million per year in absenteeism, low productivity, and employee turnover. This does not include additional millions in possible court costs, executive time, and tarnished public image, should a case end up in court."[2] Viewed this way, sexual harassment reaches a level of economic importance that grabs the attention of managers responsible for protecting their companies against such liabilities. No executive wants to be vilified within the business community or, worse, in the media, for squandering precious corporate resources propping up a man's right to demean women in his or her organization. Even in the not-for-profit world of government, the Navy continues to pay a high price for the Tailhook incident. Failure to successfully address mixed-gender workforce problems leaves management and, by association its organization, with a tarnished image and, increasingly, money and productivity problems as well. When all is said and done, management must take the blame—it runs the organization.

The June 1992 issue of *Working Woman* surveyed both its predominantly professional female readership and a group of Fortune 500 executives on sexual harassment. The study is not scholarly, but the findings reflect the experience of a sample of working women and illustrate that management must take the problem seriously:

- 60 percent of professional women (versus 25 to 40 percent of all women) reported having been harassed, and more than a third said they knew of a coworker who had been harassed

- 75 percent of the women responding to the survey viewed harassment as a serious problem

- 50 percent of sexual harassment complaints reported to management involved pressure for dates or sexual favors, and more than 34 percent were caused by touching or cornering; over two-thirds of the executives surveyed considered the complaints to be valid

- 20 percent of the women believed that companies do not provide justice for those who complain of harassment, whereas 70 percent of personnel managers think companies do provide justice

- The most common harassment scenario involves a female subordinate under 34 years of age being harassed by a male over 35 who has more power (30 percent of the incidents occur with women from 18 to 24 years old)

- Harassment is much more common in predominantly male workplaces and where women have entered male-dominated upper management

- Women respondents believed that the major reasons for harassment relate to intimidation and maintaining power rather than flirtation or sexual desire[3]

Survey results such as this reveal a major problem for business. The statistics of sexual harassment could fill a chapter in this book; they are extensive and can be derived from a variety of sources ranging from the government to popular magazines, newspapers, and books. The 60 percent figure reported by professional women experiencing harassment in the magazine survey cited above is, for example, corroborated by a 1992 study of 230 judges and 3500 lawyers of the Ninth U.S. Circuit, covering federal courts and practitioners in nine western states and the Pacific.[4] To delve deeper, look at the highly objective *Breaking with Tradition: Women and Work, The New Facts of Life* by Felice Schwartz or, for a more zealous view, the best-selling *Backlash: The Undeclared War on Women* by Susan Faludi. Whether the arguments are buttressed by dramatic statistics or statements of high social principle, management is facing liability and productivity problems, arising from gender issues, that must be taken seriously if business is to prosper.

Sexual harassment at work is not an intractable problem. Practical solutions exist. Just as the threat of a billion dollars in settlements gets the attention of corporate America, the prospect of financial loss also works wonders on the shop floor. In one case cited in the *Working Woman* survey, "A female architect, 39, from Chicago reports that one contractor deals with complaints against harassers by 'immediate dismissal, no reassignment, no second chance. Walking through the job site is like walking through an altar boy's convention. The color green is the most powerful motivation in this country.'"[5] You might say, "Only in America!" but you'd be wrong. In France sexual harassment of a subordinate at the office can land an individual in jail for up to a year and cost as much as $16,000.[6] Less radical solutions exist, of course, and 81 percent of Fortune 500 companies say that they are using training programs to address sexual harassment problems.[7] Whatever the ultimate solution in individual businesses, evidence abounds that sexual harassment is a legitimate problem and that remedies for solving it exist. Management's obligation is to acknowledge the problem and apply the remedies.

What Management Can Do about Sexual Harassment

Management can do what a *manager* cannot: it can set the tone for an entire organization and pass on to individual managers the obligation, authority, and motivation to act appropriately. Here are two examples from household names in American industry that are acting decisively to end sexual harassment in their workplaces.

Example 1

A salesman working for a supplier of Corning, Inc., in Corning, New York, no longer thinks that sexist jokes are funny. He made the mistake of telling one during a meeting with Corning employees and suffered the embarrassment of being chastised by a Corning manager. The manager then got on the phone to the salesman's company and said in no uncertain terms that Corning does not condone that kind of talk.[8]

Example 2

Joe Zimmerman (Texas Instruments' manager of corporate services in Dallas), whose responsibilities include TI real estate, was meeting with a team from a Dallas real estate group made up of four men and one woman. Each of the team members was to make a presentation, and before the woman member spoke, one of the men said, "And now the prettiest member of our team will speak." Zimmerman turned to the man and said, "That kind of remark could get you fired around here." [He explained] "We come down very hard on sexual harassment...and while this may not have been harassment, or intended as such, it was a problem. Women resent having to work in a stilted atmosphere. It stifles their abilities to work on an equal basis with men. We believe they should not have to put up with this kind of talk."[9]

Whether either of these examples rises to the level of warranting the reactions they caused is open to question, but they illustrate a point. The sexist joke and language might well have slipped by without comment. People don't like to make waves, and old cultural patterns are rarely assailed by individuals routinely doing business with their peers. But when the management of a firm lets it be known that its corporate culture will change on an issue and that individual managers are expected to accomplish that change, examples like these result. If gender bias is to end, management has to calibrate its own reaction thresholds and identify the kinds of incidents it considers worthy of intervention, make a commitment to the policies it establishes, and back up managers with the clout of upper management when it comes time for enforcement.

When management decides to take on gender bias, sexual harassment is the major issue around which policy is usually based. In an article on public personnel management, author Jeri Spann recounts the experiences of the city of Madison, Wisconsin, and provides a practical set of guidelines for a program dealing with sexual harassment. Spann suggests that management take the following steps:

1. Begin by establishing a strong antiharassment policy which takes the matter out of the realm of debatable politics and advocacy and places it squarely into the realm of law.

2. Create administrative orders which identify sexual harassment as an ordinary work rule violation and which connect such violations to disciplinary remedies.

3. Involve all managers and as many employees as feasible in the creation of basic policy and procedural documents.

4. Establish a complaint investigation and resolution process which is clearly tied to the chain of command but which utilizes specialists from core staffing functions like affirmative action, labor relations, and legal services; balance complaint resolution teams by race and sex.

5. Develop support group capabilities in departments where harassment and retaliation are difficult to see and control.

6. Develop and implement training programs at every level of the organization.

7. Establish hiring and promotional processes which specifically test candidates' attitudes toward women and minorities. Use the results of these processes to weed out potential harassers.

8. Consider the development of an Employee Assistance Program (EAP) to provide counseling and referral services to employees experiencing exceptional stress due to controlled substance abuse, alcoholism, and family problems. This stress, if ignored, may be expressed in harassing behaviors.[10]

To train personnel to make the above policies work, Spann has the following suggestions:

- Include consulting trainers on training teams as well as internal company personnel to get both internal and external perspectives
- Include high-status white males on the training teams

- Mix employees from different areas so that peer groups are broken up during training
- Make sure that women and minorities are not tokens in the training groups
- Ensure that training includes specific definitions of what the courts view as illegal harassment but broaden the discussion to include all inappropriate behavior, making the point that the intent is to stop problems before they reach the legal action stage
- Give employees a list of the kinds of behaviors that are most often the cause of complaints
- Make the complaint processing system clearly understood
- Inform the trainees that they are not being singled out for punishment but rather are exploring a cultural problem that everyone has a role in solving.[11]

Management has the wherewithal to address the problem of sexual harassment meaningfully. Ignorance about what constitutes sexual harassment, what the law requires, and how to set up and follow procedures that effectively deal with harassers is not a valid excuse for companies to sit back and do little or nothing. While the order and content may vary slightly, any number of books, articles, studies, and consultants' opinions outline the kinds of steps just enumerated. The most crucial element is management's commitment to changing the corporate culture and setting firm expectations that everyone in the company will heed new standards. It is also important to communicate management's expectations in a straightforward manner to all members of the workforce. With explicit standards in place and explained, management has to make clear in practical and unambiguous terms the consequences of violating them. It is over the consequences issue that new policy either gains acceptance or succumbs to compromises that relegate it to lip service. When management means what it says, behavior changes. Wrong attitudes and excuses may linger, but *behavior* changes if the consequences of not complying are significant. The choirboy atmosphere of the construction site described by the architect in the *Working Woman* article illustrates that management intent on effecting change can do it.[12]

Whatever the reason, an idealistic one based on heartfelt beliefs that women deserve better treatment or a pragmatic one that harassment costs the company money, if management gives clear signals that sexual harassment is wrong and will be punished, the problem for women employees will be eliminated. If sexual harassment continues to plague a workplace, management should examine how thoroughly, from the top to the bottom, it is committed to fixing the problem. Reluctant approaches to implementing resented change rarely convert productivity-robbing offenders into choirboys—whether they're wearing work boots or wingtips. Management's commitment has to be absolute and unbridled.

Managing the Glass Ceiling Problem

If sexual harassment is the most graphic illustration of mixed-gender problems in the workplace, the glass ceiling may be the most sinister. It tells women they can play but can only rarely hit a home run. Fairness and equality might appear to exist, and women might be protected from discriminatory hiring and even sexual harassment, but they can go only so far in accumulating the essential experiences needed to be top job contenders.

Management is its own problem when it comes to the glass ceiling. When not part of the problem themselves, senior managers can view sexual harassment with some detachment by looking down on their subordinates who are committing most of the offenses at the lower operating levels. This is not true with the glass ceiling. Women are being added to organizations in fair numbers at the entry level and progressing reasonably well to the lower rungs of the management ladder, but then only a handful are finding their way into senior management positions. Something almost mystical happens at the entry ramps to the senior management track. The willingness to be fair and objective that has been institutionalized at the lower levels falls by the wayside at the top in favor of less formal rites of passage, recognition, mentoring, and selection that leave women at a distinct disadvantage.

Existing rules regulating the rise of subordinates into the top ranks of management operate to the clear advantage of the people most like the people who promote them—other men on the same track. They follow the same paths to attainment and play a game of looking for and mirroring the qualities that were the standards for successful selection in the past. Young managers on the rise are most naturally apt to please if they are from the culture of the men who control the entryways to power. If you play the same games, belong to the same clubs, and have the same professional heritage, you have advantages entering the existing order. True, there are women who play the same games, belong to the same clubs (because their male counterparts have been forced to accept them), and have the same professional heritage in the company, and there are others who have made their way up the ladder by taking a new and different route. But both groups are viewed as interlopers, just as the nouveau riche are viewed as not good enough to be warmly accepted into the business and social circles made up of people from old money families. It doesn't matter that many of those with new money have more or even that they are wildly successful in business—they are kept out simply because they are attempting to enter a tightly knit closed circle.

This is the state of the predominant management culture today. Those responsible for redesigning the corporate structure to make it a fairer place in which to work are living in it very comfortably the way it is. No wonder progress mysteriously stops for outsiders who haven't partaken of the rituals and thereby qualified for entry into the select group from which top leaders are chosen. If the glass ceiling is to break, the executive management selection process as we know it has to change and accommodate a broader field of qualified aspirants.

Fundamental Problems

Based on a review of a sample of Fortune 500 companies, a Department of Labor report identified three primary barriers to the career advancement of women within businesses:

- *Recruitment practices.* Although entry-level corporate hiring was generally well-documented, consistent recruitment and tracking practices generally did not exist above a certain level. A commitment to make good faith efforts to attract a broad, diverse pool of talent from which to hire was not apparent.

- *Lack of opportunity to contribute and participate in corporate development experiences.* Often, elaborate corporate systems of early identification, career development, needs assessments, and succession planning were not monitored to ensure access for qualified minorities and women.

- *General lack of corporate ownership of equal opportunity principles.* When departmental staff discussed diversity and a commitment to take appropriate good faith measures, managers often expressed that such responsibilities were someone else's—the human resources division's, or the EEO director—but not theirs.[13]

There is no mystery as to why women are scarce at the top: (1) they aren't actively recruited for upper-level jobs in the same deliberate way men are; (2) the structuring of successor pools rarely includes any assurance that women will have been given the same opportunities as men to accumulate the key experiences that put them in the selection cluster for the top line management positions; and (3) equal opportunity obligations have been passed off to staff minions like personnel officers who have little to do with the ultimate selection of top-echelon line managers.

At an April 30, 1992, presentation before the Association of the Bar of the City of New York, the U.S. Solicitor of Labor, Marshall J. Breger, said "[T]he problem of the 1970s was bringing women and minorities into the corporation. The problem of the 1980s was keeping them there, and the challenge of the 1990s and beyond is to remove any artificial barriers impeding their upward mobility."[14] In elaborating on the glass ceiling problem, Breger mentioned that "only 6.6 percent of those in senior management were women [a]nd most of those are in the 'velvet ghetto'—staff jobs such as Human Resources and Public Relations that usually don't put them on the fast track. So after moving up the ladder a few rungs, many women...stop short and simply mark time."[15] Further evidence of the problem is shown in studies like one done at the University of Southern California that found women making up "3.1 percent of top executives at Fortune 500 companies, and 4.3 percent of senior managers at major service firms. Based on the promotion rate for women over the past 15 years, the study projects it would take 475 years—or until 2466—until half of all senior corporate executive positions statistically were filled by women."[16]

The glass ceiling problem resides at the management level and could be thought of as a white-collar crime of the mixed-gender workplace. Production line workers are not stopping women from entering the executive ranks of any business; top managers are—and they know it. Catalyst, a New York consulting firm specializing in women's employment issues, conducted a survey of CEOs and personnel officers at 1000 leading companies asking about women in management and found that:

- 79 percent of CEOs acknowledged that women face barriers to top management, especially stereotyping and unwillingness to risk promoting a woman

- 91 percent of CEOs said that companies should change their cultures to meet women's career needs

- 8 percent of the companies surveyed said that women make up more than 25 percent of senior management

- 40 percent of the companies reported that flexible work arrangements are not available to higher-level employees.[17]

A similar Catalyst survey found that "nearly half of human resource managers thought women had less initiative than men and were less willing to take risks....[W]omen are perceived as being less committed, especially if they are mothers. 'They are seen as people who will not stick around or who will not relocate.'"[18]

Solicitor Breger cited Justice Brennan's perception of the problem in the Supreme Court's ruling on *Price Waterhouse v. Hopkins:*

In the specific context of sex stereotyping, an employer who acts on the basis of a belief that a woman cannot be aggressive, or that she must not be, has acted on the basis of gender....An employer who objects to aggressiveness in women but whose positions require this trait places women in an intolerable Catch 22: out of a job if they behave aggressively and out of a job if they don't.[19]

These examples illustrate some of the barricades that block women from the top management echelons. They are viewed as not having the "right stuff" for getting to the top—they "should" or "should not" behave in certain preconceived ways—and they aren't given the same line assignments and mentoring relationships as their male counterparts to make them viable candidates for selection. "For example, one company had a requirement that, in order to become CEO, a candidate would need to have overseas experience. In that same company, however, there was also a guideline precluding women from being given overseas assignments,"[20] according to Breger.

Other subtle, closely held management perquisites mark fast-track, high-potential ("hi-pots" is the buzz word) employees identified as key contributors who should be retained for future advancement. This is done with a complex system of compensation and benefits that is a 'signal' within the corporate hierarchy.[21] Those who send and read these signals, and those who benefit from them and perpetuate the system, are a tightly knit closed "society." Women seeking equal opportunities cannot make linkages that will lead them to the top because they are not members of the groups controlling the coded behavior that designates those who will eventually rise to the top.

The *Washington Post* reports that obstacles to women are not just a matter of perception but quite real. It cites, for example, a study by researchers at Loyola University of Chicago and the Kellogg Graduate School of Management that found the career progressions of more than 1000 male and female managers in 20 Fortune 500 companies to be dramatically uneven in spite of the groups being alike in almost every way but gender. Women earned less, and there were proportionally fewer women making it to top management positions.[22]

Pipelines of Progress, Labor Department's 1992 Update on the Glass Ceiling Initiative, quoted a 1991 *Business Week* survey that highlighted the subtle screening of women from experiences that lead to the executive suite, "In regular B-school [business school] programs—usually paid for by the participants, not an employer—there are plenty of women and minorities....Yet in the prestigious programs paid for by corporations that round out a manager's credentials at a key career point, usually at age 40 or 45, companies are making only a token investment in developing female and minority executives. Only about 3 percent of the 180 executives in Stanford's recent advanced-management program were women."[23] Old boy networks are alive and well and perpetuating themselves to the detriment of those who don't qualify for membership in the club.

Solicitor Breger ended his address to the New York City Bar group with a carrot-and-stick message that symbolizes what seems like a somewhat ambivalent position taken by the federal government. He said, "The heart of the Glass Ceiling Initiative is the promotion of equal opportunity—not mandated results. We encourage the promotion of good corporate conduct through an emphasis on cooperative, not just corrective, problem solving."[24] He also brought up the Administrative Dispute Resolution Act of 1991, which requires government agencies to emphasize negotiations and conciliation in resolving glass ceiling disputes. These conciliatory remarks were punctuated with a warning note when he mentioned that state courts are settling glass ceiling suits with record monetary awards. A case in point was *Martin v. Texaco Refining and Marketing Inc.*, in which a jury award of $20.3 million was upheld by the court, which further ordered the plaintiff promoted to an executive position.[25]

Motivations for Change

Whether government officials, management consultants, or the CEOs of Fortune 1000 companies are speaking, the universal opinion is that the most effective way to crack the glass ceiling is to change the behavior of managers who curtail careers because women don't fit arbitrary molds. Adding equal opportunity to the appraisal process for their managers and holding them to positive results has been a successful tool for some companies. At Tenneco, for example, tying a portion of executive bonuses to their success in promoting women and minorities has led to a 25 percent rise in the number of women and minorities hired.[26] In some cases, managers' motives may be altruistic in that breaking the glass ceiling is the right thing to do, but the future success of their businesses is equally important, according to Labor Solicitor Breger:

> Companies…need to recognize, especially given the changing demographics of the workforce, that recruiting and developing well-trained women and minorities are essential if such companies are to remain competitive into the next century. Businesses with their eyes on the future understand the necessity of building a skilled and diverse workforce throughout every level of the company. And they

know a Glass Ceiling doesn't just prevent qualified women and minorities from reaching their full potential—it can also stunt the company's growth. If allowed to remain, it effectively cuts the pool of potential corporate leaders in half. It deprives business of new leaders, new sources of creativity and would be pioneers with entrepreneurial spirit.[27]

The same sentiment is echoed by the Towers Perrin executive recruiting firm, which in a March 1992 report entitled "Workforce 2000 Today: A Bottom-Line Concern," observed that "the single greatest factor contributing to the increase in support [of workplace diversity] is senior management's heightened awareness of workforce issues and the impact those issues have on the company's profitability and competitive position."[28] The cynics may be right—dismantling the glass ceiling may ultimately have as much to do with the corporate bottom line as altruism, social conscience, or anything else.

Self-Imposed Glass Ceilings

The emphasis for effecting significant change has to be on the role of management because it controls the organization, but an examination of glass ceiling issues should also acknowledge the personal factor. Like men, women have to take personal responsibility for their careers, and that, in the words of the Department of Labor report, includes recognizing that "[o]ftentimes workplace advancement means relocating to less than ideal localities; working long hours; taking career risks; volunteering for additional assignments; or simply moving to another division—all factors that employees must weigh, and about which they must make personal and professional decisions."[29] In other words, women have to take the bitter with the sweet of equal opportunity. Many top-level female executives will get there only after some remote tours and high-risk assignments.

Relocation is a problem for men and women, married and single, but according to executive recruiters interviewed for an article in *Management Review*: "Married women are a bit more hesitant than married men to move to a new city, although the recruiters say women are becoming less sensitive on this issue."[30] Like men, women relocate more easily if their spouses get assistance in finding work in the new city. Single women tend to avoid relocation when "the move involves a smaller city that's culturally deprived."[31] The same generalization might apply to single men, of course, but the expectation is greater that men will substitute sports such as golf or hunting or fishing (or whatever) for the missing cultural activities while spending their time in the necessary remote assignments, or simply that they won't mind as much. If they are going to be allowed into the club, women have to change the stereotypical image that they are not willing to pay the same dues as their male peers by responding when opportunity knocks—relocating when they must and making the best of the location no matter where it is.

The recruiters *Management Review* interviewed also found that women are sensitive to being hired as tokens or to fulfill quotas. They reported that "[i]f [women executives] suspect there is any hint of tokenism in their hire, they'll walk away." They want to know that companies are committed to hiring women and expect to see that women have already been promoted into higher-level jobs. "They don't want jobs because they're women; they want the jobs because the employing organizations think they can solve problems and implement programs that will drive the businesses forward."[32] This might sound like an implausible self-limitation, but it is consistent with women's overall pattern of wanting success for essentially the same reasons men do— because they deserve it.

Value of Mentoring

The brighter spots in the national equal opportunity story involve highly practical initiatives taken by companies that are truly committed to breaking the glass ceiling. Mentor programs are among the most successful because they address the fundamental problem of integrating women into the informal networks that play an important role in getting to the top levels in businesses. Ann Lindsey, an adjunct associate professor of management at Simmons College, says:

> For women to get ahead into senior positions, they must develop their own informal system. Women have moved into staff positions, but it's the senior positions that require they 'read' the corporate environment and develop sources.[33]

Gayle Kosterman, vice president of human resources at the consumer products division of S. C. Johnson Wax, benefited from a mentoring arrangement with an executive three levels above her immediate supervisor. She described its value this way: "He gave me really good feedback within the information loop, information that clearly couldn't have filtered down to me."[34] By having an assigned executive mentor, she "was privy to the kind of informal network of high-level company information passed among senior males. This can be absolutely vital to advancement—and usually not possible for women."[35] Mentoring relationships are affirmative action at its finest, compensating women for the very thing they lack through no fault of their own: not being part of the old boy network.

A similar program was put in place at Chubb and Son, Inc., part of the large insurance company, according to Jan Tomlinson, senior vice president and managing director for human resources there:

> Each member of our operating committee—all males—was assigned three or four protegees and charged with making initial contact, in person or by telephone. It was suggested that they meet individually for lunch or dinner and be available as a sounding board and a confidential ear.[36]

The sponsors were to encourage their charges to cross over into unfamiliar areas like personal computer projects. Significantly, five of those being mentored at Chubb, "four of them women—have been elevated to vice presidents, positions granted not by appointment, but by vote among the firm's 28 managing partners…unusual in our 'old-line, white male-dominated' industry," according to Tomlinson.[37]

The success secret of the mentoring programs is a simple truth long practiced in grooming promising men for top executive slots. In the words of Johnson Wax's Gayle Kosterman: "People learn best when they talk with others who have been successful."[38] Breaking the glass ceiling may in the end be no more complicated than doing the obvious—giving women the same chance to do what men do when they are qualified and want to do it.

Management and the Family

It is no longer possible to separate workers' problems, benefits, and other considerations discretely into personal and business categories. With a workforce made up of almost equal numbers of women and men, the two categories now blend in almost every dimension. One reflection of the new relationship between management and its workers' family responsibilities is a compilation of information for companies recently issued by the U.S. Department of Labor called the *Work and Family Resource Kit*. It begins with this overview of the situation:

> Increasingly, employers are being called upon to respond to their employees' needs to balance work and family responsibilities. Benefit packages, work schedules, and recruitment plans are being revised to include an innovative array of policies and programs. Dependent care options range from on-site day care centers to voucher programs, flexible benefit plans, long-term care insurance, and parental leave policies. Alternatives to the standard work week

include job sharing, voluntary reduced time, flexitime, and work-at-home options. Many companies are examining their values and style, and are responding in a variety of ways to ease work and family life conflicts of their employees.[39]

The intrusion of work on the family (and vice versa) is a growing phenomenon. According to the Bureau of Labor Statistics, women who made up only one-third of the civilian labor force in 1960[40] will account for almost half of it by the year 2000.[41] The Hudson Institute's *Workforce 2000: Work and Workers for the 21st Century*, a study done for the U.S. Department of Labor, described the change this way:

> America has become a society in which everyone is expected to work—including women with young children. But many of society's institutions were designed during an era of male breadwinners and female homemakers. What is needed is a...reform of the institutions and policies that govern the workplace, to insure that women can participate fully in the economy and that men and women have the time and resources to invest in their children.[42]

Women Have Changed the Workplace

Sweeping changes have come to the workplace in the past three decades, and management has to appreciate that adjusting business policies and practices to accommodate the new realities is not merely a gesture to a new generation of ambitious women. According to government statistics:

- More than half of working men have wives working full or part time
- 25 percent of working parents have some responsibility for an aging relative
- 37 percent of the workforce is made up of working parents with children under the age of 18
- 13 million children are in one-parent families
- 64 percent of women who maintain families work
- 56 percent of all women with children under age 6 are in the labor force.

The potential impact on worker productivity is obvious. Extensive surveys cited by the same source show that parents of children who cared for themselves "were the workers most affected on the job by missed days, lateness, interruptions, and early departures. In fact, the highest absenteeism rate for all employees was for men whose children were in self-care."[43] And the problem doesn't end when children reach adulthood. "[T]he Travelers Insurance Company found that 28% of its employees provided care for a friend or relative aged 55 or older."[44]

The term *extended family* takes on new meaning in the contemporary mixed-gender workforce. Although women are the most recent entrants to the workplace and the ones currently demanding rights, the children they bear continue to have an impact on the workforce as a whole. As women have become an integral part of working America, obligations have shifted to men and employing institutions to help shoulder the burden of caring for children and older relatives at home. Society has made its decision, and women are in the workplace to stay. This leaves us with finding ways to make broad-based adjustments in how women, men, and employers will accommodate the necessity of raising new generations and assisting with the passing of old ones without adversely affecting business productivity and profit.

Looking at the child-raising cycle of the family and its impact on women and business, Felice Schwartz, founder and former director of Catalyst, a women's interest research group, says that it is time to recognize and accommodate a very real and natural cycle that is now a part of the workplace, to:

> [L]ook more closely at the reality of maternity in the workplace, you see it is a continuum made up of four interrelated stages: pregnancy, childbirth, parental leave, and child care. The degree to which each new mother is affected by the four depends on various factors that no one can control, such as her health in pregnancy, the nature of the delivery, the health of the child, and the availability of good child care that she can afford. All four stages are multifaceted and merit a great deal of discussion and planning. As it is now, all four are obscured by the conspiracy of silence.[45]

Schwartz maintains that we have passed the point at which companies can ignore the problems and costs of working parents and their children. She believes that "[t]he experience of parenting is inseparable from the workplace experience."[46] To her, it is a question of how long it will be before management rationally integrates the cost of family accommodations into the cost of doing business. In her words, until we do:

> We'll go on treating maternity as a short-term disability and not the legitimate, lifetime commitment it is in reality. We'll also short-change business, because when you deny the reality of maternity you can't plan for it. When you don't plan, the chances are slim that you can deal with it cost-effectively.[47]

As is the case with most issues, including gender-based concerns, the ultimate arbiter of whether and when companies act is how the bottom line is affected. When it comes to family-related worker issues, the costs are becoming increasingly universal, easy to recognize, and measurable in dollars.

Workers' Needs Have Changed

The formula for success used to be predictable: The man would work himself into an early grave, and the woman would forgo a career for the sake of home and family. That picture has changed radically, and the current trend is certain to continue. Breadwinning is a shared task in many households, and the kids are getting a different kind of attention, some of it a more calculated sort of quality time made possible by careers adapted to accommodate parenting. *Client's Monthly Alert*, an accountants' client newsletter, reported in its July 1992 issue:

> *Execs want the "parent track."* A recent survey of 200 executives reveals that they feel employees want a greater balance between family and career—a trend sometimes called "parent tracking"— and believe that businesses should accommodate these desires. Ninety-two percent feel employees are more concerned with balancing family duties and jobs today than they were five years ago. Nearly half said the number of executives willing to work long hours on a fast career track has declined over the past five years, with the overwhelming reason being to spend more time with their families.[48]

The trend to "family-friendly" policies is a slowly growing one according to an article in *The Washington Post* reporting on a study of 1004 human resource professionals that found 29 percent of U.S. companies providing child care and 10 percent researching the subject.[49] The same article cites success stories like GE Medical Systems in Milwaukee, which offers flexible work arrangements that are taken advantage of by working mothers and an occasional new father. The woman coordinating the program noted that she has recruiting responsibilities too and that the policy is just a practical approach to hiring in the 1990s, when three-fifths of the new hires will be women, "41 percent of them between the ages of 26 and 36, which are the childbearing years."[50] If you need to hire women, and they need flexibility to bear and raise the next generation, then reasonable accommodations can and must be made.

Some parts of the country are further ahead than others—the Washington (D.C.) Personnel Association surveyed 355 private sector organizations and found that of those with 500 or more employees, 85 percent had child care policies and three-fourths of those with fewer than 500 employees said that they offered some kind of aid.[51] The article reported finding that family-friendly benefits are a hot topic, not only with big corporations but also with a lot of small businesses whose employees face caring for children and aging relatives. The practical origins of the movement were confirmed by the chief financial officer of a local firm who said that his company began child care because "this is something that is necessary to do. As citizens and as businesses we can make a contribution toward solving a problem."[52] But he continued, "The fact that this whole movement has continued through this recession tells us that it's here to stay. Once the economy begins to grow...there's going to be even more competition for employees."[53] The corporate bottom line speaks again.

What Companies Can Do

The following is a summary of things companies can do to help workers accommodate their family obligations and be more productive in the process. This information has been summarized from the U.S. Department of Labor's *Work and Family Resource Kit*.

Alternative Work Schedules

Flextime. With a flextime system, workers can choose the time to arrive at and leave work as long as they accumulate the required number of hours per day or per week.

Voluntary Reduced Time. Companies offer "V-time" to help employees meet family, personal, or schooling needs, and as an alternative to layoffs. Employees reduce their work time and pay by 5 to 50 percent for a specified period of 6 to 12 months while retaining their benefits and seniority status on a prorated basis.

Part-Time Work. Part-time workers may be either temporary or permanent part-time employees. Generally, temporary part-time workers do not receive benefits, whereas permanent ones often qualify for prorated vacation and sick leave but often are not eligible to receive employer contributions to health insurance.

Job Sharing. When two workers with compatible skills share the responsibilities of one full-time job, it is known as *job sharing*. Two workers sharing a position offers the potential advantage of providing a wider range of skills and experience than a single employee would and allows flexible scheduling. Continuity is also enhanced: if one employee leaves, the other generally remains. Older, experienced workers, who might leave if they had to work full-time, are retained.

Phased Retirement. A retiring employee gets the opportunity to make a gradual transition into retirement, and the company has the advantage of having that person train his or her replacement.

Flexiplace (At-Home Work). Information-based jobs in particular lend themselves to off-site working arrangements (usually at home) that can save the cost of office space for the employer and reduce child care problems for the worker.

Dependent Care Options

On-Site or Near-Site Child Care Centers. Available child care is an effective labor recruitment tool, a community relations asset for a company, and a factor in reducing employee absenteeism.

Consortium Centers. Several employers, especially smaller ones, combine their efforts to sponsor a common child care center which can have many of the same advantages as on- or near-site centers.

Resource and Referral for Child Care. These services provide counseling to employees on how to find and judge the quality of child care. They also improve the quality of care by recruiting and training the providers.

Vouchers. The company subsidizes the care selected by the parent with a voucher in the form of a flat fee or a percentage of the cost. Vouchers have the advantage of supporting existing community services and allowing the parents to make their own arrangements.

Discounts. Companies negotiate employee discounts with the child care providers. Generally, a parent saves about 20 percent—a 10 percent reduction and another 10 percent employer contribution.

Programs for Part-time or Emergency Care. These programs provide care for children during the hours before or after school when parents must be at work or during their work-related travel.

Sick-Child Care. There are a number of approaches that vary according to the circumstances and assist the parent with the cost of caring for a sick child at home or in a hospital or the cost of adding a "sick bay" facility to a regular day care center. In some cases, parents are given leave to care for sick children at home.

Elder Care Services. Estimates show that 25 to 30 percent of the workforce has care-giving responsibilities for aging relatives. Some workers take care of elderly relatives at home; others face the problem of supervising care from a distance. Employers have begun to recognize the financial and emotional strain that comes with care of the elderly and are helping with resources and referrals, on- or near-site adult day care, visiting nurse services, respite care (where the employee is given breaks in the care-giving routine), and long-term care insurance.

We have provided only a broad overview of the kinds of family-friendly resources that companies in a position to help are beginning to provide their employees. In almost every instance, the motivation of management is a combination of caring and practical concern about maintaining a productive workforce that is not distracted to a fault by its family obligations. The *Work and Family Resource Kit* is a starting point for exploring these topics more fully. It is available from the Women's Bureau, U.S. Department of Labor, Clearinghouse on Work and Family, 200 Constitution Avenue NW, Washington, D.C. 20210, (202) 523-4486.

Keeping Policies Fair and Legal

As it adapts to the needs of the modern workforce, management must not violate the law as it makes accommodations to families. *Industry Week* consulted an attorney experienced in commercial law on the pitfalls of implementing special working arrangements like the mommy track. Barbara R. Hauser, senior partner in a Minneapolis law firm, suggested caution since federal and state laws "prohibit employers—in job interviews or on employment applications—from asking about marital status, mother status, or child bearing plans." She also saw problems for any company trying to come up with a compensation system for women only. A Supreme Court ruling supporting a California law on pregnancy discrimination was quoted as saying that women workers must have "the basic right to participate fully and equally in the workforce, without denying them the fundamental right to full participation in family life." The answer to the problem lies in providing the needed flexibility for all employees, not just women; that is, the mommy track should be the parent track, and family leave provisions should apply equally to women and men.[54]

Conclusions

One's personal approach and one's institutional approach to problem solving generally arise from different perspectives, and a person who is a part of an establishment known as management should not be surprised to feel some ambivalence as he or she wrestles with mixed-gender workplace issues. Some individuals will retain twinges of less than progressive thinking—in their heart of hearts they resent some of the accommodations they know they have to make. Yet as institutional players with more than personal responsibilities, they must willingly make changes because of the ultimate benefit to both workers and business that will result.

Management plays its role by recognizing the problems of gender inequity in the professional lives of its employees and establishing unambiguous policies and expectations so that its individual managers and workers can solve them. Management does this by accepting the credibility of its workers' gender concerns, making a commitment to end sexual discrimination and harassment, resolving to shatter a glass ceiling that works to the ultimate detriment of future productivity, and giving priority to balancing the needs of business and the needs of women and men who are trying to provide quality care for their families while they pursue careers that lead to individual success and profit for the companies for whom they work.

6

A New Tomorrow at Work

To paraphrase the title of a vintage movie satirizing the Cold War, "The women are coming! The women are coming!" As a matter of fact, the women are here. Women and men have shared the planet since they first arrived on it, and in our culture at least, the process of social evolution has brought them to the verge of practical, functional equality. It was not always that way, and it is not quite that way yet, but everything indicates that it will be.

As the sexes become peers, their interaction in the workplace, where they spend more than one-third of their lives and experience so many of their satisfactions and frustrations, is *the* pivotal measure of succeeding at the task of equitably sharing. The present is not like the end of World War II. Things are not going to return to "normal," with large numbers of women putting down their tools and staying at home full time. There has been a paradigm shift of major proportions—the ways women and men live and work have changed forever. A look at the current workforce, college enrollments, or college graduates yields the same message—women do and *will* constitute a major part of the trained workforce.

Roles and relationships are changing more than the relative numbers of women and men working. Labor force projections for the years 1990–2005 indicate that women will continue to outpace men in the rate of growth, 1.3 to 0.9, but by the year 2005 will still trail them in absolute numbers, 71.4 million to 79.3 million.[1] What is changing is not the numbers—women are not on the verge of making men a minority in the workplace, as they have in the population—but they are increasingly doing the kinds of jobs men traditionally have done, and they are moving into those professions as peers, not subordinates. Each of us *can* and *must* adjust to this change if our society is going to remain productive.

As new relationships develop between working men and women, people need assistance in adapting to the change. Federal regulatory influence is the lever forcing change where it is not voluntary. Understanding the dynamics of this change is essential for anyone hoping to operate in the new environment successfully. But if regulations fuel the pressure to adopt a new balance of power institutionally, understanding each other's personal capabilities and limitations provides the basis for women and men to achieve change individually, *and* willingly. And lasting change must come at the individual level.

The editors of *Time* examined the labor force statistics for the 1990s and drew the following meaning from them:

> The U.S. is about to undergo the most wrenching shifts in the composition and quality of its workforce in more than a half-century....While most companies have yet to come to grips with the new realities, the cold, hard fact is that corporate America is facing a deepening shortage of skilled labor in the decades just ahead....For the first time in their working lives, U.S. managers are no longer able to pick and choose among an embarrassment of labor riches, but must compete harder than ever for well-educated workers...the face of the workforce is changing dramatically. While the labor force will grow slowly over the next decade, two-thirds of the increase will be women starting or returning to work....Most startling, only 9.3% of the new workers will represent the populations from which nearly all top corporate managers have sprung: white, non-Hispanic U.S.-born men.[2]

Some things we can change, and some we cannot. The number of people already in training to fill the professional workforce will not change. With women accounting for 40 percent of the students in law schools, 60 percent in journalism schools, and 40 percent of the MBAs, the future composition of these professions will include women in significant roles—that much is a given.[3]

With it established for all practical purposes that differences between the sexes are insignificant during an era in which technology compensates for lack of physical strength, equal occupational opportunity for women and men becomes inevitable. Those in favor of occupational segregation have no legitimate criteria with which to defend the status quo, so they rely on their long-held power and custom to defend their turf against an onslaught of women. However, the levees are crumbling as a flood of unstoppable change is bringing full participation for women.

With that said, keep in mind that inertia is a powerful force. Many people will still resist change simply because change of any kind is disruptive. Thus, change won't prevail universally overnight. Instead, the range of choices for women who want different lives will continue to expand over time, just as they have over the past three decades. Many women will undoubtedly choose to remain traditional wives and mothers who stay outside the workforce or enter it only intermittently as a secondary source of fulfillment. But artificial barriers will be lowered for the many others who want to depart from tradition or combine the old and the new—families and careers.

New Roles and Approaches

Smoke from ongoing battles between the sexes still clouds the view here and there, and the courts haven't seen their last sexual harassment suit. But looking back from the future, we will likely conclude that the great gender wars of the twentieth-century American workplace began to wind down with the 1990s. Dramatic moments like the Hill-Thomas hearings will be seen as exceptions.

In the future, wider-ranging changes such as new roles for women in the workplace will be a reality—they will be inside players rather than outside observers. The exercise of power, no matter how trivial the players and their circumstances, will always be evident at work as it is elsewhere. But as women are becoming and will continue to become insiders, they will be more apt to be power brokers than low-level minions, paramours, or Watergate-era secretaries dutifully covering for their male bosses' dirty deeds.

Women have come of age in the economy and in the organizations that make it work. As significant as the new female organizational politician and power broker is a trailblazing generation of women physicians drawn from pools of female talent untapped half a century ago. Each year the statistics for women in the professions increases, as this 1993 example from *The Washington Post* illustrates:

> What a difference a decade makes. This year, for the first time in its 30-year history, women outnumbered men in the graduating class at Mt. Sinai School of Medicine. In 1983, the situation at Mt. Sinai, one of six medical schools in New York City, was quite different: 43 of the 130 graduates were female. This year 67 graduates were women and 61 were men.
>
> Officials at Mt. Sinai said that their Class of 1993 marked the first time that a graduate medical program in New York, which has more medical schools than any other state, has awarded degrees to a predominately female class.

Few of the nation's 126 medical schools approach gender equity in graduating classes...[but] at virtually every medical school, newly-minted doctors are undeniably more diverse than they were in the 1970s, when most were middle-class males.
Currently...18 American medical schools had more women than men in their first-year classes. And at eight medical schools, including Harvard University, women students outnumbered men.[4]

The gender trends of the future are already set in the 1990s for top-of-line medical professionals in the twenty-first century—a lot of women will be wearing stethoscopes and having an impact on medical decisions affecting the nation. Anyone who hasn't received treatment at a major urban teaching hospital lately is in for a big surprise. Those doing the examining and prescribing the course of treatment will almost certainly include, if not be composed predominantly of, women physicians, generally young, certainly representing the future of the medical workforce.

As changes such as the predominance of women doctors become the norm rather than the rare exception, the women's movement takes on a less strident persona. Gloria Steinem, in *Revolution from Within: A Book of Self-Esteem*, now writes on self-image with as much comfort and conviction as she once focused on the injustices of a male-dominated society. Betty Friedan pens a significant book on aging after being relegated to the sidelines of the women's movement which she played such a large part in creating more than a quarter of a century ago. A feminist writer of the current generation, Susan Faludi, has even switched topics to what is wrong with men—albeit what's wrong with men relative to how they treat women.

Movements change direction as the motivations for them evolve, and the women's movement is no exception. Although salary gaps and workplace inequities are not yet history, the differences are narrowing, and some would say closing, in many important respects. In response, women are focusing more on the nitty-gritty of their immediate jobs and lives and less on sensational national movements (with the exception of abortion) and leaders. Women's interests and power are being expressed in traditional areas that were previously closed to them. The progress of women can now be measured in tangibles—a new Congress that is 11 percent women—48 members of the House of Representatives and 7 senators. The change reflects disenchantment with leadership that is not mainstream. Many ordinary women who are sensitive to gender issues have difficulty identifying with the National Organization of Women (NOW) and its leaders, who are regarded by some women as being on the fringe. They are more comfortable with the respected leaders of the movement such as Felice Schwartz, who founded Catalyst and guided it through 30 influential years of representing their interests where it counted most—with the captains of industry. Lisa Genasci, writing for the Associated Press, describes a quieter trend in the women's movement of the future:

> Catalyst considers itself a rational voice in the working woman's struggle to penetrate management levels of the corporate mainstream, a world that remains largely dominated by males. Armed with research and reason, the firm appeals to the bottom line, arguing that it makes long-term financial sense for companies to actively cultivate and promote women.
>
> Most recognize...that Catalyst has opened doors to women in corporate America.
>
> The group's $2.5 million budget is funded by corporations and private foundations. Its board is composed of seven chief executives from major American companies, led by John Bryan, CEO of Sara Lee Corp.
>
> Catalyst's underlying argument is that it's illogical for businesses to ignore women, who constitute about 46 percent of college graduates and 45 percent of the workforce.
>
> In Catalyst's view, companies must address work-family issues to retain the best women workers.
>
> By the end of the century, about two-thirds of new workers are expected to be women, and about 75 percent will become pregnant during their working years....There is a cost to companies that fail to respond to women's needs for adequate maternity leaves, flexible schedules and other allowances.
>
> Companies that don't provide maternity benefits, for example, suffer a 25 percent turnover rate, with the cost of each manager lost equal to about 150 percent of the manager's salary, Catalyst research shows...[m]any companies still only look at men for management positions to avoid these costs. But that is a throwback to a time when there were plenty of men to fill jobs—not so now.[5]

This is the businesslike and rational voice of the women's movement that is emerging as the prime mover in accomplishing change. Higher-profile leaders who grabbed national attention when that seemed necessary deserve their due, and they will continue to lead when issues demand it, but organizations like Catalyst will most likely set the tone for the future.

Changed Managers and Decision Makers

The infrastructure of leadership and decision making has changed dramatically and is only beginning to yield results. Like it or not, agree with their emphasis or not, the voices of women have been added to the national dialogue in forums where their views were seldom articulated except by males attempting to represent them. Change in society is sweeping over the managerial and governmental institutions that do much to control the state of the workplace, and new voices and perspectives are important contributors to the change.

As the proliferation of working women continues, their presence will influence the decisions being made in the councils of power. Shifts in the demographics of the powerful foretell a balance of rather than a shift in dominance that should bode well for individual men and women and the companies that employ them. With increased fairness and a greater likelihood that the broader talent pool will be exploited, the change should be toward higher productivity. Optimistic signs are apparent as women in nontraditional roles become less token and sensational. The future holds the promise of ever greater comfort with the presence of women and the influence of their ideas and even the occasional sting of their power as they force adjustments that, unless the pendulum swings too far, will be net gains for everyone involved.

Different Relationships and Attitudes

Power will shift, roles will change, new relationships will form, and attitudes will adjust to new realities. Previously uncomfortable exchanges will evolve into routine behavior and form a new business etiquette that alters how women and men approach one another, appraise their mutual potential, and interact with one another in the workplace.

Each new business encounter with the opposite sex will involve less man-woman posturing. Women and men will grow increasingly comfortable with their roles as colleagues in a never "gender-unaware" but more "gender-comfortable" mode that will ease problems of sexual harassment and stereotyping. Sexist behavior and strident feminism will become as acceptable as cigar smoking on a crowded elevator. Change occurs with time and shifts in the equations of power—the relationships and attitudes of men and women at work will move toward balance along new lines as the future unfolds.

New Expectations

The human face of change is what we see. Rising generations of women and men will model it. People cast in actual roles of gender equity will influence the future beyond the operational reach of their recently acquired influence. Consider Supreme Court Justice Ruth Bader Ginsburg, whose path to that tribunal already reads like that of a trailblazing pioneer. Imagine a time when:

- A student who was first in the graduating class of an Ivy League law school would be unable to get a job with a top law firm or even be interviewed for a Supreme Court clerkship because she was a woman

- A law professor at a prestigious university who would wear her mother-in-law's baggy clothes to conceal her pregnancy in order to avoid being denied tenure or, earlier in life, be forced to nearly the bottom of the civil service grade structure because her decision to bear a child kept her from being eligible for the training required to hold even a modest government job.[6]

In the years to come employment practices that are commonplace today will sound as anachronistic and implausible as the Ginsburg experiences sound today.

Reality is partly defined by heartfelt perceptions. Few people in the mainstream of American life today can read examples like these and respond with anything but amazement that they occurred. Fewer would advocate returning to those days. Reason and intellect are part of the rejection of the past, but emotion is a factor as well, and behavior changes more effectively when motivated by both rationality and emotion. Trends that reflect widespread gut feelings flourish, and fairness for women at work now rings a positive bell for much of the population.

The face of change is obvious wherever you look, and it promises to become even more apparent—Supreme Court justices, members of Congress, Cabinet officers, surgeons general. A first lady with legitimate professional credentials comes to the role and dramatically redefines it. Hollywood studio executives such as Sherry Lansing and producers and directors like Barbra Streisand and Penny Marshall join Steven Speilberg's longtime collaborator Kathleen Kennedy as cultural icons. Male *and* female authors and publishing industry executives are equally represented in the pages of *Publishers Weekly.* Just as readers wait for the next John Grisham or Scott Turow or Elmore Leonard novel, others eagerly await the next Mary Higgins Clark or Terry McMillan or Patricia Cornwell (who in her books happens to have a professional woman protagonist in a job once open only to men—forensic medical examiner). And on and on the examples go, as tokenism is replaced by sharing on the basis of merit, a trend that will almost certainly increase in the future.

Women's progress will not be demonstrated by a personality cult based on women as household names. It will be demonstrated in tangible ways, for example, by medical research that distinguishes between male and female biology.

Success for women in the future will be no more assured than it has been for past generations of men. Life is still a lottery in which only so many can win the top prizes. But a woman will no longer enter the workplace with one arm tied behind her back. Women will be entitled to prepare for any position, and their contributions or ascent to the top will not be quashed merely because of their gender.

Endnotes

Chapter 1

1. Anne Fausto-Sterling, *Myths of Gender: Biological Theories about Women and Men*, Basic Books, New York, 1985, p. 218.

2. Jo Durden-Smith and Diane Desimone, *Sex and the Brain*, Arbor House, New York, 1983, p. 277.

3. Anthony Astrachan, *How Men Feel*, Anchor Press/Doubleday, New York, 1986, p. 266.

4. Peter G. Filene, *Him/Her/Self: Sex Roles in Modern America*, Johns Hopkins, Baltimore, 1986, p. 33.

5. Ibid., p. 106.

6. Ibid., p. 148.

7. Ibid., pp. 162–163.

8. Felice N. Schwartz, *Breaking with Tradition: Women and Work, The New Facts of Life*, Warner Books, New York, 1992, p. 34.

9. Filene, op. cit., p. 169.

10. Filene, op. cit., p. 165.

11. Astrachan, op. cit., p. 267.

12. Filene, op. cit., p. 212.

13. Barbara Ettorre, "Breaking the Glass: Or Just Window Dressing," *Management Review*, vol, 81, issue 3, March 1992, p. 19.

14. Judi Bredemeier, "And the Surveys Say: Business & Pleasure Mix," *Business Travel News*, November 18, 1991, p. 15.

15. *DSEA*, U.S. Department of Labor, Women's Bureau, October 1991.

16. *Labor Force Statistics*, U.S. Department of Labor, Bureau of Labor Statistics, Table 5, unpublished data, 1992.

17. *The Washington Post*, May 29, 1992, p. A18.

18. *The Washington Post*, July 31, 1992, p. A15.

19. Lois R. Wise, "Social Equity in Civil Service Systems," *Public Administration Review*, vol. 50, no. 5, 1990, p. 572.

20. Kenneth K. Ahn and Michelle A. Saint-Germain, "Public Administration Education and the Status of Women," *American Review of Public Administration*, vol. 18, no. 3, 1988, pp. 297–307.

21. Rita Mae Kelly et al., "Public Managers in the States: A Comparison of Career Advancement by Sex," *Public Administration Review,* vol. 51, no. 5, September–October 1991, p. 402.

22. Ibid., p. 404.

23. Ibid., p. 411.

24. *Statistical Abstract of the United States: 1991,* U.S. Bureau of Census, no. 874, p. 533.

25. Genevieve Soter Capowski, "Be Your Own Boss? Millions of Women Get Down to Business," *Management Review,* vol. 81, issue 3, March 1992, p. 27.

26. Ibid., p. 24.

27. Ibid., p. 24.

28. Janice Castro, "On the Job, Get Set: Here They Come!" *Time* (Special Issue, Women), Fall 1990, p. 52.

29. Howard N. Fullerton, Jr., "Labor Force Projections: The Baby Boom Moves On," *Outlook: 1990–2005,* U.S. Department of Labor, Bureau of Labor Statistics, Bull. 2402, May 1992, p. 29.

30. *Projections of Education Statistics to 2001, An Update,* National Center for Education Statistics, December 1990, p. vii.

31. E. L. Dey, A. W. Astin, and W. S. Korn, *The American Freshman: Twenty-Five Year Trends,* Higher Education Research Institute, University of California at Los Angeles, 1991, p. 27.

32. Ibid., p. 15.

33. Ibid., pp. 63 and 93.

Chapter 2

1. Carol Tavris, *The Mismeasure of Woman,* Simon and Schuster, New York, 1992, pp. 94–95.

2. Douglas Stein, "Interview with Roger Gorski," *Omni,* vol. 13, no. 1, October 1990, p. 72.

3. Tavris, op. cit., p. 92.

4. Jean D. Grams and Walter B. Waetjen, *Sex: Does It Make a Difference?* Wadsworth, Belmont, California, 1975, p. 209.

5. Anne Fausto-Sterling, *Myths of Gender: Biological Theories about Women and Men,* Basic Books, New York, 1985, p. 216.

6. Ibid., pp. 215–216.

7. Ibid., p. 216.

8. Ibid., p. 217.

9. Ibid., p. 218.

10. Grams and Waetjen, op. cit., p. 19.

11. John Lancaster, "Giving Less Weight to Lean GI's," *The Washington Post,* September 4, 1992, p. A23.

12. Fausto-Sterling, op. cit., p. 218.

13. Stein, op. cit., p. 72.

14. Ibid., p. 71.

15. Kathryn Phillips, "Why Can't a Man Be More Like a Woman...and Vice Versa," *Omni,* vol. 13, no. 1, p. 48.

16. Stein, op. cit., p. 74.

17. Stein, op. cit., p. 76.

18. Stein, op. cit., p. 78.

19. Phillips, op. cit., p. 68.

20. Doreen Kimura, "How Sex Hormones Boost—or Cut—Intellectual Ability," *Psychology Today,* vol. 23, no. 11, November 1989, p. 66.

21. Ibid., p. 65.

22. Tavris, op. cit., p. 134.

23. Tavris, op. cit., p. 150.

24. Stein, op. cit., p. 71.

25. Marguerite Holloway, "Profile: Vive La Difference: Doreen Kimura Plumbs Male and Female Brains," *Scientific American,* vol. 263, no. 4, October 1990, p. 42.

26. Elizabeth Fee, "Science and the Woman Problem: Historical Perspectives," in Michael S. Teitelbaum (ed.), *Sex Differences: Social and Biological Perspectives,* Anchor Books/Doubleday, Garden City, New York, 1976, pp. 205–206.

27. Ann Gibbons, "The Brain as 'Sexual Organ,'" *Science,* vol. 253, no. 5023, August 30, 1991, p. 958.

28. Ibid., p. 957.

29. Phillips, op. cit., pp. 42–44.

30. Beryl Lieff Benderly, "Don't Believe Everything You Read: A Case Study of How the Politics of Sex-Difference Research Turned a Small Finding into a Major Media Flap," *Psychology Today,* vol. 23, no. 11, November 1989, p. 68.

31. Phillips, op. cit., p. 44.

32. Benderly, op. cit., p. 68.

33. Phillips, op. cit., p. 44–46.

34. Phillips, op. cit., p. 46.

35. Phillips, op. cit., p. 44.

36. Phillips, op. cit., pp. 44–46.

37. Holloway, op. cit., p. 42.

38. Holloway, op. cit., p. 49.

39. Constance Holden, "Is the 'Gender Gap' Narrowing?" *Science*, vol. 253, no. 5023, August 30, 1991, p. 960.

40. Phillips, op. cit., p. 44.

41. Gibbons, op. cit., p. 959.

42. Sandra Blakeslee, "Men Ask Directions? They Don't Feel Lost: Each Sex Has Its Own Way of Navigating, Study Finds," *The New York Times*, May 26, 1992, p. C-1.

43. Ibid., p. C-8.

44. Holden, op. cit., p. 960.

45. Holden, op. cit., p. 960.

46. Holden, op. cit., pp. 959–960.

47. Holden, op. cit., p. 960.

48. Tavris, op. cit., p. 42.

49. Fausto-Sterling, op. cit., p. 148.

50. Fausto-Sterling, op. cit., p. 152.

51. Betty Yorburg, *Sexual Identity: Sex Roles and Social Change*, Wiley, New York, 1974, p. 23.

52. Grams and Waetjen, op. cit., p. 44.

53. Tavris, op. cit., p. 288.

54. Michael Hutchison, "Sex on the Brain," *Playboy*, April 1990, p. 78.

55. Bruce Bower, "Darwin's Minds," *Science News*, vol. 140, no. 15, October 12, 1991, pp. 233–234.

56. Ibid., p. 233.

57. Ibid., p. 234.

58. Deborah Tannen, *You Just Don't Understand: Women and Men in Conversation*, Ballentine, New York, 1990, p. 38.

59. Ibid., p. 25.

60. Tavris, op. cit., p. 297.

61. Tavris, op. cit., p. 298.

62. Tavris, op. cit., p. 299.

63. Tavris, op. cit., p. 300.

64. Tavris, op. cit., p. 87.

65. Tavris, op. cit., p. 64.

66. Tavris, op. cit., p. 65.

67. Tannen, op. cit., p. 244.

68. Carol Stevens, "How Women Get Bad Medicine," *The Washingtonian*, June 1992, p. 75.

69. Ibid., p. 97.

204   Endnotes

70. "Gender Disparities in Clinical Decision Making," *Journal of the American Medical Association,* Council on Ethical and Judicial Affairs, American Medical Association, vol. 266, no. 4., July 24–31, 1991, p. 559.

71. Phillips, op. cit., p. 68.

72. Stevens, op. cit., p. 77.

73. "Gender Disparities in Clinical Decision Making," op. cit., p. 560.

74. "Gender Disparities in Clinical Decision Making," op. cit., p. 561.

75. Stevens, op. cit., p. 77.

76. Bernadine Healy, "Women's Health, Public Welfare," *Journal of the American Medical Association,* vol. 266, no 4., July 24–31, 1991, p. 566.

77. Ibid., p. 567.

78. Stevens, op. cit., p. 98.

79. "Gender Disparities in Clinical Decision Making," op. cit., p. 559.

80. "Gender Disparities in Clinical Decision Making," op. cit., p. 560.

81. John Poppy, "It's All in Your Head? Men and Women Don't Feel Pain Differently—We Just Think They Do," *Esquire,* vol. 113, no. 4, April 1990, p. 87.

82. Judy B. Rosener, "Ways Women Lead," *Harvard Business Review,* vol. 68, no. 6, November–December, 1990, p. 120.

83. Ibid., p. 124.

84. Cynthia Fuchs Epstein, "Ways Men and Women Lead," *Harvard Business Review,* vol. 69, no. 1, January–February 1991, p. 150.

85. Felice N. Schwartz, *Breaking with Tradition: Women and Work, The New Facts of Life,* Warner Books, New York, 1992, p. 154.

86. "Ways Men and Women Lead," op. cit., pp. 154–155.

87. Yorburg, op. cit., p. 154.

88. Phillips, op. cit., p. 68.

89. Tavris, op. cit., p. 54.

90. Karen Matthes, ed., "Facts on Women," *Management Review,* vol. 81, issue 3, March 1992, p. 61.

91. Patricia Madoo Lengermann and Ruth A. Wallace, *Gender in America: Social Control and Social Change,* Prentice-Hall, Englewood Cliffs, New Jersey, 1985, p. 210.

92. Oren Harari, "What Do Women Want, Anyway?" *Management Review,* vol. 81, issue 3, March 1992, p. 43.

93. John Money and Patricia Tucker, *Sexual Signatures: On Being a Man or a Woman,* Little, Brown, Boston, 1975, pp. 202–203.

94. Matthes, op. cit., p. 60.

95. Schwartz, op. cit., p. 196.

96. U.S. Bureau of Census, *1991 Statistical Abstract of the United States*, no. 648, p. 393.

97. U.S. Bureau of Census, *1991 Statistical Abstract of the United States*, no. 650, p. 394.

98. "Employee Tenure and Occupational Mobility in the Early 1990's," *News*, U.S. Department of Labor, Bureau of Labor Statistics, Washington, June 26, 1992, pp. 1–2.

99. Money and Tucker, op. cit., p. 199.

100. Tavris, op. cit., p. 88.

101. Tavris, op. cit., p. 333.

102. Phillips, op. cit., p. 68.

103. Phillips, op. cit., p.68.

104. Fausto-Sterling, op. cit., p. 221.

Chapter 3

1. *Policy Guidance on Current Issues of Sexual Harassment*, Equal Employment Opportunity Commission, no. N-915-050, March 19, 1990, p. 3.

2. Ibid., p. 30.

3. 631 *Federal Reporter*, 2d Ser. 1094 (1980), p. 1099.

4. *Time of Change: 1983 Handbook on Women Workers*, Bull. 298, U.S. Department of Labor, Office of the Secretary, Women's Bureau, pp. 144–145.

5. Jack Gordon, "Rethinking Diversity," *Training Magazine*, vol. 29, no. 1, January 1992, p. 27.

6. *A Working Woman's Guide to Her Job Rights*, U.S. Department of Labor, Office of the Secretary, Women's Bureau, August 1992, p. 6.

7. *Time of Change: 1983 Handbook on Women Workers*, op. cit., pp. 146–147.

8. §1604.11 Sexual Harassment [45 FR 74677, November 10, 1980].

9. *A Working Woman's Guide to Her Job Rights*, op. cit., pp. 26–27.

10. *Policy Guidance on Current Issues of Sexual Harassment*, op. cit., p. 2.

11. "Civil Rights Act of 1991," Special Supplement No. 218, The Bureau of National Affairs, Inc., Washington, D.C., November 12, 1991, p. S-1.

12. Ibid., p. S-1.

13. Ibid., pp. S2–S3.

14. Ibid., p. S-3.

15. Ibid., p. S-4.

16. 563 *Federal Reporter*, 2d Ser. 553 (1977).

17. Ibid., p. 356.

18. Ibid., p. 356.

19. Ibid., p. 357.

20. 620 *Federal Reporter,* 2d Ser. 228 (1980).

21. Ibid., p. 230.

22. 631 *Federal Reporter,* 2d Ser. 1094 (1980).

23. 563 *Federal Reporter,* 2d Ser. 553 (1977), p. 355.

24. 631 *Federal Reporter,* 2d Ser. 1094 (1980), p. 1108.

25. Ibid., pp. 1114–1115.

26. 101 *Supreme Court Reporter* 2242 (1981).

27. Ibid., p. 2246.

28. Ibid., p. 2253.

29. 713 *Federal Reporter,* 2d Ser. 1127 (1983).

30. Ibid., p. 1134.

31. 578 *Federal Supplement* 846 (1983).

32. Ibid., p. 849.

33. Ibid., p. 861.

34. Ibid., p. 850.

35. Ibid., p. 867.

36. Ibid., p. 871.

37. Ibid., p. 871.

38. 709 *Federal Reporter,* 2d Ser. 251 (1983).

39. 106 *Supreme Court Reporter* 2399 (1986).

40. 685 *Federal Supplement* 1269 (D.D.C. 1988).

41. 875 *Federal Reporter,* 2d Ser. 468 (5th Cir. 1989).

42. 895 *Federal Reporter,* 2d Ser, 1469 (3d Cir. 1990).

43. Ibid., p. 1486.

44. 924 *Federal Reporter,* 2d Ser. 872 (9th Cir. 1991).

45. Ibid., p. 877.

46. Ibid., p. 878.

47. Ibid., p. 880.

48. *Policy Guidance on Current Issues of Sexual Harassment,* op. cit., p. 2.

49. Ibid., p. 2.

50. Ibid., p. 3.

51. 875 *Federal Reporter,* 2d Ser. 468 (5th Cir. 1989), op. cit., p. 875.

52. *Policy Guidance on Current Issues of Sexual Harassment,* op. cit., p. 6.

53. Ibid., pp. 7–9.

54. Ibid., p. 16.
55. Ibid., p. 17.
56. Ibid., p. 6.
57. Ibid., pp. 10–11.
58. Ibid., p. 16.
59. Ibid., p. 9.
60. Ibid., p. 14.
61. Ibid., p. 15.
62. Ibid., p. 15.
63. Ibid., p. 17.
64. 924 *Federal Reporter*, 2d 872 (9th Cir. 1991), pp. 879–880.
65. *Policy Guidance on Current Issues of Sexual Harassment*, op. cit., p. 19.
66. Ibid., p. 20.
67. Ibid., p. 23.
68. Ibid., pp. 25–26.
69. Ibid., p. 19.
70. Ibid., p. 4.
71. 685 *Federal Supplement* 1269 (D.D.C. 1988), p. 1270.
72. *Policy Guidance on Current Issues of Sexual Harassment*, op. cit., p. 5.
73. Ibid., p. 24.

Chapter 4

1. Ellen Wright, "Incriminating Data," *Hemispheres,* June 1993, pp. 32–33.

Chapter 5

1. Ronni Sandroff, "Sexual Harassment: The Inside Story," *Working Woman,* June 1992, p. 51.
2. Jane Walstedt, social science adviser, Women's Bureau, U.S. Department of Labor, "Remarks on Sexual Harassment in the Workplace," unpublished speech before the Hotel Human Resources Directors of Northern Virginia, March 10, 1992, pp. 7–8.
3. Sandroff, op. cit., pp. 48–49.
4. Saundra Torry, "Study Finds Sexual Harassment Prevalent in Western U.S. Courts," *The Washington Post,* August 5, 1992, p. A2.
5. Sandroff, op. cit., p. 51.

6. "Sexual Harassment Abroad," *Parade Magazine,* January 12, 1992, p. 14.

7. Sandroff, op. cit., p. 51.

8. "Managing Diversity," *Management Letter,* no. 413, Bureau of Business Practice, Waterford, Connecticut, July 10, 1991, p. 4.

9. Ibid., p. 4.

10. Jeri Spann, "Dealing Effectively with Sexual Harassment: Some Practical Lessons from One City's Experience," *Public Personnel Management,* vol. 19, no. 1, Spring 1990, pp. 67–68.

11. Ibid., p. 66.

12. Sandroff, op. cit., p. 51.

13. *Pipelines of Progress, Labor Department's 1992 Update on the Glass Ceiling Initiative,* Bureau of National Affairs, Washington, D.C., p. 33.

14. Marshall J. Breger, solicitor, U.S. Department of Labor, unpublished speech on "The Glass Ceiling" before the Association of the Bar of the City of New York, Special Committee on Women in the Profession, April 30, 1992, p. 2.

15. Ibid., p. 3.

16. Larry Reynolds, "Translate Fury into Action," *Management Review,* March 1992, p. 38.

17. "Can the Feds Bust through the 'Glass Ceiling'?" *Business Week,* no. 3211, April 29, 1991, p. 33.

18. Susan B. Garland, "How to Keep Women Managers on the Corporate Ladder," *Business Week,* no. 3229, September 2, 1991, p. 64.

19. Breger, op. cit., p. 4.

20. Breger, op. cit., p. 9.

21. Breger, op. cit., p. 7.

22. Carol Kleiman, "'All the Right Stuff' Often Goes Wrong for Female Managers," *The Washington Post,* Sunday, January 12, 1992, p. H2.

23. *Pipelines of Progress, Labor Department's 1992 Update on the Glass Ceiling Initiative,* op. cit., p. 8.

24. Breger, op. cit., p. 20.

25. Breger, op. cit., p. 19.

26. Garland, op. cit., p. 64.

27. Breger, op. cit., pp. 21–22.

28. *Pipelines of Progress, Labor Department's 1992 Update on the Glass Ceiling Initiative,* op. cit., p. 11.

29. Ibid., p. 40.

30. Don Nichols, "Job Candidates Wanted: Talented Women Please Apply," *Management Review,* March 1992, p. 41.

31. Ibid., p. 41.

32. Ibid., p. 41.

33. Barbara Ettorre, "Breaking the Glass: Or Just Window Dressing," *Management Review*, vol. 81, issue 3, March 1992, p. 21.

34. Ibid., p. 21.

35. Ibid., p. 21.

36. Ibid., p. 21.

37. Ibid., p. 21.

38. Ibid., p. 22.

39. "Work and Family Life: An Introduction," *Work and Family Resource Kit*, U.S. Department of Labor, Women's Bureau.

40. *Employment and Earnings*, U.S. Department of Labor, Bureau of Labor Statistics, January 1991, Tables 1 and 2.

41. *Facts on Working Women*, U.S. Department of Labor, Women's Bureau, No. 92-1, January 1992, p. 1.

42. *Workforce 2000: Work and Workers for the 21st Century*, a study by the Hudson Institute for the U.S. Department of Labor, 1987.

43. "Work and Family Life: An Introduction," op. cit.

44. "Work and Family Life: An Introduction," op. cit.

45. Felice N. Schwartz, *Breaking with Tradition: Women and Work, The New Facts of Life*, Warner Books, New York, 1992, p. 42.

46. Ibid., p. 50.

47. Ibid., p. 48.

48. *Client's Monthly Alert*, July 1992, p. 4.

49. Carol Kleiman, "GE Finds Its Family Policies Bring Good Things to Employees' Lives," *The Washington Post*, September 27, 1992, p. G2.

50. Ibid., p. G2.

51. Marianne Kyrakos, "Learning to Be Family Friendly: Small Company Child-Care Benefits Gain in Popularity," *Washington Business*, November 2, 1992, p. 8.

52. Ibid., p. 8.

53. Ibid., p. 8.

54. Tom Brown, "The Mommy Track: Is it Legal?" *Industry Week*, October 2, 1989, vol. 238, no. 19, p. 24.

Chapter 6

1. Howard N. Fullerton, Jr., "Labor Force Projections: The Baby Boom Moves On," *Outlook 1990–2005*, U.S. Department of Labor, Bureau of Labor Statistics, Bull. 2402, May 1992, p. 37.

2. Janice Castro, "On the Job, Get Set: Here They Come!" *Time* (Special Issue, Women), Fall 1990, p. 52.

3. David Sheff, "Playboy Interview: Betty Friedan," *Playboy*, vol. 39, no. 9, September 1992, p. 149.

4. Sandra G. Boodman, "Medical School Grads: More Women than Men," *The Washington Post*, July 6, 1993, p. 5.

5. Lisa Genasci, "Her Firm's Name Also Defines Felice Schwartz's Corporate Legacy: Catalyst," *The Washington Post*, June 27, 1993, p. H2.

6. David Von Drehle, "Ruth Bader Ginsburg: Her Life and Her Law. Conventional Roles Hid a Revolutionary Intellect, *The Washington Post*, July 18, 1993, pp. A1, A14.

Bibliography

Ahn, Kenneth K. and Michelle A. Saint-Germain: "Public Administration Education and the Status of Women," *American Review of Public Administration,* vol. 18, 1988, no. 3, pp. 297–307.

Astrachan, Anthony: *How Men Feel,* Anchor Press/Doubleday, New York, 1986.

Benderly, Beryl Lieff: "Don't Believe Everything You Read: A Case Study of How the Politics of Sex-Difference Research Turned a Small Finding into a Major Media Flap," *Psychology Today,* vol. 23, no. 11, November 1989, pp. 67–69.

Blakeslee, Sandra: "Men Ask Directions? They Don't Feel Lost: Each Sex Has Its Own Way of Navigating, Study Finds," *The New York Times,* May 26, 1992, pp. C-1 and C-8.

Boodman, Sandra G.: "Medical School Grads: More Women than Men," *The Washington Post,* July 6, 1993, p. 5.

Bower, Bruce: "Darwin's Minds," *Science News,* vol. 140, no. 15, October 12, 1991, pp. 232–234.

Bredemeier, Judi: "And the Surveys Say: Business & Pleasure Mix," *Business Travel News,* November 18, 1991, p. 15.

Breger, Marshall J., Solicitor, U.S. Department of Labor: unpublished speech on "The Glass Ceiling" before the Association of the Bar of the City of New York, Special Committee on Women in the Profession, April 30, 1992.

Brown, Tom: "The Mommy Track: Is it Legal?" *Industry Week,* October 2, 1989, vol. 238, no. 19.

"Can the Feds Bust through the 'Glass Ceiling?'" *Business Week,* no. 3211, April 29, 1991, p. 33.

Capowski, Genevieve Soter: "Be Your Own Boss? Millions of Women Get Down to Business," *Management Review,* vol. 81, issue 3, March 1992, pp. 24–30.

Castro, Janice: "On the Job, Get Set: Here They Come!" *Time* (Special Issue, Women), Fall 1990, pp. 50–52.

"Civil Rights Act of 1991," Special Suppl. no. 218, Bureau of National Affairs, Inc., Washington, D.C., November 12, 1991.

Client's Monthly Alert, July 1992.

Dey, E. L., A. W. Astin, and W. S. Korn: *The American Freshman: Twenty-Five Year Trends,* Higher Education Research Institute, University of California at Los Angeles, 1991.

Durden-Smith, Jo and Diane Desimone: *Sex and the Brain,* Arbor House, New York, 1983.

Equal Employment Opportunity Commission: *Information for the Private Sector and State and Local Governments*, Washington, D.C.

————: *Policy Guidance on Current Issues of Sexual Harassment*, no. N-915-050, March 19, 1990.

Epstein, Cynthia Fuchs: "Ways Men and Women Lead," *Harvard Business Review*, vol. 69, no. 1, January–February, 1991, pp. 150–160.

Ettorre, Barbara: "Breaking the Glass: Or Just Window Dressing," *Management Review*, vol. 81, issue 3, March 1992, pp. 16–22.

Eyler, David R. and Andrea P. Baridon: *More than Friends, Less than Lovers: Managing Sexual Attraction in the Workplace*, Tarcher, Los Angeles, 1991.

Faludi, Susan: *Backlash: The Undeclared War against American Women*, Crown, New York, 1991.

Fausto-Sterling, Anne: *Myths of Gender: Biological Theories about Women and Men*, Basic Books, New York, 1985.

563 *Federal Reporter*, 2d Ser. 553 (1977).

620 *Federal Reporter*, 2d Ser. 228 (1980).

631 *Federal Reporter*, 2d Ser. 1094 (1980).

709 *Federal Reporter*, 2d Ser. 251 (1983).

713 *Federal Reporter*, 2d Ser. 1127 (1983).

875 *Federal Reporter*, 2d Ser. 468 (5th Cir. 1989).

895 *Federal Reporter*, 2d Ser. 1469 (3rd Cir. 1990).

924 *Federal Reporter*, 2d Ser. 872 (9th Cir. 1991).

578 *Federal Supplement* 846 (1983).

685 *Federal Supplement* 1269 (D.D.C. 1988).

Fee, Elizabeth: "Science and the Woman Problem: Historical Perspectives," in Michael S. Teitelbaum (ed.): *Sex Differences: Social and Biological Perspectives*, Anchor Books/Doubleday, Garden City, New York, 1976.

Filene, Peter G: *Him/Her/Self: Sex Roles in Modern America*, Johns Hopkins, Baltimore, 1986.

Fullerton, Howard N., Jr.: "Labor Force Projections: The Baby Boom Move On," *Outlook: 1990–2005*, U.S. Department of Labor, Bureau of Labor Statistics, Bulletin 2402, May 1992, pp. 29–42.

Garland, Susan B.: "How to Keep Women Managers on the Corporate Ladder," *Business Week*, no. 3229, September 2, 1991, p. 64.

Genasci, Lisa: "Her Firm's Name Also Defines Felice Schwartz's Corporate Legacy: Catalyst," *The Washington Post*, June 27, 1993, p. H2.

"Gender Disparities in Clinical Decision Making," *Journal of the American Medical Association*, Council on Ethical and Judicial Affairs, American Medical Association, vol. 266, no. 4., July 24–31, 1991, pp. 559–562.

Gibbons, Ann: "The Brain as 'Sexual Organ,'" *Science*, vol. 253, no. 5023, August 30, 1991, pp. 957–959.

Gordon, Jack: "Rethinking Diversity," *Training Magazine*, vol. 29, no. 1, January 1992.

Grams, Jean D. and Walter B. Waetjen: *Sex: Does It Make a Difference?* Wadsworth, Belmont, California, 1975.

Harari, Oren: "What Do Women Want, Anyway?" *Management Review*, vol. 81, issue 3, March 1992, pp. 42–43.

Healy, Bernadine: "Women's Health, Public Welfare," *Journal of the American Medical Association*, vol. 266, no. 4, July 24–31, 1991, pp. 566–568.

Holden, Constance: "Is the 'Gender Gap' Narrowing?" *Science*, vol. 253, no. 5023, August 30, 1991, pp. 959–960.

Holloway, Marguerite: "Profile: Vive La Difference: Doreen Kimura Plumbs Male and Female Brains," *Scientific American*, vol. 263, no. 4, October 1990, pp. 40–42.

Hutchinson, Michael: "Sex on the Brain," *Playboy*, April 1990, pp. 77, 154.

Kelly, Rita Mae, et al.: "Public Managers in the States: A Comparison of Career Advancement by Sex," *Public Administration Review*, vol. 51, no. 5, September–October 1991, p. 402.

Kimura, Doreen: "How Sex Hormones Boost—or Cut—Intellectual Ability," *Psychology Today*, vol. 23, no. 11, November 1989, pp. 62–66.

Kleiman, Carol: " 'All the Right Stuff' Often Goes Wrong for Female Managers," *The Washington Post*, Sunday, January 12, 1992, p. H2.

———: "GE Finds Its Family Policies Bring Good Things to Employees' Lives," *The Washington Post*, September 27, 1992, p. G2.

Kyrakos, Marianne: "Learning to Be Family Friendly: Small Company Child-Care Benefits Gain in Popularity," *Washington Business*, November 2, 1992, p. 8.

Lancaster, John: "Giving Less Weight to Lean GI's," *The Washington Post*, September 4, 1992, p. A23.

Lengermann, Patricia Madoo, and Ruth A. Wallace: *Gender in America: Social Control and Social Change*, Prentice-Hall, Englewood Cliffs, New Jersey, 1985.

"Managing Diversity," *Management Letter*, issue no. 413, the Bureau of Business Practice, Waterford, Connecticut, July 10, 1991.

Matthes, Karen (ed.): "Facts on Women," *Management Review*, vol. 81, issue 3, March 1992, pp. 60–61.

Money, John and Patricia Tucker: *Sexual Signatures: On Being a Man or a Woman*, Little, Brown, Boston, 1975.

National Center for Education Statistics, *Projections of Education Statistics to 2001, An Update*, December 1990.

Nichols, Don: "Job Candidates Wanted: Talented Women Please Apply," *Management Review*, March 1992, pp. 39–41.

Phillips, Kathryn: "Why Can't a Man Be More Like a Woman...and Vice Versa," *Omni*, vol. 13, no. 1, pp. 42–48, 68.

Pipelines of Progress, Labor Department's 1992 Update on the Glass Ceiling Initiative, Bureau of National Affairs, Inc., Washington, D.C.

Poppy, John: "It's All in Your Head? Men and Women Don't Feel Pain Differently—We Just Think They Do," *Esquire*, vol. 113, no. 4, April 1990, pp. 86–87.

Reynolds, Larry: "Translate Fury into Action," *Management Review*, March 1992, pp. 36–38.

Rosener, Judy B: "Ways Women Lead," *Harvard Business Review*, vol. 68, no. 6, November–December, 1990, pp.119–125.

Sandroff, Ronni: "Sexual Harassment: The Inside Story," *Working Woman*, June 1992, pp. 47–51, 78.

Schwartz, Felice N.: *Breaking with Tradition: Women and Work, The New Facts of Life*, Warner, New York, 1992.

"Sexual Harassment Abroad," *Parade Magazine,* January 12, 1992.

§1604.11 Sexual Harassment [45 FR 74677, November 10, 1980].

Sheff, David: "Playboy Interview: Betty Friedan," *Playboy,* vol. 39, no. 9, September 1992, pp. 51–62, 149.

Spann, Jeri: "Dealing Effectively with Sexual Harassment: Some Practical Lessons from One City's Experience," *Public Personnel Management,* vol. 19, no. 1, Spring 1990, pp. 53–69.

Stein, Douglas: "Interview with Roger Gorski," *Omni,* vol. 13, no. 1, October 1990, pp. 70–134.

Stevens, Carol: "How Women Get Bad Medicine," *The Washingtonian,* June 1992, pp. 74–77, 94, 96, 98.

101 *Supreme Court Reporter* 2242 (1981).

106 *Supreme Court Reporter* 2399 (1986).

Tannen, Deborah: *You Just Don't Understand: Women and Men in Conversation,* Ballentine, New York, 1990.

Tavris, Carol: *The Mismeasure of Woman,* Simon and Schuster, New York, 1992.

Tiger, Lionel and Robin Fox: *The Imperial Animal,* Henry Holt, New York, 1989.

Torry, Saundra: "Study Finds Sexual Harassment Prevalent in Western U.S. Courts," *The Washington Post,* August 5, 1992.

U.S. Bureau of Census: *Statistical Abstract of the United States: 1991,* nos. 247, 253, 255, 648, 650, 672, 874.

U.S. Department of Labor, Bureau of Labor Statistics: "Employee Tenure and Occupational Mobility in the Early 1990's, *News,* June 26, 1992.

——: Employment and Earnings, January 1991.

——: Labor Force Statistics, Table 5, unpublished data, 1992.

U.S. Department of Labor, Women's Bureau: *DSEA,* October 1991.

——: Facts on Working Women, no. 92-1, January 1992.

——: *Time of Change: 1983 Handbook on Women Workers,* Bull. 298.

—— *Work and Family Resource Kit.*

——: *A Working Woman's Guide to Her Job Rights,* August 1992.

U.S. Department of Labor: *Workforce 2000: Work and Workers for the 21st Century* (study by the Hudson Institute), 1987.

Von Drehle, David: "Ruth Bader Ginsburg: Her Life and Her Law. Conventional Roles Hid a Revolutionary Intellect, *The Washington Post,* July 18, 1993, pp. A1, A14.

Walstedt, Jane, social science adviser, Women's Bureau, U.S. Department of Labor: "Remarks on Sexual Harassment in the Workplace," unpublished speech before the Hotel Human Resources Directors of Northern Virginia, March 10, 1992.

The Washington Post, May 29, 1992, p. A18.

The Washington Post, July 31, 1992, p. A15.

Wise, Lois R.: "Social Equity in Civil Service Systems," *Public Administration Review,* vol. 50, no. 5, 1990, pp. 567–575.

Wright, Ellen: "Incriminating Data," *Hemispheres,* June 1993, pp. 32–33.

Yorburg, Betty: *Sexual Identity: Sex Roles and Social Change,* Wiley, New York, 1974.

Index

Administrative Dispute Resolution Act of 1991, 181
Administrative positions, women in, 22–26
Aggressive behavior, 68, 70
American Council on Education, 39–41
American Federation of State, County, and Municipal Employees v. State of Washington, 103–104
American Freshman, The (Dey et al.), 40–41
American Management Association, 28
American Medical Association, 73–75
American Society of Travel Agents, 20
Andrews v. City of Philadelphia, 112–114
Anxiety, 78
Apparent authority, concept of, 119
Arthur Anderson & Company, 19–20
Astin, Alexander W., 40–41
Astrachan, Anthony, 11, 16
Attractiveness, and power in work relationships, 151–153

Backlash: The Undeclared War on Women (Faludi), 21, 173
Behavioral differences, 67–70
Benbow, Camilla, 65
Bernbaum, Sheri, 58
Bever, Thomas, 64
Bilateralization, of brain, 61
Birth control pill, 11, 16
Body differences, 52, 54–56
  and medical treatments, 73
  nature of, 54–56
  and occupational and social inequalities, 77–78
  significance of, 56
Body fat, 55, 56
Body size, 56, 60
Bower, Bruce, 69–70
Bowman Gray School of Medicine, 62

Brain differences, 10, 51–52, 57–67
  hormonal, 57–59
  and occupational and social inequalities, 77–78
  significance of, 66–67
  structural, 59–66
Brain Research Institute, 57
Breaking with Tradition: Women and Work, The New Facts of Life (Schwartz), 2, 15, 78–79, 173
Breger, Marshall J., 179–182
Broderick v. Ruder, 110–111
Brown University, 61
Business ownership, by women, 27–29
Business Week magazine, 180–181
Buss, David M., 69

Catalyst, 2, 76, 179, 186, 195–196
Center for Urban Affairs and Policy Research, 76–77
Child care centers, 189
Christensen v. The State of Iowa, 96–97, 98
Chubb and Son, Inc., 184
Circadian rhythm, 61–62
City University of New York, 76
Civil Rights Act of 1866, 93
Civil Rights Act of 1964, 96, 98, 107
  Bennett Amendment, 99, 105, 106
  Title VII, 89–90, 91, 92, 96–104, 113, 114, 116–118, 120
Civil Rights Act of 1991, 92–94, 171
Civil rights movement, 14, 16, 17, 90
Code switching, 71
Cognitive ability, 58–59, 60, 62, 63, 64–66
Columbia University, 61, 95
Common-law agency principles, 109, 118
Communication:
  compliments in, 161–163
  criticism in, 163–166

Communication (*Cont.*):
 gender differences in, 70–72
 and handling unpleasant tasks, 142–146
Comparable worth, concept of, 105
Competition, and workplace etiquette,
 139–142
Compliments, and workplace etiquette,
 161–163
Constructive discharge, 119
Corning, Inc., 174
Corpus callosum, 61
County of Washington v. Gunther, 100–101,
 102, 103
Crichton, Michael, 86
Criticism, and workplace etiquette, 163–166
Cultural differences, 66, 67–80

Daddy track, 135, 187
de Lacoste, Christine, 61
Demographic trends, 20–47
 education of women, 29–41, 193
 future projections of, 19
 population, roles of men and women in,
 41–45
 women in the workforce, 21–29
Dependency, of women, 13, 15–16
Dependent care options, 189–190
Depression, emotional, 78
DES, 57–58
Desimone, Diane, 10
Dey, Eric L., 40–41
Differences, gender (*see* Gender
 differences)
Disclosure (Crichton), 86
Discounts, for dependent care, 189
Division of labor, 11, 12–15, 68
Durden-Smith, Jo, 10

Earnings, of women, 21
 (*See also* Equal Pay Act of 1963; Equal
 pay for equal work)
Education, of women, 29–41
 attitudes toward, 39–41
 degrees conferred, 31–39
 enrollment trends, 29–30, 193
Elder care services, 189–190
Ellis, Albert, 2
Ellison v. Brady, 114–115
Emergency care for dependents, 189

Emotional differences, 67–70
Emotional disorders, 78
Empathy, 71–72
Employee Assistance Program (EAP), 175
Employment, of women, 11
 in American frontier, 13
 court cases on, 94–115
 and demographic trends, 19, 20–47
 and the Depression, 14
 and education, 29–41
 and equal pay (*see* Equal pay for equal
 work)
 and family responsibilities, 78–79,
 91–92, 134–136, 156, 184–190
 in government, 26–27
 and identity, 79–80
 impact on workplace, 185–187, 196–197
 laws regulating, 87–94
 and misunderstanding, 17–19
 and occupational differences, 75–80
 in the overall workforce, 21–26
 and sexual harassment (*see* Sexual
 harassment)
 and workplace etiquette (*see* Workplace
 etiquette)
 during World War II, 14–15
Entrepreneurship, of women, 27–29
Epstein, Cynthia Fuchs, 76
Equal Employment Opportunity Act of
 1972, 91
Equal Employment Opportunity
 Commission (EEOC), 89
 filing charges with, 120–122
 *Guidelines on Discrimination because of
 Sex*, 91, 92, 109
 *Policy Guidance on Current Issues of
 Sexual Harassment*, 85, 86, 115–120
 Policy on Remedies and Relief for
 Individual Cases of Unlawful
 Discrimination, 121
Equal Pay Act of 1963, 89, 95–96, 99–100,
 102, 105, 107
 filing charges, 121
Equal pay for equal work, 89, 105
 court cases on, 95–107
 laws regulating, 88–94
 lessons for managers, 104–107
Estradiol, 57–58
Estrogen, 58
Etiquette, workplace (*see* Workplace
 etiquette)

Executive Order 11246, 90–91
Executive Order 11375, 91
Executive positions, women in, 22–26,
    177–184, 194–197
Expectations, changes in, 197–199

Fair Labor Standards Act of 1938, 89, 95
Faludi, Susan, 17, 21, 173, 195
Family responsibilities, 78–79, 184–190
    and alternative work schedules, 79, 187,
        188–189
    and dependent care options, 189–190
    and gender stereotypes, 134–136
    impact on workplace, 185–187
    and "meeting people" etiquette, 156
    and needs of workers, 187–188
    and Pregnancy Discrimination Act of
        1978, 91–92
    and self-imposed glass ceiling, 78–79,
        182–183
Fausto-Sterling, Anne, 55, 56, 61, 68, 81
Feminine Mystique, The (Friedan), 89
Fennama, Elizabeth, 65
Field, Pauline, 60–61
Filene, Peter G., 13–14, 15
Flexible work schedules, 79, 187, 188
Flexiplace (at-home work), 189
Flextime, 188
Fortune 500 companies, 172, 178–181
Fox, Robin, 69
Friedan, Betty, 89, 195

Gaulin, Steven I. C., 63
GE Medical Systems, 187
Genasci, Lisa, 196
Gender differences, 10–19
    anthropological bases for, 12–13
    body, 52, 54–56, 73, 77–78
    brain, 10, 51–52, 57–67, 77–78
    dependency of women, 13, 15–16
    discrimination in workplace, 16–17
    kinds of, 49
    misunderstanding in, 17–19
    psychological and cultural, 66, 67–80
    recognition of, 50–52
    and sex roles, 11, 12–15, 68
    and stereotypes (see Stereotypes)
Gender in America: Social Control and Social
    Change (Lengermann and Wallace), 78

General Motors, 90
Ginsburg, Ruth Bader, 198
Glass, Lillian, 2
Glass ceiling, 93–94, 167, 177–184
    change, motivation for, 181–182
    described, 28, 177–178
    and mentoring, 183–184
    self-imposed, 78–79, 182–183
Glass Ceiling Act of 1991, 93–94, 180–181
Gorski, Roger, 51–52, 57–58, 60, 77
Government, employment of women in,
    26–27
Grams, Jean D., 53, 55–56, 68
Growth patterns, 55
Gumbel, Bryant, 163

Halpern, Dian, 65
Hamilton, Jean, 73
Hampson, Elizabeth, 58–59
Handedness, 62
Harari, Oren, 78
Harris v. Forklift, 95
Harvard Business Review, 2
Harvey, George, 29
Hauser, Barbara R., 190
Hayes system, 96
Health differences, 72–75
Healy, Bernadine, 72, 74
Heart disease, 73, 74
Higher Education Research Institute, 39–41
Hill-Thomas hearings, 86, 122, 194
Him/Her/Self: Sex Roles in Modern America
    (Filene), 13–14, 15
Hines, Melissa, 57, 77
Hippocampus, 63–64
Hormonal differences, 55, 57–59, 68
Hubbard, Ruth, 81
Hudson Institute, 185
Hutchison, Michael, 69
Hyde, Janet, 65
Hypothalamus, 58, 60–62

Industry Week magazine, 190
International Paper Company, 111–112
International Union of Electrical, Radio and
    Machine Workers, AFL-CIO-CLC v.
    Westinghouse Electric Corporation,
    98–100
Intuition, 71–72

218

Jealousy, 12, 69
Job mobility, 79
Job sharing, 188–189
Johns Hopkins University, 65
Johnson, Lyndon, 90–91
Journal of the American Medical Association, 73–75

Kanter, Rosabeth Moss, 79–80
Kariban v. Columbia University, 95
Katz v. Dole, 107–108
Kellogg Graduate School of Management, 180
Kimura, Doreen, 58–59, 60, 62
Korn, William S., 40–41
Kosterman, Gayle, 183, 184

Lakeoff, Robin, 1, 71
Lamon, Susan, 65
Language (*see* Communication)
Lateralization, of brain, 61
Leadership style, 76–77, 80
Lemons v. City and County of Denver, 97–98
Lengermann, Patricia Madoo, 78
Levy, Jerre, 61
Lindsey, Ann, 183
Linn, Marica, 65
Lohman, David, 63
Loyola University, 180
Lubinsky, David, 65
Lung cancer, 73

McGill University, 75
McMaster University, 62, 65, 81
Male standards, in workplace etiquette, 153–155
Management Review, 28, 78, 182, 183
Management style, 76–77, 80
Managers:
  and "boys will be boys" syndrome, 133
  and equal pay cases, 104–107
  and gender stereotypes, 133, 135–136, 138–139, 148
  and handling of unpleasant situations, 145–146
  and "male standard" etiquette, 155
  and "meeting people" etiquette, 157–158
  and "no fraternization" rules, 151

Managers (*Cont.*):
  and private comments at work, 136–139, 163–166
  and required socializing, 160–161
  and "saying it right" problems, 165–166
  and sexual harassment, 115–120, 171–177
  and sharing behavior, 168
  team building behavior of, 141–142, 157–158, 168
  use of power and attractiveness, 153
  women as, 22–26, 177–184, 194–197
Mansbridge, Jane, 76–77
Martin v. Texaco Refining and Marketing Inc., 181
Mathematics skills, 64–66
Mating behavior, 68–69
Mead, Margaret, 55
Medical differences, 72–75
Meeting people, etiquette of, 155–158
Melzack, Ronald, 75
Menstrual cycle, 58–59, 73
Mentor programs, 183–184
Meritor Savings Bank, FSB v. Vinson, 92, 108–110, 116
Mismeasure of Woman, The (Tavris), 50, 66
Mixed-motive cases, 93
Mommy track, 2, 134, 135, 187
Money, John, 78, 79
Motor coordination, 63
Myths of Gender (Fausto-Sterling), 55

National Academy of Sciences, 56
National Institutes of Health (NIH), 72
National Organization of Women (NOW), 195
Navigation skills, 63–64
Naylor, Cecile, 62
Netherlands Institute for Brain Research, 60

Occupational differences, 75–80
Oxford University, 60–61

Packwood, Robert, 122
Pain, response to, 75
Parent track, 2, 134, 135, 187
Part-time care for dependents, 189

Part-time work, 188
Pearson, Karl, 60
Peters, Tom, 78
Physical differences (*see* Body differences; Brain differences)
Pipelines of Progress, Labor Department's 1992 Update on the Glass Ceiling Initiative, 180–181
Pitney Bowes, 29
Plemer v. Parsons-Gilbane, 101–103
Power, 11
    and attractiveness in work relationships, 151–153
    and coercive sexual relationships, 126–128, 131, 132
    and gender stereotypes, 147
    and the glass ceiling, 177–178
    and language, 71
    and required socializing, 158–161
    and sexual harassment, 86
    shifts in, 197
Pregnancy Discrimination Act of 1978, 91–92
Price Waterhouse v. Hopkins, 93, 180
Psychological differences, 66, 67–80
Public Administration Review, 27
Pygmalion (Shaw), 50–51

Racism, and workplace etiquette, 136–139, 163–166
Raisman, Geoffrey, 60–61
Rational-emotive therapy, 2
Relocation, 182–183
Retirement, phased, 189
Revolution from Within: A Book of Self-Esteem (Steinem), 195
Romantic interests, at work, 127–128, 148–151
Rosener, Judy, 76
Rucker, Patricia, 78

S. C. Johnson Wax, 183
Sapolsky, Robert M., 66
SAT verbal and mathematics scores, 64–66
Schwartz, Felice N., 2, 15, 76, 78–79, 173, 186, 195–196
Science News, 69–70
Scott, Willard, 163
SDN (sexually dimorphic nucleus), 58

Securities and Exchange Commission (SEC), 110–111
Sex: Does It Make a Difference? (Grams and Waetjen), 53, 68
Sex and the Brain (Durden-Smith and Desimone), 10
Sex-based discrimination, 106
    (*See also* Equal pay for equal work; Glass ceiling; Sexual harassment)
Sex roles, 11, 12–15, 68
Sexism, and workplace etiquette, 136–139, 163–166, 197
Sexual harassment, 85–87
    continuing-violation sexual harassment, 116
    court cases on, 107–120
    damages for, 171–172, 173
    disparate impact charges, 93
    EEOC guidelines, 91, 92, 109
    and employer liability, 118–119, 171–172, 173
    filing charges, 120–122
    hostile environment harassment, 92, 108, 109, 110, 116, 118
    lessons for managers, 115–120, 171–177
    quid pro quo harassment, 92, 108, 116, 117
    and reasonable person standard, 117–118
    and unwelcome conduct, 116–117
    by women, 86, 127
Sexual Identity: Sex Roles and Social Change (Yorburg), 68
Sexual revolution, 11, 51
Sexual Signatures: On Being a Man or a Woman (Money and Tucker), 79
Sexuality:
    and birth control, 11, 16
    and gender stereotypes in the workplace, 126–128, 130–136
    and hormones, 57–58
    and jealousy, 69
    mating behavior, 68–69
    and required socializing, 158–161
    and romantic interests at work, 127–128, 148–151
Sharing:
    job, 188–189
    and workplace etiquette, 166–168
Shaw, George Bernard, 50–51
Sick-child care, 189

Simmons College, 183
Socializing, etiquette of, 158–161
Spann, Jeri, 175–176
Spatial perception skills, 58–59, 60, 61, 63–64
Sperry, Roger, 61
Spiegel, David, 75
Sports, 55–56, 63
Stanford University, 181
Stanley, Julian, 65
State Farm Insurance, 90
Steinem, Gloria, 195
Stereotypes, 9, 52, 68, 75
    and workplace etiquette, 126–128, 133–136, 138–139, 140, 146–148
Stevens, Carol, 73
Structural differences, in brain, 59–66
Study of Mathematically Precocious Youth (SMPY), 65
Swaab, Dick, 60

Tailhook incident, 172
Talking Power: The Politics of Language (Lakeoff), 1
Tannen, Deborah, 1, 18, 70–72
Tavris, Carol, 50, 52, 59, 62–63, 66, 68, 71, 72, 77–78, 79–80, 81
Team building:
    and competition mentality, 139–142
    and "meeting people" etiquette, 157–158
    sharing in, 166–168
Tenneco, 181
Test scores, 64–66
Testosterone, 57–58, 58
Texaco Refining and Marketing Inc., 181
Texas Instruments, 174
Thomas, Clarence, 86, 122, 194
Tiger, Lionel, 69
Time magazine, 127, 193
Tomlinson, Jan, 184
Toy preference tests, 57–58
Travelers Insurance Company, 186
Tucker, Patricia, 79

U.S. Bureau of the Census, 26, 29, 36, 37, 39, 40, 43–46, 64, 65
U.S. Constitution:
    Fourteenth Amendment, 88, 98
    Nineteenth Amendment, 88–89

U.S. Department of Education, National Center for Education Statistics, 30–35
U.S. Department of Labor, 29, 80
    Bureau of Labor Statistics, 21, 23–25, 29, 185
    Current Population Survey, 79
    and glass ceiling, 178–181, 182
    Office of Federal Contract Compliance Programs (OFCCP), 91
    Women's Bureau, 42, 89, 172
    Work and Family Resource Kit, 184–185, 188–190
University of California at Berkeley, 65
University of California at Irvine, 76
University of California at Los Angeles, 57–58, 77
University of Chicago, 61
University of Iowa, 63, 65
University of Michigan, 69
University of Northern Iowa, 96–97
University of Pittsburgh, 63
University of Rochester, 64
University of San Francisco, 78
University of Southern California, 65, 179
University of Texas, 73
University of Utah, 63
University of Western Ontario, 62
University of Wisconsin, 65
USX Corporation, 90

Verbal skills, 58–59, 60, 62, 63, 64–66
Visual-spatial skills, 58–59, 60, 61, 63–64
Voluntary reduced time, 188
Voting, by women, 44, 45, 85, 88–89
Vouchers, for dependent care, 189

Waetjen, Walter B., 53, 55–56, 68
Wallace, Ruth A., 78
Walstedt, Jane, 172
Waltman v. International Paper Company, 111–112
Wards Cove Packing Co. v. Atonio, 93
Washington (D.C.) Personnel Association, 187–188
Westinghouse Electric Corporation, 98–100
Witelson, Sandra, 62, 65, 81
Women's movement, 11, 17, 21, 70, 89, 173, 195–196
Work and Family Resource Kit, 184–185, 188–190

Workforce, 21–29
  government, women in, 26–27
  and occupational differences, 75–80
  overall, women in, 21–26
*Workforce 2000: Work and Workers for the
  21st Century,* 185
Working Woman magazine, 172–173
Workplace:
  and body differences, 56
  impact of women on, 185–187, 196–197
  laws regulating gender issues in, 87–94
  sexual revolution in, 51
Workplace etiquette, 125–169
  of attractiveness and power, 151–153
  and "boys will be boys" syndrome,
    130–133
  and competition mentality, 139–142
  and compliments, 161–163
  and criticism, 163–166

Workplace etiquette (*Cont.*):
  and gender stereotypes, 126–128,
    133–136, 138–139, 140, 146–148
  of handling unpleasant tasks, 142–146
  male standard in, 153–155
  of meeting people, 155–158
  and nature of working relationships,
    127–129
  of private comments, 136–139, 163–166
  and required socializing, 158–161
  and romantic interests, 127–128, 148–151
  of sharing, 166–168
World War I, 13–14
World War II, 14–15, 29

Yorburg, Betty, 68, 77
You Just Don't Understand (Tannen), 1,
  70–72

About the Authors

Andrea P. Baridon and David R. Eyler are both senior staff members at the National Center for Higher Education in Washington, D.C. In this capacity they serve as program managers and professional trainers for the Servicemembers Opportunity Colleges project of the American Association of State Colleges and Universities. They are the authors of *More than Friends, Less than Lovers: Managing Sexual Attraction in Working Relationships.*